The following study guides by Dawn Apgar are also available to assist social workers with studying for and passing the ASWB® examinations.

Bachelors

The Social Work ASWB® Bachelors Exam Guide: A Comprehensive Guide for Success, Second Edition

Test focuses on knowledge acquired while obtaining a Baccalaureate degree in Social Work (BSW). A small number of jurisdictions license social workers at an Associate level and require the ASWB Associate examination. The Associate examination is identical to the ASWB Bachelors examination, but the Associate examination requires a lower score in order to pass.

Masters

The Social Work ASWB® Masters Exam Guide: A Comprehensive Guide for Success, Second Edition

Test focuses on knowledge acquired while obtaining a Master's degree in Social Work (MSW). There is no postgraduate supervision needed.

Clinical

The Social Work ASWB® Clinical Exam Guide: A Comprehensive Guide for Success, Second Edition

Test focuses on knowledge acquired while obtaining a Master's degree in Social Work (MSW). It is usually taken by those with postgraduate supervised experience.

Advanced Generalist

The Social Work ASWB® Advanced Generalist Exam Guide: A Comprehensive Guide for Success, Second Edition

Test focuses on knowledge acquired while obtaining a Master's degree in Social Work (MSW). It is usually taken by those with postgraduate supervised nonclinical experience.

Dawn Apgar, PhD, LSW, ACSW, has helped thousands of social workers across the country pass the ASWB® examinations associated with all levels of licensure. In recent years, she has consulted in numerous states to assist with establishing licensure test preparation programs.

Dr. Apgar has done research on licensure funded by the American Foundation for Research and Consumer Education in Social Work Regulation and has served as chairperson of her state's social work licensing board. She is a past President of the New Jersey Chapter of NASW and has been on its National Board of Directors. In 2014, the Chapter presented her with a Lifetime Achievement Award. Dr. Apgar has taught in both undergraduate and graduate social work programs and has extensive direct practice, policy, and management experience in the social work field.

Social Work ASWB® Masters Practice Test

170 Questions to Identify Knowledge Gaps

Second Edition

Dawn Apgar, PhD, LSW, ACSW

SPRINGER PUBLISHING COMPANY

Springer Publishing Company, LLC
11 West 42nd Street
New York, NY 10036
www.springerpub.com

Acquisitions Editor: Debra Riegert
Compositor: diacriTech

ISBN: 978-0-8261-4722-6
ebook ISBN: 978-0-8261-4723-3

20 21 22 / 13 12

Publisher's Acknowledgment: Springer Publishing Company recognizes that the ASWB® is a registered service mark of the Association of Social Work Boards and has applied this service mark to the first mention of the association in each of the chapters in the book and its cover. The Association of Social Work Boards neither sponsors nor endorses this product.

The author and the publisher of this Work have made every effort to use sources believed to be reliable to provide information that is accurate and compatible with the standards generally accepted at the time of publication. The author and publisher shall not be liable for any special, consequential, or exemplary damages resulting, in whole or in part, from the readers' use of, or reliance on, the information contained in this book. The publisher has no responsibility for the persistence or accuracy of URLs for external or third-party Internet websites referred to in this publication and does not guarantee that any content on such websites is, or will remain, accurate or appropriate.

Library of Congress Cataloging-in-Publication Data
Names: Apgar, Dawn, author. | Association of Social Work Boards.
Title: Social work ASWB masters practice test : 170 questions to identify
    knowledge gaps / Dawn Apgar, PhD, LSW, ACSW.
Description: Second edition. | New York, NY : Springer Publishing Company, LLC, [2018]
Identifiers: LCCN 2017034878 | ISBN 9780826147226 | ISBN 9780826147233 (ebook)
Subjects: LCSH: Social workers—Certification—United States. | Social
    service—United States—Examinations—Study guides. | Social
    service—United States—Examinations, questions, etc.
Classification: LCC HV40.52 .A743 2018 | DDC 361.3076—dc23 LC record available at
https://lccn.loc.gov/2017034878

Contact us to receive discount rates on bulk purchases.
We can also customize our books to meet your needs.
For more information please contact: sales@springerpub.com

Publisher's Note: **New and used products purchased from third-party sellers are not guaranteed for quality, authenticity, or access to any included digital components.**

Printed in the United States of America.

To Bill, Ryan, and Alex

You remind me what is important, support me so I can do it all, and always inspire me to be a better person

Contents

Introduction

Despite social workers' best efforts to study for and pass the Association of Social Work Boards (ASWB®) examinations for licensure, they can encounter difficulties answering questions correctly that can ultimately lead to challenges in passing. Social workers who struggle with standardized test taking or have failed the ASWB examinations find themselves at a loss in finding resources to assist them in identifying the mistakes they made and strategies for correcting these errors. The focus of test preparation courses and guides is usually the review of the relevant content and supplying some study and test-taking tips. However, when these resources do not result in passing the ASWB examinations, social workers do not know where to turn for help.

Often, social workers will turn to taking practice tests in an effort to gauge their readiness for the ASWB examinations. In addition, they will try to use them to identify gaps in knowledge and errors in problem solving that prevent desired outcomes. Such an approach is understandable because there has been a void in available diagnostic resources. However, for several reasons, use of existing practice examinations is not usually helpful.

First, it is difficult to identify specific content that is used by test developers to formulate actual questions. For example, many practice tests do not provide the rationales for the correct and incorrect answers. In addition, they usually do not let social workers know which specific ASWB® content areas were being tested (e.g., Human Development, Diversity, and Behavior in the Environment; Assessment and Intervention Planning; Interventions With Clients/Client Systems; or Professional Relationships, Values, and Ethics). In addition, the ASWB competencies and corresponding Knowledge, Skills, and Abilities statements (KSAs) that form the basis for question development are also not included. Thus, when questions are answered incorrectly, social workers do not know which knowledge in the ASWB content areas, competencies, and KSAs is lacking so they can go back and review relevant source materials.

Based on a practice analysis conducted by ASWB, which outlines the content to be included on the exam, content areas, competencies, and KSAs are created. Content areas are the broad knowledge areas that are measured by each exam. The content areas structure the content for exam construction and score reporting purposes. When receiving exam scores, failing candidates are given feedback on their performance on each content area of the exam. Competencies describe meaningful *sets* of abilities that are important to the job of a social worker within each content area. Finally, KSAs structure the content of the exam for item development purposes. The KSAs provide further details about the nature and range of exam content that is included in the competencies. Each KSA describes a discrete knowledge component that is the basis for individual exam questions that may be used to measure the competency.

Having ASWB content areas, competencies, and KSAs identified is critical in order to make practice tests useful for diagnosing knowledge weaknesses. The following example illustrates the usefulness of having this material explicitly stated.

SAMPLE QUESTION

A social worker at a community mental health agency is doing a home visit to a client as he has not gotten his medication refilled as prescribed. The social worker learns that he has not been taking it for several weeks due to a belief that it is not helping alleviate his thought to "just end things." In order to assist the client, the social worker should FIRST:

- **A.** Accompany the client to his next appointment with the psychiatrist to see if another medication can be prescribed
- **B.** Explain to the client the importance of taking the medication as prescribed
- **C.** Conduct a suicide risk assessment
- **D.** Ask the client if he has suggestions for other strategies that may assist him

ANSWER

1. C

Rationale

Social workers have an ethical duty to respect and promote the right of clients to self-determination. However, there are times when **social workers' responsibility to the larger society** or specific legal obligations supersedes their commitment to respecting clients' decisions or wishes. These instances are when, *in the social workers' professional judgment*, clients' actions or potential actions pose a serious, foreseeable, and imminent risk to themselves (including the risk of suicide) or others (in general or aimed at identifiable third parties—duty to warn).

The client's thoughts to "just end things" may be an indicator of suicide risk. The social worker should FIRST assess the degree of risk that is present to determine whether the client is safe without use of the medication and can wait to discuss his concerns with his psychiatrist at a future appointment or needs to be treated immediately, voluntarily or involuntarily.

Knowledge Area

Unit II—Assessment and Intervention Planning (Content Area); Assessment Methods and Techniques (Competency); The Indicators and Risk Factors of the Client's/Client System's Danger to Self and Others (KSA)

If this answer was missed, social workers need the rationale for the correct response choice in order to identify the need to review materials related to assessment and intervention planning, which is the content area being assessed. Specifically, this question focused on determining competency with regard to identifying indicators of client danger to self or others (KSA). Reviewing the risk factors and signs associated with suicide would be a useful place to start. In addition, refined literature searches on behavioral, emotional, and psychological warning signs would produce more targeted information to fill this information gap.

Most practice tests will not help direct social workers toward these resources as they do not provide the ASWB content areas, competencies, and KSAs being tested. They also do not give valuable information on the topics as a way for social workers to understand the rationales for the correct answers and why the others are incorrect.

Second, practice tests rarely explicitly identify the test-taking strategies that must be used in order to select the correct answers from the others provided. Even when rationales are provided on practice tests, the test-taking strategies that should be generalized to other questions are often not explicitly stated. This void makes it difficult for social workers to see problems that they may be having in problem solving, outside of content gaps.

For example, in the sample question, social workers must be keenly aware of the client's thoughts to "just end things" as delineated by quotation marks. These thoughts may be an indication of suicide risk.

There is also a qualifying word—FIRST—used, which is capitalized in the question. The use of this qualifying word indicates that more than one of the provided response choices may be correct, but selecting the one that precedes the others is what is being asked. When clients are potentially suicidal, social workers must FIRST assess for risk.

This tool was developed to assist social workers in identifying their knowledge gaps and difficulties in problem solving by providing critical information including the knowledge area being assessed and the test-taking strategies required in order to answer questions correctly.

Social workers should use this diagnostic practice test to identify:

- Question wording that is important to selecting correct answers
- Key social work concepts that are being assessed
- Useful problem-solving strategies and themes
- Mistakes in logic
- Content areas, competencies, and/or KSAs that require additional study

This test is not intended to be a study guide, but does contain important social work content related to the KSAs. This diagnostic practice test helps social workers who are struggling to find answers about what mistakes they are making and what they need to study more. It can be used in conjunction with existing study guides that provide an overview of needed social work material, such as the second edition of *Social Work ASWB® Masters Exam Guide: A Comprehensive Guide for Success* by this author.

Social workers must understand their learning styles and use available resources to fill in existing content gaps through the use of visual, auditory, and/or hands-on materials. Most social work content is available for little or no cost. There is no need to purchase expensive products as there are many educational materials available for free. However, it is important that social workers make sure that these resources are rooted in the values and knowledge base of the profession, as well as produced by those providing legitimate instruction. There are no tricks or fast facts for the examination that can replace learning and understanding a topic. The application of material requires being able to relate it to various case scenarios or vignettes.

Recommendations for Using This Practice Test

Actual ASWB test results are based on 150 scored items and an additional 20 questions that are not scored because they are being piloted. These pilot items are intermixed with the scored ones and not distinguished in any way. Social workers never find out which ones are scored and which questions are being piloted.

In an effort to make this diagnosis as similar to the examination as possible, it contains 170 questions, the same number as the actual exam, proportionately distributed within the four domains—Human Development, Diversity, and Behavior in the Environment (46 questions); Assessment and Intervention Planning (41 questions); Intervention With Clients/Client Systems (41 questions); and Professional Relationships, Values, and Ethics (42 questions). These proportions mirror the distribution of questions across these domains on the actual ASWB® examination.

The best way for social workers to use this practice test is to:

- Complete it after you have studied yet are still feeling uncertain about problem areas
- Finish it completely during a 4-hour block of time as a way of gauging fatigue and length of time it will take to complete the actual examination
- Avoid looking up the answers until after you have finished completely

■ Generate a listing of content areas in which you experienced problems and use it as the basis of a study plan employing other source materials to further review the concepts

■ Generalize the test-taking strategies for future use on the actual examination

This practice test is to be used as a diagnostic tool, so social workers should not worry about getting incorrect answers, but should view them as learning opportunities to avoid common pitfalls and pinpoint learning needs. On the actual ASWB examination, the number of questions that social workers need to correctly answer generally varies from 93 to 106 of the 150 scored items. Since this diagnostic practice test is 170 items, 20 questions would need to be randomly removed (5 from Unit I, 5 from Unit II, 5 from Unit III, and 5 from Unit IV) to determine if the overall number correct falls into this range.[1] Since many social workers who do not pass find themselves "just missing" these pass points, the value of identifying content gaps and difficulties in problem solving is tremendous because it can result in additional correct answers on the actual test.

---

[1] Because different test takers receive different questions, raw scores on the actual exam—the actual number of correctly answered questions—go through an "equating process" to make sure that those receiving more difficult questions are not placed at a disadvantage. Equating adjusts the number of items needed to answer correctly up or down depending on the difficulty levels. This diagnostic practice test has not gone through the equating process, which is why the number of correct answers needed to "pass" using ASWB standards cannot be determined.

170-Question Diagnostic Practice Test

1. Upon intake, a client who professes to be "health conscious" reports that she smokes cigarettes. When asked by the social worker if she is aware of the health risks associated with smoking, the client states that "the reports are filled with misinformation and the hazards are not that great." The client's assertion MOST likely results from:

   A. Cognitive dissonance
   B. Metacommunication
   C. Displacement
   D. Intellectualization

2. A social worker who retired more than a year ago from private practice runs into a former client whom she has not seen in years. The former client received grief counseling from the social worker for several years after her mother died. The former client also recently retired and suggests that the social worker join a local group for retirees to which she belongs. The social worker, who has been looking for ways to stay active, agrees to attend the next meeting. The social worker's actions are:

   A. Justified as she has not served the client for years
   B. Unprofessional because the social worker is using the former client for her own gain
   C. Problematic as she is knowingly creating a conflict of interest or dual relationship
   D. Acceptable because the interaction will be in a group context and not intimate in nature

3. A client reports that he was recently in a serious accident at work that has resulted in limitations in his mobility. In this situation, a social worker should FIRST:

   A. Assist with making a workers' compensation claim to help the client pay for medical expenses and lost wages
   B. Refer the client for vocational rehabilitation services to determine whether modifications are needed to his home and work environments
   C. Discuss the psychological impacts of trauma and disability that will need to be addressed in order for the client to make a full recovery
   D. Conduct a biopsychosocial assessment to determine the impact of the client's physical changes on his other life domains

4. Which is NOT an appropriate reason for a social worker to conduct a needs assessment?

   A. Detection of barriers preventing service or resource access
   B. Identification of clients impacted by problems that require services or resources
   C. Documentation of critical needs identified by service agencies
   D. Recognition of an ongoing social problem

5. Universalism as a basis of social allocation is BEST defined as:

   A. Resources that adequately meet all existing needs of clients
   B. Benefits made available to an entire population as a basic right
   C. Services that are consistently provided regardless of geographic locale
   D. Distribution of assistance that disproportionately benefits those in power

6. Which of the following is TRUE about child sexual abuse?

   A. Perpetrators are male in the majority of reported cases of sexual abuse.
   B. Sexual abuse is a cultural or socioeconomic problem.
   C. Most victims do not know their perpetrators prior to the sexual abuse first occurring.
   D. Victims of sexual abuse will have physical signs of their abuse.

7. Absent client consent to release records or a recognized legal exception, what ethical duty do social workers have with regard to releasing client information?

   A. Social workers must release information only if subpoenaed to do so.
   B. Social workers must provide only material that they feel will directly benefit clients.

    C. Social workers must keep all records confidential while clients are living.

    D. Social workers must claim privilege on behalf of clients.

8. When children are not emancipated, their ability to legally consent to treatment may depend on all of the following EXCEPT:

    A. Their age

    B. The services requested

    C. Their service utilization history

    D. The state in which they are seeking assistance

9. A school social worker is contacted by the parents of a 12-year-old boy as they would like to see his educational records based on the belief that they contain inaccurate information about his academic achievements. Under federal law, these records are:

    A. Public information, making them accessible to any party for justified purposes

    B. Open to inspection and review by the parents at any time

    C. Available to the parents only if the assent of the child is obtained prior to their release

    D. Strictly confidential, only to be released to the parents if ordered by a court

10. Which of the following behaviors is NOT an indicator that a client is resistant or lacks readiness to fully participate in services?

    A. Engaging in small talk about irrelevant topics

    B. Regularly missing or being late for appointments

    C. Limiting the amount of information revealed about the problem

    D. Asking in detail about confidentiality practices and procedures

11. An example of cultural blindness in social work practice is:

    A. Viewing the needs of all clients, not just those in the dominant culture, as equally important

    B. Identifying cultural norms that have impacted on clients' presenting problems

    C. Advocating for the rights of all clients regardless of culture, race, and/or ethnicity

    D. Applying helping approaches universally to all clients without considering cultural diversity

12. Which criterion does not need to be met for social workers to be able to terminate clients for nonpayment of fees?

    A. The clinical and other consequences of the nonpayment have been discussed with clients.
    B. The financial contractual arrangements have been made clear to clients, preferably in writing.
    C. Social workers have used sliding scales to make fees affordable for clients.
    D. Clients do not pose imminent danger to self or others.

13. A client is upset about the breakup of his marriage. He feels distraught and does not think that he will ever have another intimate relationship. In this situation, the social worker can BEST demonstrate empathy by:

    A. Discussing similar events in the social worker's life that have been resolved successfully
    B. Telling the client that many people in this situation feel similarly
    C. Listening attentively while looking at the client as he describes his feelings
    D. Helping the client to find ways to cope with his emotions during this difficult time

14. A social worker receives a request for "all mental health records" of a client. The social worker maintains psychotherapy notes of sessions in a separate locked location. After reviewing all of the records and notes, the client signs a single authorization releasing all mental health information. Based on this consent, the social worker should:

    A. Provide copies of both the record and psychotherapy notes
    B. Advise the client that the decision is poor and no information should be sent
    C. Send a summary of diagnoses, treatment dates, and fees collected
    D. Release only the information in the record and not the psychotherapy notes

15. A social worker has just implemented a new agency practice to resolve an existing ethical issue. According to the principles of ethical problem solving, the social worker should NEXT:

    A. Ensure that the new practice is formally incorporated in agency documents and trainings
    B. Examine the key social work values and principles that support the new procedure

    C. Explore if other practices need to be updated to incorporate new trends in the field

    D. Monitor the procedure to see if the problem is resolved and any new concerns emerge

16. A social worker organizes and joins a group of community members for a "sit in" at a government building. This demonstration, which is against the law, aims to put political pressure on officials to act on pending legislation. The strategy employed is known as:

    A. Community advocacy

    B. Indirect casework

    C. Civil disobedience

    D. Social planning

17. A client who was hospitalized for hallucinations is being discharged with medication to address these symptoms. The client is MOST likely being prescribed:

    A. Paxil (paroxetine)

    B. Tegretol (carbamazepine)

    C. Risperdal (risperidone)

    D. Klonopin (clonazepam)

18. A female social worker is part of a multidisciplinary team working with a Muslim male client. When interacting with the client, the social worker should be aware that physical touch is generally:

    A. Prohibited in all public and nonpublic interactions unless occurring between spouses

    B. Limited to handshaking if occurring between members of the opposite gender

    C. Encouraged to demonstrate empathy and compassion in all formal and informal relationships

    D. Not accepted between members of the opposite gender unless they are nonpublic interactions between close family members

19. A client is very concerned about information that has been shared with a social worker over the years being "used against her." The client is trying to be appointed guardian of her elderly father by the court despite the objections of her siblings. In this situation, the social worker should:

    A. Advise the client to work out the disagreement with her siblings amiably so they can provide mutual support to one another during this difficult time

    B. Suggest that the client speak to a lawyer to better understand what is admissible in such proceedings

    C. Ask the client what has been revealed that causes her concern so that the social worker can better understand why she is fearful

    D. Review confidentiality procedures and their limits in order to alleviate the client's concerns

20. A client is upset because a boy whom she recently kissed broke up with her. The client states that she does not understand why the breakup occurred as the kiss indicated that he had strong feelings toward her. The social worker explains that kissing may not have the same meaning for the boy. The social worker's statement is rooted in which theoretical perspective?

    A. Self psychology

    B. Symbolic interactionism

    C. Operant conditioning

    D. Object relations

21. A social worker is assisting a community to develop a program to treat adolescent drug addiction. Neighborhood citizens are very concerned as several youth have died due to overdoses in the last few weeks. In order to ensure that services are developed using the principles of social justice, the social worker should:

    A. Advocate for community members to have decision-making power in the planning process

    B. Use evidence-based practices as the foundation for treatment of this hard-to-serve population

    C. Integrate substance use and mental health treatment due to the prevalence of co-occurrence of these disorders

    D. Gain support from community leaders to increase the likelihood of successful implementation

22. Within social work practice, action research is distinguished from other scientific methods due to the:

    A. Mandate that investigation occur as urgent injustice is currently occurring

    B. Commitment of resources to take action on the findings in order to realize change

    C. Focus on social problems that have been identified as needing immediate attention

    D. Processes of collaborative problem solving and inquiry occurring simultaneously

23. A client is discharged from the hospital with a medication that must be taken four times a day. Which of the following abbreviations will appear on the client's medication order?

    A. qid
    B. prn
    C. bid
    D. qh

24. A client who is making substantial progress in treatment learns that her insurance has authorized only two more sessions. The social worker and client feel that additional therapy is needed in order to achieve stated treatment goals. In order to BEST assist the client, the social worker should:

    A. Identify the most critical topics to be discussed so they can be covered in the remaining sessions

    B. Inform the client of the insurance company's appeals process while providing support through the process

    C. Provide the insurance company with information on additional problems experienced by the client and services needed in order to justify continued payment

    D. Set an affordable fee that the client can pay privately once the insurance company stops paying

25. A decision about whether a social worker must disclose privileged information without a client's consent is NOT legally influenced by:

    A. Relevant statutes
    B. Professional experience
    C. Judicial opinion
    D. State and federal regulations

26. A child who is receiving services from a child protection agency due to physical abuse is referred to a school social worker because of bullying behavior. In the last month, the child has hit several of his peers while in school. The child is MOST likely using which defense mechanism?

    A. Compensation
    B. Incorporation

    C. Rationalization

    D. Displacement

27. A client is discouraged as her siblings have received many academic awards and she is a very poor student. The client works hard to get the lead in the high school play in order to earn the praises of others. This client is using the defense mechanism of:

    A. Sublimation

    B. Compensation

    C. Substitution

    D. Conversion

28. A school social worker receives a referral for a fifth-grade girl who is having trouble getting along with classmates. This behavior may result in her being placed in a resource room with one-on-one instruction. The nature of the problem is BEST understood by:

    A. Reviewing her past academic records

    B. Determining whether similar behavior is occurring in the home

    C. Observing classroom interactions between the girl and her peers

    D. Interviewing the child to find out her thoughts about being moved

29. When intense subgroup attraction interferes with group functioning, the social worker should employ all of these strategies EXCEPT:

    A. Examining whether the group as a whole is sufficiently attractive to members

    B. Engaging in exercises that separate subgroup members

    C. Promoting norms that emphasize group cohesion

    D. Dismissing subgroup members from the larger group

30. Ecomaps are BEST defined as visual tools to:

    A. Understand where natural resources are scarce and conservation must occur

    B. Explore clients' relationships with other people and entities in their environments

    C. Guide environmental justice advocacy efforts on the micro, mezzo, and macro levels

    D. Show sources of power within all types of environmental systems

31. A client reports that she was recently fired from her job based upon her religious beliefs. She is intimidated by the thought of taking action against her former employer as she does not believe that she will be successful in fighting the bias against her. She feels depressed and hopeless. In formulating treatment goals, the social worker should:

    A. Identify whether antidepressant medication may be needed
    B. Determine the impacts of her current emotional state
    C. Complete a suicide risk assessment
    D. Assist the client in fighting the discriminatory practices of the agency

32. A social worker is supervising a student intern and would like to ensure that the intern considers the social work core values in all agency decision making. The BEST method for the student to learn about these values is to:

    A. Read the agency policies and procedures manual
    B. Speak to employees of the agency about their experiences
    C. Review the professional code of ethics
    D. Receive regular supervision to discuss client issues and progress

33. A social worker completes a sexual history with an adolescent client. The social worker asks about the number of partners that she has had and the methods, if any, that she is using to prevent pregnancy and sexually transmitted diseases. The social worker then puts the sexual history in the client's file. The social worker's supervisor would consider this sexual history to be inappropriate because it:

    A. Included protected health information about sexually transmitted diseases
    B. Was placed in an adolescent client's file instead of stored separately
    C. Lacked important information about the gender of her partners and sexual practices
    D. Should have been completed by another professional who is licensed in this area

34. During acculturation, which of the following statements describes the responsibilities of those in the dominant and nondominant cultures?

    A. Individuals in both the majority and minority have an equal responsibility to change in order to work together cooperatively.
    B. Individuals in majority groups must teach those in the minority about their customs and traditions.

    C. Individuals in the minority must advocate for inclusion to ensure equal access to societal rewards by those in the majority.

    D. Individuals in the minority must decide which majority practices they will follow for integration to occur.

35. A social worker who was recently hired by a large agency sees that services are delivered in a very bureaucratic manner with employees at the lowest organizational levels having their tasks overseen by supervisors who, in turn, are overseen by managers. There is also a strong expectation that workers perform tasks according to specific procedures designed to maximize levels of service. This agency is MOST likely operating according to the principles of:

    A. Human relations theory

    B. Systems theory

    C. Scientific management theory

    D. Contingency theory

36. Which statement is NOT true about the distinction between grief and depression?

    A. Painful feelings caused by grief come in waves while mood and ideation, which are almost constantly negative, are associated with depression.

    B. Feelings of worthlessness, suicidal ideas, and impairment of overall function are symptoms of grief rather than depression.

    C. When grief and depression coexist, grief is more severe and prolonged than grief without depression.

    D. In grief, self-esteem is usually preserved while corrosive feelings of worthlessness and self-loathing are more common when depressed.

37. Asking clients closed-ended, instead of open-ended, questions assists social workers with:

    A. Ensuring that clients are in charge of the helping process

    B. Focusing the social work interview

    C. Learning how client experiences have been perceived

    D. Using positive regard in the problem-solving approach

38. A social work administrator agrees to meet with a group of employees who are concerned about the impact of an agency policy on client services. After expressing appreciation to the employees for raising the issue, the social worker should NEXT:

A. Explain the reasons why the policy was originally implemented
B. Identify alternatives which can address the concerns raised
C. Determine the nature and length of the employees' distress
D. Obtain information from clients on the issue to see whether they view it as a concern

39. A client who is a member of an American Indian tribe states that he is "two-spirited" during an assessment. This information likely means that he:

A. Recognizes the impact of elders, including deceased relatives, on his life circumstances
B. Views the good and bad in his own decisions and actions, as well as those of others
C. Has encountered difficulties assimilating into broader society due to ethnic differences
D. Identifies both masculine and feminine parts of his sexual, gender, and/or spiritual identity

40. A couple in their mid-50s makes an appointment to see a social worker due to recent sexual dysfunction. During the first session, they report that they have recently had a lot of life changes due to their children entering college. The husband reports decreased sexual desire that has made physical intercourse difficult. In this situation, the social worker should FIRST:

A. Explore how having their children leave the house has affected their relationship
B. Determine when changes in their sexual activities first began
C. Refer the couple for physical examinations to rule out medical etiology
D. Arrange to meet with each spouse separately to find out if other issues exist

41. The PRIMARY criterion for selecting an intervention modality should be that it is:

A. Applied consistently to ensure reliability of service provision
B. Sanctioned and monitored by agency administration to ensure quality
C. Approved by third-party payers so that reimbursement for services will occur
D. Supported by research and professional values for treating the presenting problem

42. A social worker observes a steady decline in a client's mobility as he has refused to get a needed hip replacement. The doctor has assured the client that the surgery is low risk and will greatly enhance his quality of life. In order to best assist the client, the social worker should:

   A. Urge the client to get the surgery based upon the doctor's advice
   B. Speak to the client's family so that they can assist in helping the client change his mind
   C. Provide the client with materials that clearly articulate the benefits of having the procedure
   D. Assist the client to prioritize his concerns about having the surgery

43. What is the MOST important factor in the development of an effective helping relationship?

   A. Social worker's training and experience in working with similar client problems
   B. Client's willingness to view a social worker as a resource for change
   C. Nonverbal and verbal communication between a social worker and client
   D. Agency policies that clearly articulate the roles of both a social worker and client

44. Echolalia is associated with which of the following *DSM-5* diagnoses?

   A. Catatonia
   B. Autism Spectrum Disorder
   C. Bipolar Disorder
   D. Major Depression

45. A hospital social worker is working with a client who has suffered a traumatic brain injury that has damaged his cerebellum. The social worker would expect this impairment to affect his:

   A. Problem-solving abilities
   B. Coordination and balance
   C. Feelings and emotions
   D. Breathing and heart rate

46. A social worker attends a new-employee orientation that reviews the mission of the agency and its programs. It is designed to assist

employees in their work with clients. The supervisor documents attendance in the social worker's personnel file. Which function of supervision is represented by the supervisor's action?

A. Supportive
B. Bureaucratic
C. Educational
D. Administrative

47. A social work supervisor finds that a supervisee is having trouble advocating for the needs of clients when participating in interdisciplinary team meetings. The supervisee states that he often feels intimidated speaking in front of other members of the team and bringing up his concerns. In order to best assist the supervisee, the social worker should:

A. Accompany the supervisee to future team meetings to provide support
B. Explain the importance of representing the client's perspective in team meetings
C. Role play team meetings with the supervisee to strengthen his assertiveness skills
D. Clarify the social worker's role within the team so he understands his unique contribution

48. A hospital social worker will be working with a woman who is getting a percutaneous endoscopic gastrostomy (PEG) tube. Based on this information, it is likely that the needs of the client will focus on:

A. Improving mobility for maximum ambulation and independence
B. Ensuring sufficient specialized liquid nutrition for ongoing sustenance
C. Enhancing cardiopulmonary functioning to increase oxygen intake
D. Monitoring urine output to guarantee waste is being eliminated from the body

49. A client in his early 20s meets with a social worker to discuss his decision to have predictive testing for Huntington's disease, which occurs later in life. It is not curable, but he thinks it will be useful in making decisions about getting married and starting a family. He states that he does not want anyone to have to care for him so he would not get married or have children if it is found that he will

eventually develop the disease. In order to best assist the client, the social worker should:

A. Discourage him from undergoing testing because marrying and having children are important life tasks

B. Ask him about his risk factors so that a better recommendation about testing can be made

C. Encourage testing so that he can make informed choices now and in the future

D. Discuss the implications of the testing for him and his family

50. A client seeing a social worker for weekly counseling for her anxiety feels that her symptoms are worsening. She would like to be voluntarily hospitalized to address her problem, but has been told by her insurance company that inpatient services will not be covered since appropriate services can be delivered in the community. In order to formulate a treatment plan, the social worker should:

A. Assess her current symptoms so an appropriate level of care can be established

B. Obtain a listing of the criteria for medical necessity from the insurance carrier

C. Contact the inpatient program to see if charity care funding is available

D. Explain the medical necessity requirement for inpatient hospitalization

51. Hypomania can be characterized as:

A. Extreme manic episode with psychotic features

B. Inflation in mood that does not result in significant impairment in work or family/social life

C. Elevated mood that is subtle and not noticeable to family members or friends

D. Any manic episode that does not meet the diagnostic criteria for a mental disorder

52. A social worker has an involuntary client who has been court-ordered to receive counseling. Since intake, the client has expressed her belief that meeting with the social worker will not be helpful and has repeatedly threatened not to come in the future. During the next session, the social worker stops the client when she is complaining and says, "You are correct that talking with me does not appear to

be helpful and I don't think that you should come next week." The social worker's statement is an example of a:

A. Paradoxical directive
B. Cognitive distortion
C. Double bind
D. Manifest message

53. A client is referred to a social worker by her employer due to many absences. She is a single mother with three small children. Financial troubles have resulted in her home being placed in foreclosure. She has had many different jobs in the last few years with few lasting more than several months. In order to best assist this client, the social worker should FIRST:

A. Develop strategies to address issues that led to the work absences
B. Help the client to identify her underlying problems
C. Ascertain the client's earnings and expenses to find existing financial gaps
D. Determine if she qualifies for subsidized housing assistance

54. A client has been seeing a social worker to deal with the grief associated with the recent death of his elderly mother. The client lived with his mother for his entire life and was her primary caregiver just prior to her passing. The client informs the social worker that he has recently been diagnosed with cancer and will begin treatment immediately. The social worker should respond to this disclosure by:

A. Assessing whether current goals need to be altered given a change in his physical well-being
B. Adjusting his appointments in order to work around needed medical appointments
C. Mobilizing the client's natural support network to assist him during treatment
D. Reassuring him that there are many effective medical treatments for cancer

55. A client who is discriminated against due to his or her national origin and/or culture is being judged based on:

A. Nondominant ancestry
B. Race

C. Ethnicity
D. Minority status

56. A social worker is a field supervisor for a student in an agency. As her internship ends, the student confides to the social worker that she thinks that she could benefit from counseling to assist with some unresolved issues. The student would like to receive those services at the agency, preferably from the social worker. In this situation, the social worker should:

    A. Explore the reasons for the request as a method of professional development for the student
    B. Make an appointment for the student to see another social worker in the agency
    C. Inform the student that her request would violate professional boundaries and provide contact information for several other counseling agencies
    D. Agree to see the student for counseling after she completes all the requirements for the internship

57. Using the *DSM-5*, symptoms of Borderline Personality Disorder include all of the following EXCEPT:

    A. Marked impulsivity
    B. Obsessive tendencies
    C. Suicidal ideation
    D. Affective instability

58. A social worker is using a single-subject design to assess the impact of an intervention on client functioning. Prior to implementing the intervention, it is essential that the baseline measurements are:

    A. Decreasing
    B. Increasing
    C. Stable
    D. Variable

59. Reversal methods in single-subject research designs are unethical when:

    A. Baseline measurements have not occurred to determine clients' functioning prior to treatment
    B. Costs of treatments are very expensive given clients' financial situations

    C. Alternative treatments are available to clients to address presenting problems

    D. Withdrawal of treatment could result in clients' risk of harm

60. A social worker who has been helping a client for more than a year to deal more effectively with unconscious conflicts, including understanding how adverse childhood experiences have impacted on adult functioning, is MOST likely engaged in:

    A. Dialectic behavioral therapy

    B. Psychoanalysis

    C. Task-centered treatment

    D. Crisis intervention

61. A client uses racist language when describing an incident that occurred at work resulting in his termination. The social worker is helping the client locate another job as outlined in his service plan. While the comments are not related to the reasons why he was fired, they are deeply troubling and offensive to the social worker. The social worker feels that the client is ethnocentric and discriminates against others. In this situation, the social worker should:

    A. Modify the client's service plan to include increasing his knowledge about other cultures

    B. Process feelings with a supervisor while continuing to work with the client on locating employment

    C. Ask that the client be transferred to another social worker in the agency as it is impossible for the social worker to be objective in assisting this client

    D. Explore the underlying basis for the client's discriminatory attitudes

62. Which is NOT true of diagnosing Schizophrenia using the *DSM-5*?

    A. Symptoms must have been present for 6 months.

    B. Clients must exhibit at least two of the specified symptoms.

    C. Symptoms must be active for at least 1 month.

    D. The predominant symptom should define the subtype.

63. During an assessment, a client admits to regularly using drugs. When asked about attempts to seek treatment, the client states that he is

fearful of being "dope sick." Based on this statement, the client is MOST likely using:

A. Cocaine
B. Heroin
C. Marijuana
D. Stimulants

64. A social worker is contacted by a former client who received follow-up services from another agency after termination. The former client reports that his confidentiality was breached by this agency's staff and recommends that the social worker not refer to this agency in the future. In order to best assist, the social worker should:

A. Inform the agency director about the incident so that no referrals are made in the future
B. Educate the client about methods for filing licensing and other complaints
C. Ask the client if he would like to meet to discuss the situation further
D. Contact the follow-up agency staff to see if they are aware of the allegations

65. A social worker learns that his daughter's boyfriend has made an appointment to see him at his agency to discuss problems that the youth is having at home. The social worker contacts the boyfriend by phone and learns that fighting with his parents has become destructive. The boyfriend states that he trusts the social worker who has interacted with the boy and his parents for several months. In this situation, the social worker should:

A. Arrange to see the boy at the agency immediately to assess whether he is in danger
B. Offer suggestions that may be helpful before telling him that being served by the agency would pose a conflict
C. Explain prohibitions about meeting with the boy while providing names and contact information of other clinicians who can help
D. Recommend that the boy meet with the social worker's supervisor so that a determination can be made about how to best assist

66. A social worker who was recently hired as an executive director of a large mental health agency notices that the racial composition of the administration does not reflect that of the overall organizational staff. There are few individuals of color in leadership positions. In this situation, the social worker should FIRST:

    A. Encourage minority staff to apply for supervisory positions in the future
    B. Review the hiring process and practices of the agency
    C. Raise the concern at the next executive staff meeting
    D. Implement a program to attract and develop qualified job candidates of color

67. A client who attributes his illness to the "evil eye" is likely going to seek intervention through:

    A. Medication administration
    B. Educational group work
    C. Spiritual rituals
    D. Medical treatment

68. Positive regard is BEST defined as:

    A. Unconditional acceptance of clients' actions and feelings
    B. Acknowledgment of clients' strengths in assessments
    C. Constant reinforcement of clients' progress toward change
    D. Use of language that is free of pejorative terms

69. During the sixth session, a client becomes angry as she feels that a social worker is judging her behavior. She leaves abruptly, sending a written request several days later for a copy of her record. In the request, the client states that she will not be returning for services. The social worker does not feel that the information in the record would be harmful to the client, but is concerned about the abrupt termination. The social worker should:

    A. Tell the client that she can receive a copy only if she meets with the social worker again
    B. Provide a copy with an offer to assist with interpreting the information if needed
    C. Refuse to release the information as the client did not terminate appropriately
    D. Refer the client to her insurance company for all relevant service information

70. In recent weeks, a school social worker has developed a reasonable suspicion that a teenage student is being physically abused at home. When asking the child about the injuries, she reports child protective services has already interviewed her and found that "everything is fine." She states that she frequently gets injured in sports and that accounts for the cuts, scrapes, and bruises. In this situation, the social worker should:

    A. Report the suspicion immediately to the abuse hotline
    B. Monitor the situation to see if the signs continue when she is not engaged in sports
    C. Document the conversation in the student record
    D. Speak to a supervisor to determine if a report is still needed since child protective services has already investigated the allegations

71. Trauma bonding helps to explain why victims of abuse:

    A. Stay in relationships with their perpetrators
    B. Benefit from providing mutual support to one another
    C. Are likely to be abusers themselves
    D. Experience long-term psychological issues

72. Upon intake, a client reports that she would like to end her marriage, but it is prohibited in her religion. Her relationship with her husband has deteriorated over the years and he has told her that he is unwilling to change the situation. She feels "torn" between respecting her religious doctrine and her strong desire to leave her husband due to her unhappiness. She begins to cry and says, "Maybe I am just a bad person and supposed to live my whole life in misery." After reflecting the client's unhappy feelings, the social worker should NEXT:

    A. Use universalization to reassure the client that many people in her situation would feel this way
    B. Suggest that the client ask her husband if he would be willing to attend the next session as a way of determining if he is truly not willing to change
    C. Ask about the reasons that the client feels that she is being punished
    D. Help the client to identify and weigh all costs and benefits of leaving the marriage to assist in her decision making

73. Upon intake, a client tells a social worker that she cannot wait "to be told how to fix the problem." The client's statement is BEST representative of role:

    A. Ambiguity
    B. Reversal
    C. Conflict
    D. Complementarity

74. Which of the following is a dynamic risk factor for predicting the likelihood that perpetrators of sexual assault will reoffend?

    A. History of antisocial behavior
    B. Prior criminal history
    C. Use of force in prior assaults
    D. Abuse of substances

75. A social worker learns from a client that his wife's company is going to open a corporate site in a neighboring town that will dramatically increase property values in that area. The social worker tells this information to a colleague who is struggling financially and looking to invest in order to improve his situation. The social worker does not reveal the source of the information. In this situation, the social worker's actions are:

    A. Unethical, since the social worker used client information for a personal interest
    B. Ethical, since the social worker protected the confidentiality of the client
    C. Unethical, since the social worker cannot ensure that the colleague's investment will grow
    D. Ethical, since the social worker assisted a colleague and did not personally benefit from the information

76. A client confides to a social worker that she feels overwhelmed as she does not know where to begin addressing her many problems. She recently lost her job and has increasing demands being placed on her by her aging parents. Which of the following statements by the social worker will BEST convey empathy to the client?

    A. "We need to figure out together which problem is most pressing so we can come up with some strategies to help make things better."
    B. "It is a pity that you are experiencing so many problems at the same time, but we can work together to make your situation better."
    C. "Perhaps your job loss can be viewed as a positive as you will now have more time to meet the demands placed on you by your parents."

D. "Feeling overwhelmed is understandable given the issues that you have mentioned and your acknowledgment of these feelings is important."

77. Negative entropy in a system occurs when order is:

A. Decreased or eliminated
B. Maintained or increased
C. Directed at maladaptive purposes
D. Not controlled in any way

78. A client is experiencing severe financial hardship and working outside the home will greatly enhance the financial well-being of her family. She refuses to seek employment, citing the need to stay home and care for her small child as the reason. This decision will likely result in the eviction of her family in the near future. To effectively serve this client, the social worker must:

A. Locate affordable housing options in case the client needs to move quickly
B. Help the client to see the urgency of her situation
C. Acknowledge the effects of values on the client's attitudes and behaviors
D. Explore with the client employment opportunities that may be done at home

79. A family comes to see a social worker as their relationships have become strained. The teenage son has a group of good friends, but never brings them home and spends most of his time in his room. The parents engage in destructive patterns of fighting that usually result in them not speaking to each other. The family is experiencing financial difficulties due to underemployment and the son threatens to leave the house if "things do not get better." In order to best assist, the social worker should:

A. Model effective communication strategies that can be used by family members
B. Begin individual counseling with the son to assist him with dealing with the stress in the household
C. Help the parents look for additional work to alleviate their financial demands
D. Determine the outcomes desired by the family to assist them with prioritizing their concerns

80. Which Personality Disorder is MOST closely associated with attention-seeking behavior?

    A. Schizoid
    B. Histrionic
    C. Obsessive-Compulsive
    D. Narcissistic

81. A client meets with a social worker as he has been estranged from his parents and feels an emotional loss at not having a relationship with them. He reports that he would like to contact them and does not know why it has been so long since they talked. In order to discuss the available options, the social worker should FIRST:

    A. Ask the client about his family history and relationships before the split occurred
    B. Obtain more information about the last contact that the client had with his family
    C. Discuss the feelings of grief that have resulted from this family breakup
    D. Help the client contact his parents with the goal of meeting to discuss the situation

82. When doing treatment planning, a social worker asks a client, "If you woke up tomorrow and the change you want had happened, how would you know? What would be different?" These questions aim to:

    A. Help define the roles of the client and social worker in the planned change process
    B. Identify which interventions or techniques are best suited to address the problem
    C. Develop an evaluation strategy for monitoring progress
    D. Specify the concrete, observable goal which will be the focus of treatment

83. A client who was not selected valedictorian of her high school class describes herself "as a failure." Her grade point average was one of the highest in the graduating class, but she states that she is "a loser." This client is MOST likely using the cognitive distortion of:

    A. Jumping to conclusions
    B. Polarized thinking

    C. Catastrophizing

    D. Blaming

84. Which of the following statements BEST supports the need for mental health parity?

    A. Mental health treatment should be done by those with specialized education and experience.

    B. Mental health clinicians should be compensated commensurate with other health care professionals.

    C. Physical and mental health are not distinct as one is not possible without the other.

    D. Mental health screening is essential to detect psychological issues that may negatively impact on quality of life.

85. A social worker is hired by an organization to increase employee recruitment and retention due to a problem with staff turnover. Immediately upon starting, the social worker is pressured by the administrator to "get something in place." The BEST response for the social worker is to:

    A. Ask the administrator to identify what would be helpful

    B. Begin implementing some strategies that can be built upon incrementally over time

    C. Explain the pitfalls of not spending time understanding the root cause of the problem

    D. Inquire about getting assistance in designing a strategy that will be acceptable to all employees

86. During a session, a couple is told by a social worker to enact a problem so the social worker can observe interaction patterns and confront maladaptive behaviors. This social worker is MOST likely using which type of family therapy?

    A. Behavioral

    B. Bowenian

    C. Strategic

    D. Structural

87. Crisis intervention for clients who have just experienced trauma or violence is NOT focused on:

    A. Instilling hope that equilibrium and mastery of their current circumstances will occur

B. Implementing strategies to prevent further incidents from occurring in the future
C. Providing education about the events that occurred and the supports available to assist
D. Meeting immediate needs to ensure safety and further adverse outcomes

88. During an assessment, a social worker MOST likely obtains a family history from a client in order to:

A. Assist the client to see how problems can be multigenerational
B. Learn how the client's problems emerged and are influenced by his or her larger system
C. Reveal any past traumas that may have inhibited optimal functioning
D. Identify informal supports that can be helpful in addressing issues or problems

89. Self-actualization is BEST defined as:

A. Practicing mindfulness and staying in the moment by concentrating on tasks at hand
B. Monitoring progress toward goal attainment
C. Understanding the consequences of one's actions when engaging in maladaptive behavior
D. Realizing one's potential through personal growth and peak experiences

90. A 24-year-old client wants to move out of her family home and live with several friends. The social worker has concerns as the family provides a lot of financial and emotional support to the client. In addition, the friends are having problems paying the rent and have received an eviction notice. Though the client reports that her financial support toward the bills will address the issue, the social worker strongly believes that the client is making a poor choice. In this situation, the social worker should FIRST:

A. Acknowledge that the client has the right to make this decision
B. Determine the main reason that the client wants to move
C. Suggest that the client further discuss her decision with her family
D. Assess whether the client is being financially exploited by her friends

91. A client with Anorexia Nervosa, who believes her eating habits are normal, takes pride in her excessive exercise, and does not want to change, views her disorder as:

    A. Ego alien
    B. Ego-dystonic
    C. Ego-syntonic
    D. Egocentric

92. Which theory of prejudice explains hiring a worker of a minority group at a lower wage?

    A. Scapegoating
    B. Authoritarian personality
    C. Exploitation
    D. Normative

93. In the *DSM-5*, the multiaxial system was:

    A. Eliminated completely
    B. Expanded to include additional areas
    C. Reduced to only those of clinical priority
    D. Not changed from the *DSM-IV-TR*

94. Personality Disorders are MOST often diagnosed during:

    A. Middle childhood
    B. Puberty
    C. Infancy
    D. Adulthood

95. Couples counseling for those who are currently in battering relationships should:

    A. Accompany concurrent individual counseling of both parties to enhance effectiveness
    B. Occur only if there is assurance that no violence will occur after the onset of treatment
    C. Commence only after reporting requirements under "duty to warn" legislation are made clear
    D. Not be selected as a therapeutic intervention due to safety concerns

96. A social worker is promoting a social policy that will make treatment readily available to an underserved group. Given opposition from several

special interest groups, it is unlikely that the policy will be adopted as currently proposed. The social worker invites leaders from each of these groups to work on an amended policy, agreeing to incorporate elements of their competing proposals if they support the collaborative plan. The social worker is using which technique to influence social policy?

A. Cooptation
B. Advocacy
C. Planning
D. Mobilization

97. Upon intake, a social worker learns that a client needs to be referred to another agency for nutrition assistance. After verifying the need for the service, the social worker should NEXT:

A. Assist the client to gather all financial documents needed for an eligibility determination
B. Contact nutrition assistance programs to see if there are any openings
C. Determine which agencies, if any, already provide other services to the client
D. Educate the client about the importance of healthy eating in maintaining good health

98. Upon intake, a social worker learns that a client has been successfully managing her Bipolar Disorder for several years. The client is MOST likely using which of the following interventions?

A. Psychopharmacology
B. Individual psychotherapy
C. Support group counseling
D. Peer recovery

99. A client is admitted to an inpatient setting for substance abuse detoxification. The social worker learns that the client is addicted to a prescription medication with a very short half-life. Based upon this information, the social worker can predict that the withdrawal symptoms will likely:

A. Increase significantly over time, peaking weeks or months after initial detox
B. Be life-threatening, needing careful medical monitoring to ensure health and safety

  C. Occur quickly after admission, causing the desire to use again to happen immediately
  D. Consist of psychological, rather than physical, effects which require psychopharmacological intervention

100. Social workers who use a humanistic approach:

  A. Promote scientific inquiry based in sound qualitative research methods
  B. Value the study of animals as knowledge generated can be applied to human behavior
  C. Acknowledge that people are basically good and have free will to make themselves better
  D. View objective reality as more important than subjective perception and understanding

101. Which is NOT explicitly stated as a social work core value in the professional code of ethics?

  A. Service
  B. Importance of human relationships
  C. Integrity
  D. Professional capacity

102. A social worker is meeting with a client who has a very different racial and cultural background from his own. What will be MOST critical in ensuring effective service delivery?

  A. Learning about the customs and traditions of the client's heritage
  B. Confirming that the client feels comfortable working with the social worker
  C. Understanding by the social worker of how such differences impact the problem-solving process
  D. Completing a thorough biopsychosocial–spiritual–cultural assessment to drive treatment planning

103. At about what age does Freud state that the superego begins to emerge?

  A. 6 months
  B. 5 years
  C. 16 years
  D. 10 years

104. Object permanence is BEST defined as:

   A. The need for a child to live in a stable home with caregivers who are consistent role models
   B. A behavioral technique used with a child to reinforce positive actions
   C. The ability of a child to understand that objects exist even if they cannot directly be sensed
   D. The belief that change will not occur in a child until the rewards of making the modification exceed the risks

105. A client who is a cancer survivor reports that she feels nauseous every time that she returns to the hospital where she received chemotherapy last year. The hospital is acting as a(n):

   A. Conditioned response
   B. Unconditioned stimulus
   C. Conditioned stimulus
   D. Unconditioned response

106. A social worker is designing a discharge plan for a client leaving the hospital. Due to a chronic medical condition, the client will need ongoing services to maintain his current functioning. The PRIMARY focus of discharge planning should be:

   A. Documenting the reasons for the current hospitalization and inpatient services delivered
   B. Providing education about the long-term effects and prognosis of the medical problem
   C. Ensuring continuity of care as the client moves from an inpatient to outpatient setting
   D. Addressing psychological and emotional needs associated with living with a chronic illness

107. Which component of a mental status exam is LEAST likely to be solely assessed through direct observation?

   A. Mood
   B. Appearance
   C. Speech
   D. Affect

108. A social work administrator is worried about the productivity of agency employees. Using human relations management theory, the social worker should motivate staff through the provision of:

    A. Increased wages
    B. Strengthened employee relationships
    C. Comprehensive medical and dental benefits
    D. More paid leave days

109. When a client who has successfully completed treatment is contacted by a social worker for follow-up, she requests a meeting to discuss a new presenting problem. In order to most appropriately address this situation, the social worker should:

    A. Facilitate a referral to a colleague as the client is experiencing a different presenting problem
    B. Explore with the client whether the request is related to difficulties with termination
    C. Schedule a session to see the client in person to do an assessment as soon as possible
    D. Ask the client more about the situation over the phone so that appropriate action can be taken

110. According to force field analysis, the status quo in organizations is promoted by which type of forces?

    A. Marginal
    B. Driving
    C. Permanency
    D. Restraining

111. A social worker is providing grief counseling to an older man whose wife recently died. During a session, the client becomes angry at his deceased wife for not attending to health concerns that he feels led to her death. The social worker gets upset by these emotions as her own mother's health is failing. In order to appropriately deal with these feelings, the social worker should:

    A. Acknowledge the emotion and discuss it later with a supervisor
    B. Attempt to calm the client so that the session can shift to another topic

C. Explain the situation to the client so he knows that the social worker understands how he feels
D. Tell the client that anger is a step in the grieving process and his emotions are typical

112. When acting as a mandatory reporter by reporting a client for child abuse, a social worker is PRIMARILY fulfilling which core human service function?

    A. Habilitation
    B. Social control
    C. Social care
    D. Rehabilitation

113. Cognitive behavioral techniques are NOT contraindicated for use with clients who are: *CBT is not*

    A. Psychotic
    B. Cognitively impaired
    C. Anorexic
    D. Suicidal

114. Grant-in-aid that provides state and local governments with a specified amount of funding to assist in addressing broad purposes is called a:

    A. Federal match
    B. Voucher program
    C. Categorical grant
    D. Block grant

115. An amicus brief is a:

    A. Document that aims to advise a court, submitted by a party not involved in the litigation
    B. Method for becoming certified as an expert prior to testifying in a court case
    C. Ruling by a court that client records will remain confidential and cannot be used as evidence
    D. Structured summary of progress made toward goal attainment by a court-mandated client

116. Which active listening skill is MOST effective in demonstrating that a social worker understands a client's perspective?

   A. Listening attentively without any verbal communication by the social worker
   B. Paraphrasing what a client says back to him or her using similar words and phrases
   C. Repeating a client's words back to him or her using the same phrases
   D. Reflecting what a client says back to him or her using the social worker's own words and sentence structure

117. A social worker who has been seeing a couple for conjoint therapy sessions can release a copy of their record when:

   A. Either party consents to its release
   B. Subpoenaed by the court
   C. Both parties consent to its release
   D. Requested by the insurance company of either party

118. Linguistic competence is BEST defined as:

   A. Conveying information in a manner that is easily understood by diverse audiences
   B. Having proficiency in speaking multiple languages
   C. Being able to read and write at a level that addresses basic needs
   D. Possessing oral communication abilities that exceed expressive writing skills

119. Psychological abuse is usually NOT characterized by:

   A. Unexplained bruises or abrasions
   B. Extreme humiliation or embarrassment
   C. Domination and control
   D. Hypercriticism or blame

120. A client who is a local contractor has been receiving substance abuse treatment for several months. He has made substantial progress and both the social worker and client believe that continued service is needed. However, the client's work hours have been substantially reduced and he no longer can pay his insurance copayment. The client suggests performing basic carpentry repairs as his

contribution to treatment. In order to meet the needs of the client, the social worker should:

A. Collect payment from the insurance company and waive the copayment for the client
B. Serve the client pro bono until he is able to pay his copayment
C. Ask the client to determine what would be a fair bartering arrangement
D. Provide him with self-help and other free resources to temporarily assist while he cannot pay

121. A social worker is conducting an intake with a client who is deaf. The client uses American Sign Language to communicate and a qualified interpreter is being used. The social worker sits across from the client at a table in the social worker's office. In order to effectively facilitate communication, the interpreter should be:

A. Standing next to the client across from the social worker
B. Sitting next to the client across from the social worker
C. Standing away from both the social worker and client
D. Sitting next to the social worker across from the client

122. A social worker has begun serving an 8-year-old girl who was recently removed from her parents' home due to physical abuse. The child has not mentioned the abuse or the subsequent removal despite being asked about her family situation. In this situation, the social worker should:

A. Tell the child that it is important to discuss her feelings with others
B. Ask her open-ended questions about the abuse so she can answer in her own words
C. Focus on discussion topics of interest to the child
D. Evaluate the severity of the abuse by gathering information from others involved in her care

123. Upon intake, a client informs a social worker that he abruptly stopped therapy after having received it for a long period of time. When asked about the reason, the client states that he does not want to talk about it and will not consent for his treatment records to be released from the prior provider. In response, the social worker should:

A. Inform the client that the records are needed for continuity of care

B. Ask the client why he is reluctant to discuss what has occurred in the past

C. Acknowledge to the client that consent for treatment and release of records are his decisions

D. Complete a detailed treatment history to determine if other such terminations have occurred in the past

124. "Use of self" is best defined as social workers:

A. Being aware of how their values, beliefs, experiences, and heritage influence work with clients

B. Monitoring how working with traumatized clients affects their own well-being

C. Employing the therapeutic alliance as the major agent of change in helping relationships

D. Putting the interests of clients above their own in order to provide objective feedback

125. A client states that his fear of dogs has prevented him from leaving his house most of the time. The social worker recommends that he accompany her to a local animal shelter so that he can be exposed to many dogs with her support. The behavioral technique used by the social worker is:

A. Extinction
B. Modeling
C. Aversion therapy
D. Flooding

126. Which intervention is MOST appropriate based on a client having a concrete cognitive–emotional–developmental style?

A. Mind–body complementary therapy
B. Behavioral intervention
C. Psychoanalysis
D. Dream analysis

127. Which of the following is TRUE about Dementia?

A. Many Dementias are progressive, meaning symptoms start out slowly and gradually get worse.

B. Dementia is a disease which is characterized by substantial deficits in activities of daily living.

C. All of the causes of Dementia are irreversible so services should not be focused on treatment.

D. Dementia is characterized by neurological malady, rather than physical damage to brain cells.

128. A social worker is part of a team conducting an ethics audit in an agency setting. The ethics audit is LEAST likely to reveal:

A. Improvements in morale which will result from implementing ethically sound procedures

B. Resources (time, financial, etc.) needed to improve agency practices

C. Internal and external policies that place workers and their clients at risk

D. Priorities of changes to be made based upon risks (high, moderate, and low) and resources

129. A social worker employed in a long-term care facility is helping a client who is creating an advance directive, including appointing a health care proxy. The social worker assists the client to consider potential scenarios, evaluate options for care, and cope with the emotions that are arising during the process. Once the documents are prepared, the client asks the social worker to sign them as a witness signatory. In this situation, the social worker should:

A. Sign the documents, as the social worker was critical in assisting with their preparation

B. Not sign the documents, as the social worker has no legal responsibility over the client's decisions

C. Sign the documents, as they are beneficial to ensuring the self-determination of the client

D. Not sign the documents, in order to avoid the appearance of a conflict

130. When obtaining informed consent from a client who is not literate, a social worker must:

A. Provide a detailed verbal explanation of service purpose, risks, limits, and so on

B. Get written authorization from an appointed guardian

C. Complete a competency evaluation to ensure comprehension

D. Obtain assent from the client and legal consent from an appropriate third party

131. A hospital social worker is planning for the discharge of a 10-year-old Hispanic/Latino boy. During his stay, she observes "familismo" present within the family unit. In order to meet this client's needs, the social worker should:

    A. Ensure that the boy's medical prognosis is understood by members of the immediate family
    B. Hold family meetings which are open to extended kin to discuss follow-up recommendations
    C. Include goals about family functioning and communication patterns in the discharge plan
    D. Determine which family member will be primarily responsible for the boy's care after discharge

132. A client has an initial meeting with a social worker as she is having problems dealing with her anxiety. In this meeting, the social worker will MOST likely not:

    A. Discuss the limits of confidentiality
    B. Discuss options for treatment
    C. Explain the helping process, including the role of the social worker
    D. Ask about the problem and the reasons for seeking help now

133. Behaviors which are the hardest to extinguish are those that result from:

    A. Consistent punishment
    B. Intermittent reinforcement
    C. Consistent reinforcement
    D. Intermittent punishment

134. Which is NOT a new diagnosis in the *DSM-5*?

    A. Hoarding Disorder
    B. Substance/Medication-Induced Obsessive-Compulsive and Related Disorder
    C. Trichotillomania
    D. Excoriation Disorder

135. When adapting an intervention for use with a different community, it is BEST for a social worker to understand the cultural beliefs and practices of the target group by:

A. Reviewing government and legislative documents
B. Speaking directly with members of the community
C. Reading newspaper articles about important events and issues
D. Spending time with key officials within the community

136. A client experiences rejection from her family after telling them that she is a lesbian and in a committed relationship with another woman. The client feels upset at her family's reaction and cannot believe that they would not be happy about her relationship. She feels lonely, stating that "no other family would act this way." In order to best address the client's isolation, the social worker should use:

A. Confrontation
B. Clarification
C. Universalization
D. Reflection

137. A social worker is the co-owner of a private mental health therapy practice with another social worker who passes away unexpectedly. In order to BEST manage the client records of the deceased partner, the social worker should:

A. Make them available to clients upon request while securely maintaining them for any period specified by law
B. Immediately destroy them to ensure confidentiality
C. Send them via certified mail to clients so they can be shared, if desired, with subsequent treatment professionals
D. Review them to see if immediate action is needed, such as making appointments for ongoing treatment

138. Munchausen syndrome by proxy is defined as a:

A. Metabolic condition that impairs physical functioning if not managed through diet and exercise
B. Progressive cognitive decline in older adults that impairs short-term memory recall
C. Genetic disorder that results in significant developmental delays in all areas of functioning
D. Mental health problem in which adults make up or cause illnesses or injuries to those under their care

139. When engaged in cross-cultural communication with clients, social workers must recognize that nonverbal behaviors:

    A. Adhere to set standards that are universal regardless of race and/or ethnicity
    B. Require self-reflection to challenge assumptions that are culturally based
    C. Often come in conflict with expressive communication
    D. Must be thoroughly analyzed after verbal messages are clearly understood

140. During which step in the problem-solving process is a working alliance initiated?

    A. Planning
    B. Assessment
    C. Engagement
    D. Intervention

141. Which of the following is NOT true about elder abuse?

    A. There is currently a federal law protecting elders from abuse.
    B. Abandonment is considered a type of abuse.
    C. Social workers do not need to prove that abuse is occurring prior to reporting it.
    D. The majority of abusers are family members, most often adult children or spouses.

142. A young child states that he did not engage in a behavior as he "did not want to get in trouble." This child is MOST likely in which stage of moral development?

    A. Maintaining social order
    B. Obedience and punishment
    C. Social contract and individual rights
    D. Universal principles

143. A social worker receives a referral for a family that is having trouble meeting its basic needs. During the assessment, the social worker wants to identify external supports that may be available to assist this family. In order to learn about family members' relationships with community resources, the social worker should complete a(n):

A. Ecomap
B. Mental status exam
C. Genogram
D. Psychological assessment

144. Which of the following is NOT true about empathic communication between a social worker and client?

    A. Empathic communication includes both verbal and nonverbal messages.
    B. Empathic communication must be based on sound logic and reasoning.
    C. Empathic communication defuses anger that can be a barrier to progress.
    D. Empathic communication is based on respect and acceptance of feelings and experiences.

145. When a problem arises in interdisciplinary collaboration, a social worker is more likely to reach an acceptable solution by:

    A. Understanding the professional values and norms of the other disciplines involved
    B. Educating others about the ethical standards that guide the social work profession
    C. Evaluating each alternative option with his or her supervisor
    D. Ensuring that the decision-making process is clearly outlined to all members of the team

146. All of the following should be in client termination letters EXCEPT:

    A. Summaries of treatment provided
    B. Therapeutic information, including diagnoses
    C. Dates when treatment began and ended
    D. Reasons for termination

147. Which is NOT a reason that community participation is needed in the social planning process?

    A. Effective solutions to problems are more likely to be generated by community members.
    B. Most state and federal grants require community participation as a stipulation for funding.

C. Relationships are strengthened by members of the community working together.

D. Positive change will continue once community members see their accomplishments.

148. According to the *DSM-5*, clients with Bipolar I Disorder who have moods that simultaneously contain both manic/hypomanic and depressive symptoms should receive which specifier?

A. Not otherwise specified
B. With mixed features
C. With anxious distress
D. Other specified

149. A client is suing a social worker who he alleges collected payments for services which were not delivered. In order to address the matter ethically, the social worker should:

A. Inform the court that professional confidentiality standards prohibit discussing the services, including billing
B. Provide the court with copies of all treatment documents so the nature of and reasons for services delivered are known
C. Disclose billing records and redacted case notes that document the services in question
D. Contact the client to see if there are financial or other issues which may have motivated the lawsuit

150. A social worker who is providing mental health services to a 21-year-old client is contacted by her family. While the client sought treatment on her own, the services are paid for by her father's health insurance as she is enrolled in college. The family is extremely distraught as the client committed suicide over the weekend. They are trying to understand the reasons for her death and ask the social worker for a copy of her record. The social worker should:

A. Offer to meet with the family to discuss the client's problems instead of sending the file
B. Send a copy of the record to the father, whose insurance was paying for treatment
C. Ask them to put their request in writing so that it can be considered
D. Explain that confidentiality laws preclude releasing the file or discussing the client's treatment

151. A social worker is developing a service plan with an elderly client who has two main concerns. She faces eviction due to safety issues related to leaving the stove on for extended periods and she is estranged from her family, causing her to be isolated. The social worker writes that "the stove will be off consistently, when it is not in use." There are problems raised in supervision about this goal statement because:

    A. There is no time frame for evaluation to check progress or see whether it has been achieved.

    B. The focus of service should be on the isolation because it is adversely affecting her well-being.

    C. Other issues that may be causing the eviction are unknown.

    D. It does not include the actions that should occur if the goal is not achieved.

152. A social worker is contacted by an ex-girlfriend as she is having trouble dealing with the recent death of her father. She knows that the social worker facilitates a group on grief and would like to attend to discuss her feelings with others who have experienced similar loss. The ex-girlfriend has no concerns about seeking treatment with the social worker as the romantic relationship ended years ago, but contacted the social worker to make sure that her participation would not be distracting to the group. In this situation, the social worker should:

    A. Provide information about other qualified service providers who can address her concern

    B. Encourage individual counseling with the social worker to avoid questions by group members

    C. Facilitate group participation immediately given her pressing need for treatment

    D. Assess what has been done since the loss to address the grief experienced

153. The use of a biopsychosocial assessment to understand clients' presenting problems is supported by:

    A. Transpersonal theory

    B. Rational choice theory

    C. Systems theory

    D. Social learning theory

154. A social worker employed by a child welfare agency suspects that a child who is a member of an American Indian tribe is being physically abused by her mother and needs to be removed from her home while an investigation occurs. According to federal legislation, what unique factor must be considered in this situation?

   A. The administrative office of the child's tribe is involved in decision making.
   B. Children who are American Indian can be placed only with biological family members.
   C. Child abuse is defined differently for children who are American Indian.
   D. Reports of abuse by children who are American Indian do not require additional investigation.

155. When selecting intervention goals for clients who will be receiving time-limited treatment, the PRIMARY focus should be:

   A. Making sure there is ongoing access to services in the event the problem reoccurs
   B. Working to identify goals that are based on client priorities
   C. Identifying supports needed to sustain progress after treatment has concluded
   D. Ensuring that desired results can be achieved within the period specified

156. A client who has been talking to a social worker about ending her marriage states that she is upset as her husband does not want to have a special ceremony to renew their vows on their anniversary in several months. The client is very disappointed as she wants to have a big party to celebrate her marriage. When responding, the social worker should:

   A. Help the client to find other ways to celebrate that may be more acceptable to her husband
   B. Suggest the client stress to her husband the importance of the ceremony and party
   C. Comfort the client by explaining that it is understandable that she is disappointed given the circumstances
   D. Confront the client about her emotions given past discussions about her marriage

157. Using an ecological perspective, social workers explain differences in social roles for men and women by:

A. Physical attributes that are present at birth
B. Biological, cultural, and social influences that affect one another
C. Socialization that occurs throughout the life course
D. Environmental factors that impact on development

158. The primary aim of clinical supervision is to:

A. Make certain that clients' issues are reviewed with more experienced practitioners
B. Improve social workers' skills and knowledge through professional development
C. Ensure that clients receive the most efficient and effective services possible
D. Prepare social workers to serve as mentors of new professionals in the future

159. The PRIMARY reason for using structured decision making in child welfare service delivery is:

A. Consistency
B. Advocacy
C. Transparency
D. Homogeneity

160. A social worker receives a request from an insurance company for a copy of the intake assessment from a client's record. Which of the following will BEST assist the client in deciding whether the assessment should be released?

A. Providing the client with a copy of the document for review
B. Explaining to the client what services are paid for by the insurance company
C. Reviewing the release of information form used by the social worker
D. Obtaining a copy of the insurance company's confidentiality policy

161. Which is NOT a criterion when evaluating risk associated with client decisions in order to limit the right to self-determination?

A. The potential negative consequences are serious.
B. The harm is foreseeable (e.g., a reasonable person would be able to predict the outcome).

    C. The damaging action violates the rights of another person or persons.

    D. The adverse outcome is imminent or will happen right away.

162. When developing a Child and Family Team for a youth entering the child welfare system, a social worker should include informal supports, other than biological relatives, when they are:

    A. Identified by the family as familiar with its strengths and needs

    B. Believed by treating professionals to be supportive of the child's well-being

    C. Knowledgeable about the alleged abuse or neglect suffered

    D. Committed to being present at all case conferences

163. A social worker who is the director of an adolescent service agency routinely posts announcements of agency fundraising and community awareness events on her own social networking site. She receives a "friend" request from the parent of an agency client who is eager to support the agency. The social worker should:

    A. Accept the request as a method of engaging the parent and providing information about volunteer activities

    B. Refrain from accepting the request until after meeting with the parent to discuss ways in which she can provide assistance to the agency

    C. Refrain from accepting the request to avoid boundary confusion

    D. Accept the request with the understanding that information cannot be shared with the client to avoid a dual relationship

164. Using the *DSM-5*, an 8-year-old child with persistent and frequent irritable episodes of behavioral outbursts that are grossly out of proportion in intensity or duration to the situation is MOST likely to be diagnosed with:

    A. Bipolar Disorder

    B. Oppositional Defiant Disorder

    C. Autism Spectrum Disorder

    D. Disruptive Mood Dysregulation Disorder

165. During which step in the problem-solving process is the Cultural Formulation Interview (CFI) MOST helpful?

    A. Assessment

    B. Planning

C. Engagement

D. Intervention

166. A "black box warning" on a psychotropic medication indicates:

A. Appropriate usage is limited to adults

B. An adverse reaction may lead to death or serious injury

C. Need for ongoing medical monitoring if preexisting health conditions exist

D. Effectiveness for only a small number of mental health disorders

167. Upon intake, a client reveals that she just left an abusive relationship that she was in for many years. She feels ashamed of having stayed in it for so long and has many physical and emotional problems due to her trauma. She feels alone and is scared to trust others. In order to best meet this woman's needs, the social worker should FIRST:

A. Determine why she stayed in this abusive relationship for so long

B. Refer her to a physician to treat medical difficulties, which may have resulted from the abuse

C. Assure her that it is safe to tell the social worker anything about her experiences

D. Help her to deal with the psychological consequences of the abuse

168. A mother who has recently divorced brings her 13-year-old son in for counseling as he is having trouble adjusting in school. She feels that he would benefit from speaking to a social worker. The social worker asks to see the mother's divorce and child custody decrees in order to determine whether the mother's consent is sufficient for treatment. The documents indicate that both parents have legal custody, but do not contain information on each parent's decision-making authority for health care decisions, including mental health. In this situation, the social worker should NEXT:

A. Request written consent from both parents before beginning treatment

B. Begin treatment immediately as the mother is a legal guardian and has already consented

    C. Ask the mother to sign a statement that consent is needed from only one parent

    D. Refuse to serve the child until decision-making authority is included in the divorce documents

169. A social worker is experiencing a lot of personal issues including the ending of her marriage. Her marital separation has led to financial troubles which have caused her to file for bankruptcy. In order to appropriately protect clients, the social worker should:

    A. Temporarily limit her practice to the treatment of single adults and children to minimize countertransference

    B. Seek professional help and take remedial action as needed to ensure self-care during this period of distress

    C. Suppress thoughts and feelings about her current situation so that they do not interfere with her practice

    D. Work with her supervisor to address her financial issues which may include minimizing spending and/or maximizing earnings

170. Culturally competent social work practice views informal supports as:

    A. Central to understanding the root causes of problems experienced by clients and their families

    B. Supplemental resources that should be ancillary to formal services

    C. Important when used in conjunction with clinical services to address distress and dysfunction

    D. Necessary for meeting the ongoing unique needs of clients and their families

Answer Key

1. A	18. D	35. C	52. A
2. C	19. D	36. B	53. B
3. D	20. B	37. B	54. A
4. C	21. A	38. C	55. C
5. B	22. D	39. D	56. C
6. A	23. A	40. C	57. B
7. D	24. B	41. D	58. C
8. C	25. B	42. D	59. D
9. B	26. D	43. C	60. B
10. D	27. B	44. B	61. B
11. D	28. C	45. B	62. D
12. C	29. D	46. D	63. B
13. C	30. B	47. C	64. B
14. D	31. D	48. B	65. C
15. D	32. C	49. D	66. B
16. C	33. C	50. A	67. C
17. C	34. A	51. B	68. A

69. B	95. D	121. D	147. B
70. A	96. A	122. C	148. B
71. A	97. C	123. C	149. C
72. A	98. A	124. A	150. D
73. A	99. C	125. D	151. A
74. D	100. C	126. B	152. A
75. A	101. D	127. A	153. C
76. D	102. C	128. A	154. A
77. B	103. B	129. D	155. D
78. C	104. C	130. A	156. D
79. D	105. C	131. B	157. B
80. B	106. C	132. B	158. C
81. A	107. A	133. B	159. A
82. D	108. B	134. C	160. A
83. B	109. C	135. B	161. C
84. C	110. D	136. C	162. A
85. C	111. A	137. A	163. C
86. D	112. B	138. D	164. D
87. B	113. C	139. B	165. A
88. B	114. D	140. C	166. B
89. D	115. A	141. A	167. B
90. A	116. D	142. B	168. A
91. C	117. C	143. A	169. B
92. C	118. A	144. B	170. D
93. A	119. A	145. A	
94. D	120. B	146. B	

Answers With Analytic Rationales

1. A

Rationale

Psychologist Leon Festinger (1957) proposed a theory of **cognitive dissonance** centered on how people try to reach internal consistency. Clients have an inner need to ensure that their beliefs and behaviors are consistent. Inconsistent or conflicting beliefs lead to disharmony, which clients strive to avoid. As the experience of dissonance is unpleasant, clients are motivated to reduce or eliminate it and achieve consonance (e.g., agreement).

For example, clients who smoke might continue to do so, even though they know it is bad for their health. They might decide that they value smoking more than their health, deeming the behavior "worth it" in terms of risks versus rewards. Another way to deal with this dissonance is to minimize the potential drawbacks. *Smokers might convince themselves that the negative health effects have been overstated.* They might also rationalize health concerns by telling themselves that they cannot avoid every possible risk out there. Lastly, smokers might try to convince themselves that if they do stop smoking then they will gain weight, which also presents health risks. By using such explanations, smokers are able to reduce the dissonance and continue the behavior.

There are three key strategies to reduce or minimize cognitive dissonance: (1) focus on more supportive beliefs that outweigh the dissonant belief or behavior, (2) reduce the importance of the conflicting belief, and (3) change the conflicting belief so that it is consistent with other beliefs or behaviors.

Metacommunication is the context within which to interpret the content of a message (such as nonverbal communication, body language, tone, etc.).

Displacement and **intellectualization** are both defense mechanisms. Displacement is directing an impulse or feeling toward a less threatening target and intellectualization is focusing on the facts and logic to avoid uncomfortable emotions.

Test-Taking Strategies Applied

The question contains a qualifying word—MOST. While the client may be using a defense mechanism, it is likely that her statement results from cognitive dissonance as she has minimized the health risks in an attempt to justify her continued smoking.

Knowledge Area

Unit I—Human Development, Diversity, and Behavior in the Environment (Content Area); Human Growth and Development (Competency); Communication Theories and Styles (KSA)

2. C

Rationale

Social workers must ensure that they do not engage in **dual or multiple relationships with current or former clients**. In addition, social workers should be alert to and avoid conflicts of interest. In instances when dual or multiple relationships are unavoidable, social workers should take steps to protect clients and are responsible for setting clear, appropriate, and culturally sensitive boundaries. Dual or multiple relationships occur when social workers relate to clients in more than one relationship, whether it is professional, social, or business. *Dual or multiple relationships can occur simultaneously or consecutively.*

Test-Taking Strategies Applied

This is a recall question that relies on social workers understanding the ethical issues that relate to conflicts of interest and dual relationships. While the specifics of the case scenario are not explicitly mentioned in the 2008 *NASW Code of Ethics* the social worker's actions are concerning. Perhaps the former client might need counseling again. Asking the social worker to serve as her therapist would not be possible if both were socializing as members of this retirement group. To avoid this problem and others, social workers should treat former clients in the same way that they do current ones ("once a client, always a client"). Many ethical standards, such as confidentiality, do not cease when the therapeutic relationship ceases between a social worker and client.

Knowledge Area

Unit IV—Professional Relationships, Values, and Ethics (Content Area); Professional Development and Use of Self (Competency); Ethical Issues Related to Dual Relationships (KSA)

3. D

Rationale

Social workers view client problems using a systems perspective. A system is a whole comprising component parts that work together. **Systems theory** views human behavior through larger contexts. It illustrates that clients are members of families, communities, and broader society. Thus, a change to an individual client brings about adjustments in these larger structures. Contrarily, family, community, and societal modifications impact on individual client functioning.

Systems theory also recognizes an individual client has his or her own system—with physiological, psychological, social, spiritual, and cultural components. If there is a change in one domain, it is likely to affect the others.

In this case scenario, the client has had a physiological change resulting from an accident at work. The social worker may ultimately take one of the actions described in the incorrect response choices, but he or she must initially determine the impact that this decline in mobility has had on client well-being in all other areas. A complete assessment must be done to determine the client's short- and long-term needs in each life domain. These needs would then require prioritization so that those that necessitate immediate attention are addressed first.

Test-Taking Strategies Applied

The question contains a qualifying word—FIRST. There may be more than one appropriate response choice, but the order in which they are to occur is critical. The problem-solving process states that assessment must occur before treatment planning and intervention. According to systems theory, social workers know that physiological changes will impact psychological and social functioning. Thus, it is necessary to assess the needs in these areas before taking action. The incorrect response choices are interventions which can be done only *after* all needs have been assessed and prioritized.

Knowledge Area

Unit I—Human Development, Diversity, and Behavior in the Environment (Content Area); Human Growth and Development (Competency); Systems and Ecological Perspectives and Theories (KSA)

4. C

Rationale

Social workers are often called upon to assist with developing or navigating **service networks**, as well as creating community resources where they are lacking. **Needs assessments** are concerned with discovering the characteristics and extent of a particular social situation to determine the most appropriate response. There are a number of different reasons for conducting a needs assessment including to determine

- Whether services exist in the community
- Whether there are enough clients
- Who uses existing services
- What barriers prevent clients from accepting services
- The existence of an ongoing social problem

A key ethical issue with needs assessment is ensuring that the needs documented are expressed by those in a community affected by a problem, rather than the needs that an agency would like to see met. Recommendations should not be based on the services that an agency feels are important and wants to provide. Agencies sometimes have their own "agendas" that may be different from the "true" needs of a community.

Test-Taking Strategies Applied

The question contains a qualifying word—NOT—that requires social workers to select the response choice that is not an appropriate reason for conducting a needs assessment. Ethical issues must be considered when deciding whether to use this method to document a social problem and appropriate solutions. The needs, and services or resources to meet them, must be expressed by those affected, rather than what agency personnel feel are important or services they want to provide. The correct response choice bases the critical need as that "identified by service agencies"—which is not proper.

When NOT is used as a qualifying word, it is often helpful to remove it from the question and eliminate the three response choices that are appropriate rationales. This approach will leave the one response choice which is NOT a reason for conducting a needs assessment.

Knowledge Area

Unit III—Interventions With Clients/Client Systems (Content Area); Intervention Processes and Techniques for Use With Larger Systems (Competency); Methods to Establish Service Networks and Community Resources (KSA)

5. B

Rationale

A critical aspect of **social policy analysis** is determining the **social allocation** methodology. Social allocation concerns who shall benefit and the manner in which entitlement is defined. Attempts to develop principles of eligibility traditionally begin with the distinction between universalism and selectivity. *Universalism denotes benefits made available to an entire population as a basic right.* Examples are Social Security for those who are elderly and public education for youth. Contrarily, selectivity denotes benefits made available based on individual need, usually determined by a test of income. Examples include public assistance and public housing. Universalism, consistent with institutional welfare practice, takes the approach that needs are a part of everyday life and that welfare should be provided as a public service. Institutional social work focuses on giving each person equal opportunity to be supported, whatever his or her circumstances may be.

Test-Taking Strategies Applied

This is a recall question that relies on social workers understanding the meaning of social allocation and the difference between social welfare eligibility approaches—universal versus selective.

The question contains a qualifying word—BEST. While some of the response choices mention widespread needs or application, they are not optimal descriptions of universalism as these statements do not contain the critical element of this allocation strategy, which is provision to all as an entitlement.

Knowledge Area

Unit III—Interventions With Clients/Client Systems (Content Area); Intervention Processes and Techniques for Use With Larger Systems (Competency); Concepts of Social Policy Development and Analysis (KSA)

6. A

Rationale

Male perpetrators tend to be the majority of reported cases of abuse. However, women are also capable of child sexual assault. Reports of female perpetrators are on the rise, and female offenders have been reported in cases of abuse involving both male and female children.

Sexual abuse is not a problem plaguing only certain families or people with a certain level of family income and education. Sexual abuse crosses all socioeconomic, neighborhood, race, and class barriers. It happens in large and small families; in cities and in rural areas; in wealthy and lower income neighborhoods; and in homes, schools, churches, and businesses.

The people most likely to abuse children are the ones with the most opportunity, most access, and most trust. Abusers can be parents, stepparents, uncles, aunts, siblings, babysitters, tutors, and family friends. Most reported cases of child molestation involve a child and a known perpetrator.

Frequently, an absence of physical evidence is used as support that a perpetrator must be innocent of an alleged sexual assault. However, abnormal genital findings are rare, even in cases where abuse has been factually proven by other forms of evidence. Many acts leave no physical trace. Injuries resulting from sexual abuse tend to heal very quickly, and many times exams of child victims do not take place on the same day as the alleged act of abuse.

Test-Taking Strategies Applied

The question contains a qualifying word—TRUE. It is even capitalized to assist with identifying the distinguishing factor of the correct response from the rest. Each statement must be read carefully and evaluated as to its accuracy. The correct answer is identified through a process of elimination, with each false assertion being excluded.

Knowledge Area

Unit I—Human Development, Diversity, and Behavior in the Environment (Content Area); Concepts of Abuse and Neglect (Competency); Indicators and Dynamics of Abuse and Neglect Throughout the Lifespan (KSA)

7. D

Rationale

Absent client consent to release records or a recognized legal exception, social workers have a duty to claim **privilege** on behalf of their clients before releasing any information. The *NASW Code of Ethics, 2008—1.07(j)*, states that social workers should protect the confidentiality of clients during legal proceedings to the extent permitted by law.

Subpoenas may be issued by judges, clerks of the court, or attorneys. Social workers should not assume that attorney subpoenas requesting client records have legal authority requiring the release of records unless they are accompanied by court orders signed by judges—not judges' clerks. Acceptance of subpoenas does not mean social workers consent to complying with them. Objections to subpoenas can be made with "Motions to Quash," which is a legal procedure to block or modify subpoenas. Judges review the legal issues and determine if the client records or information should be disclosed.

Social workers are mandated to keep information confidential unless told by clients to release it or due to legal exceptions. They cannot release confidential information even when they think doing so will directly benefit clients. Confidentiality extends past client death. Thus, deceased clients have the same rights to confidentiality as those who are living.

Test-Taking Strategies Applied

The question requires social workers to be aware of their ethical duties with regard to confidentiality and releasing client information. When answering questions about ethical mandates, response choices should be judged against standards that appear in the 2008 *NASW Code of Ethics*. The answer that most closely resembles the wording of the *Code* should be selected. Each of the incorrect response choices are not accurate as information cannot be released if only subpoenaed (it must be court-ordered), social workers feel it is beneficial to do so, or clients die.

Knowledge Area

Unit IV—Professional Relationships, Values, and Ethics (Content Area); Confidentiality (Competency); Legal and/or Ethical Issues Regarding Confidentiality, Including Electronic Information Security (KSA)

8. C

Rationale

The **ability of children to legally consent** to their own treatment depends on

- Their age
- The services requested
- The state in which assistance is sought

If children have been legally deemed emancipated (either due to maturity or automatically because they are parents themselves), they are able to consent for treatment. Otherwise, the age of majority at which an individual is deemed to be sufficiently mature to make adult decisions is 18 years of age in most states. However, some states have statutes that increase the age to 19, 20, or 21.

In addition, certain treatment requests, including for mental health treatment, can be made by minors in a number of states. For example, in one state, a minor who is 16 years or older has the same capacity as an adult to consent to consultation, diagnosis, and treatment of a mental or emotional disorder. Discretion is given to the health care provider concerning notice to the parent, guardian, or custodian of the minor. In another, any minor who is 12 years or older may request and receive counseling services or psychotherapy of up to five sessions on an outpatient basis without the consent of the parent or guardian, but the parent or guardian will not be responsible for the costs of the services.

Test-Taking Strategies Applied

The question contains a qualifying word—EXCEPT. Three of the four response choices are factors that must be considered when determining if those under the age of majority can seek treatment without parental consent. The correct answer, service utilization history, is not a factor in deciding whether children can legally consent for treatment, though it may be considered in deciding the need for services. Once need has been established, social workers must follow legal standards with regard to obtaining proper consents for the delivery of services to children.

Knowledge Area

Unit IV—Professional Relationships, Values, and Ethics (Content Area); Confidentiality (Competency); The Principles and Processes of Obtaining Informed Consent (KSA)

9. B

Rationale

Social welfare legislation has an important impact on many areas of social work practice, including confidentiality. The **Family Educational Rights and Privacy Act (FERPA)** is a federal law that protects the privacy of student education records. The law applies to all schools that receive funds under an applicable program of the U.S. Department of Education.

FERPA gives parents certain rights with respect to their children's education records. These rights transfer to the student when he or she reaches the age of 18 or attends a school beyond the high school level. Students to whom the rights have transferred are "eligible students."

Parents or eligible students have the right to inspect and review the students' education records maintained by schools. Schools are not required to provide copies of records unless, for reasons such as great distance, it is impossible for parents or eligible students to review the records. Schools may charge a fee for copies. *Parents or eligible students also have the right to request that schools correct records which they believe to be inaccurate or misleading.* If a school decides not to amend a record, the parent or eligible student then has the right to a formal hearing. After a hearing, if the school still decides not to amend the record, the parent or eligible student has the right to place a statement with the record setting forth his or her view about the contested information.

Generally, schools must have written permission from the parent or eligible student in order to release any information from a student's education record. However, FERPA allows schools to disclose those records, without consent, to certain parties or under certain conditions.

Test-Taking Strategies Applied

This is a recall question that relies on social workers being fully informed of existing laws, policies, practices, and procedures that impact or govern service delivery, including confidentiality of records. The age of the child is included in the case scenario to indicate that he is not 18 years or older and, therefore, not considered an "eligible student." Thus, his parents have the right to inspect his education record and request changes be made if information is inaccurate and/or misleading. A formal hearing and written statement by the parents may be needed if the school does not agree to their changes.

Knowledge Area

Unit III—Interventions With Clients/Client Systems (Content Area); Intervention Processes and Techniques for Use With Larger Systems (Competency); The Effects of Policies, Procedures, Regulations, and Legislation on Social Work Practice and Service Delivery (KSA)

10. D

Rationale

Social workers should not assume that clients are ready or have the skills needed to make changes in their lives. Clients may be oppositional, reactionary, noncompliant, and/or unmotivated. These attitudes or behaviors are often referred to as **resistance**.

There are indicators that a social worker should use as evidence that a client may be resistant or not ready/able to fully participate in services. These indicators include engaging in small talk with a social worker about irrelevant topics, not keeping appointments, and limiting the amount of information communicated to a social worker.

Additional indicators of resistance include

- Silence/minimal talking during sessions
- Engaging in intellectual talk by using technical terms/abstract concepts or asking questions of a social worker that are not related to client issues or problems
- Being preoccupied with past events instead of current issues
- Discounting, censoring, or editing thoughts when asked about them by a social worker
- False promising
- Flattering a social worker in an attempt to "soften" him or her so that the client will not be pushed to act
- Payment delays or refusals

Test-Taking Strategies Applied

The question contains a qualifying word—NOT—that requires social workers to select the response choice which is not an indicator of resistance. When NOT is used as a qualifying word, it is often helpful to remove it from the question and eliminate the three response choices which are indicators. This approach will leave the one response choice which does NOT signify that clients lack readiness to change.

Asking in detail about confidentiality practices and procedures is expected by clients, especially when they want to reveal sensitive information about themselves. Such questioning can actually be an indication of a willingness to fully engage in the process and not withhold information that is deeply personal.

Knowledge Area

Unit II—Assessment and Intervention Planning (Content Area); Assessment Methods and Techniques (Competency); Methods to Assess Motivation, Resistance, and Readiness to Change (KSA)

11. D

Rationale

Cultural blindness is a point on the cultural proficiency continuum that is characterized by a well-intentioned desire to be unbiased. The continuum begins with cultural destructiveness and progresses to cultural incapacity, cultural blindness, cultural precompetence, and cultural competence, respectively, before ultimately reaching cultural proficiency. The hallmark of cultural blindness is that all people are the same and that color or culture should make no difference. This attitude leads to **ethnocentrism** in the delivery of services. Ethnocentric helping approaches and other dominant-culture attitudes and values are deemed universally applicable, with little regard for their relevancy to minority populations. Cultural blindness, like views that promote assimilation, degrades the unique strengths and capabilities of diverse groups. Examples of cultural blindness include exhibiting little motivation to learn more about diverse groups or pretending not to notice the race or other diversity characteristics of a client. Cultural blindness leads to the incapacity to comprehend how specific situations may be seen differently by clients belonging to other cultures. There is a strict alignment with the viewpoints, outlooks, and morals of social workers' own societies or cultures.

Test-Taking Strategies Applied

The question is assessing social workers' knowledge about cultural proficiency and the steps in the process. Obtaining the correct answer requires familiarity with the hallmark of cultural blindness, which is a failure to consider the influences of culture, race, and/or ethnicity on behaviors and attitudes. It is not appropriate to function with the belief that color or culture makes no difference and that all clients are the same. Helping approaches traditionally used by the dominant culture should not be seen as universally applicable, effective, or optimal.

Knowledge Area

Unit I—Human Development, Diversity, and Behavior in the Environment (Content Area); Diversity, Social/Economic Justice, and Oppression (Competency); The Principles of Culturally Competent Social Work Practice (KSA)

12. C

Rationale

According to the *NASW Code of Ethics, 2008—1.16 Termination of Services*, before social workers begin **termination of services for nonpayment of fees**, the following criteria should be met:

- The financial contractual arrangements have been made clear to clients, preferably in writing

- Clients do not pose an imminent danger to self or others

- The clinical and other consequences of the nonpayment (e.g., disruption of treatment/interruption of services) have been discussed with clients

When setting fees, social workers should ensure that they are fair, reasonable, and commensurate with the services performed (*NASW Code of Ethics*, 2008—*1.13 Payment for Services*). Consideration should be given to clients' ability to pay. However, social workers do not need to institute sliding scales or set fees based on clients' incomes.

Test-Taking Strategies Applied

While many social workers are employed in agency settings and not responsible for the collection of payments, they must be knowledgeable about fee setting and payment issues. Terminating client services for nonpayment of fees must be done ethically.

The question contains a qualifying word—NOT. Unlike other questions, the qualifying word in this question is not capitalized. Qualifying words may or may not be capitalized, so it is important to read questions carefully. Three of the response choices represent criteria that are required by the 2008 *NASW Code of Ethics*. The correct answer is the one that is not mandated.

Sliding scales also do not inherently make fees affordable. Fees can still be unfair and unreasonable even when differentials are used to account for income.

Knowledge Area

Unit IV—Professional Relationships, Values, and Ethics (Content Area); Professional Values and Ethical Issues (Competency); Ethical Issues in Supervision and Management (KSA)

13. C

Rationale

There are many methods that social workers use to facilitate communication with clients. Central to the formation of a therapeutic alliance is displaying empathy. **Empathy** is distinguished from sympathy as the latter denotes pity or feeling bad for a client, whereas the former means that a social worker understands the ideas expressed, as well as the feelings of a client. To be empathic, a social worker must accurately perceive a client's situation, perspective, and feelings, as well as communicate this understanding in a helpful (therapeutic) way.

In order to facilitate change through the problem-solving process, a social worker must use various verbal and nonverbal communication techniques to assist clients to understand their behavior and feelings. In addition, to ensure clients are honest and forthcoming during this process, social workers must build trusting relationships with clients. These relationships develop through effective verbal and nonverbal communication. Social workers must be adept at using both forms of communication successfully, as well as understanding them, because verbal and nonverbal cues will be used by clients throughout the problem-solving process. Insight into their meaning will produce a higher degree of sensitivity to clients' experiences and a deeper understanding of their problems.

There are many verbal and nonverbal communication methods, including

Active listening, in which social workers are sitting up straight and leaning toward clients in a relaxed and open manner, can involve commenting on clients' statements, asking open-ended questions, and making statements that show listening is occurring.

Silence by social workers shows acceptance of clients' feelings and promotes introspection or time to think about what has been learned.

Reframing by social workers shows clients that there are different perspectives and ideas that can help to change negative thinking patterns and promote change.

Test-Taking Strategies Applied

The question contains a qualifying word—BEST. While telling the client that his feelings are typical in this situation and helping him cope with his emotions will be helpful, the correct answer is the one that "can BEST demonstrate empathy." Central to empathy is understanding a client's situation and the feelings expressed. Showing a client that his or her experiences and perceptions are important can be achieved with nonverbal communication techniques like active listening and eye contact/posture.

The incorrect response choices focus on the social worker intervening by "discussing," "telling," or "helping." Often empathy is established by more passive actions such as listening, attending, and suspending value judgments.

Most therapeutic situations require little to no self-disclosure by a social worker and any self-disclosure must be thoroughly evaluated in supervision before it is used as it can be an indication of a professional boundary violation.

Knowledge Area

Unit I—Human Development, Diversity, and Behavior in the Environment (Content Area); Human Growth and Development (Competency); Communication Theories and Styles (KSA)

14. D

Rationale

The Health Information Portability and Accountability Act (HIPAA) affords **psychotherapy notes** more **confidentiality protection** in certain circumstances. The term "psychotherapy notes" is specifically defined in the HIPAA medical privacy regulations as the "notes of a mental health provider documenting or analyzing the conversation during a counseling session" that are *maintained separately* from the client record.

Social workers should understand that *a general consent or authorization to release all mental health information in the record is not sufficient to disclose separately maintained psychotherapy notes*. If a clinical social worker possesses separate therapy notes, they may be released only if a second, separate signed authorization is provided by the client. If a separate authorization from the client to release "psychotherapy notes" is not provided, the separate notes should be withheld when responding to a request for records.

A social worker should not make the decision that information should not be sent unless there is a compelling professional reason why such a disclosure may be harmful to the client, which is not indicated in this case scenario. In addition, sending only a summary of diagnoses, treatment dates, and fees collected is not honoring the client's authorization that all mental health information be released.

Test-Taking Strategies Applied

Social workers must be aware of the confidentiality or privacy standards that are dictated by social welfare legislation, such as HIPAA, and the 2008 *NASW Code of Ethics*. Social workers must be knowledgeable about what information should be released when client consent is given for all mental health records. Without understanding the provisions of HIPAA with regard to psychotherapy notes, social workers may inadvertently release information that is afforded extra protection. This is a recall question that relies on having substantive knowledge in this content area.

Knowledge Area

Unit IV—Professional Relationships, Values, and Ethics (Content Area); Confidentiality (Competency); The Elements of Client/Client System Reports (KSA)

15. D

Rationale

While all of the response choices may occur and be useful on a practical level, the question asks for the response choice which occurs next according to the principles of **ethical problem solving**. There are six sequential steps in ethical problem solving: (1) identifying the ethical standards, as defined by the professional code of ethics, that are being compromised; (2) determining whether an ethical issue or dilemma exists; (3) weighing ethical issues in light of the social work values and principles as defined by the professional code of ethics; (4) suggesting modifications in light of prioritized ethical values and principles; (5) implementing modifications in light of prioritized ethical values and principles; and (6) *monitoring for new ethical issues and dilemmas.*

As the new practice has just been implemented (step 5), the social worker should monitor the situation to determine if the problem has been rectified and any new ethical issues emerge (step 6).

Test-Taking Strategies Applied

The question contains a qualifying word—NEXT. Its use indicates that the order in which the response choices should occur is critical. Knowledge of the sequential steps in the ethical problem-solving process is needed in order to identify where the social worker is in this process as outlined in the case scenario.

Realizing that modifications have already been implemented to resolve the problem makes clear that the only step left involves monitoring the situation.

Some of the incorrect response choices may be practically useful (such as incorporating the new practice into documents and training or reviewing other procedures to make sure they are based on current knowledge), but they are not directly related "to the principles of ethical problem solving" as specified in the question. Also, justifying the procedure in light of professional values and principles comes before implementation—not after or "next," making it incorrect.

Knowledge Area

Unit IV—Professional Relationships, Values, and Ethics (Content Area); Professional Values and Ethical Issues (Competency); Techniques to Identify and Resolve Ethical Dilemmas (KSA)

16. C

Rationale

Influencing social policy often requires mobilizing those who either traditionally have little power in society—the poor, minorities, or people with disabilities, for example—and/or groups that feel their concerns are being ignored. By working together, members of these groups can exercise power collectively because of their numbers, using the media, their votes, boycotts, and other types of social, political, and economic pressure to convince those in power to rethink their positions. There are many techniques to draw attention to social problems.

Civil disobedience is a particular kind of action in which group members intentionally break a law. They might do so because they are protesting a law, want to make a strong statement about an issue, and/or desire a particular action to be taken. Civil disobedience is effective as a strategy only if those who practice it are willing to accept the consequences of their actions, and face arrest, trial, and possible punishment. Otherwise, they are simply lawbreakers, and their protest loses its moral force.

Often an act of civil disobedience involves a protest or a "sit-in," which occurs when a group occupies a space in order to make a moral point, to assert its right to use the space, or to spur desired action. The act becomes civil disobedience if the group is trespassing on the space it occupies.

Test-Taking Strategies Applied

Selecting the correct answer requires social workers to be familiar with the terms listed as response choices. While the case scenario described is associated with advocacy for legislative change, community advocacy, as well as the other response choices, are not the best answers as the question is looking for a specific "strategy." Civil disobedience is a tool or method in which law breaking is used to draw attention to or urge action.

Community advocacy is a broad social mandate and most advocacy techniques are not rule violating, such as the one described.

Indirect casework may be considered as those administrative and other tasks associated with assisting clients such as travel, waiting at court, preparing monthly reports or a court report, reading documents, and attending meetings. This is a macro activity, but not associated with the actions mentioned in the question.

Social planning is a process through which needs or problems become known. Meeting those needs or solving those problems involves generating and evaluating alternative solutions before choosing the one that is best. Planning also involves evaluating the effectiveness of the implementation effort. These steps are not mentioned in the case scenario.

Knowledge Area

Unit III—Interventions With Clients/Client Systems (Content Area); Intervention Processes and Techniques for Use With Larger Systems (Competency); Techniques to Inform and Influence Organizational and Social Policy (KSA)

17. C

Rationale

Social workers must have knowledge of psychotropic medications as **psychopharmacology** is the treatment of choice for some mental disorders. Antipsychotic medicines are used primarily to manage psychosis. The word "psychosis" is used to describe conditions that affect the mind, and in which there has been some loss of contact with reality, often including delusions (false, fixed beliefs) or hallucinations (hearing or seeing things that are not really there). It can be a symptom of a physical condition, drug abuse, or a mental disorder such as Schizophrenia.

Test-Taking Strategies Applied

The question contains a qualifying word—MOST. While the client may be prescribed any of the medications for other symptoms, the correct answer must be a medication that addresses the symptoms mentioned—hallucinations. Risperdal is the only **antipsychotic medication** listed.

Paxil is an **antidepressant** used to address signs of sadness, lethargy, hopelessness, and so on. Tegretol is a **mood stabilizer**, often used for the treatment of Bipolar Disorder. Klonopin is an **antianxiety drug**, which is prescribed for nervousness and panic disorders.

While social workers are not expected to know every psychotropic medication, they should be familiar with popular medications within each category as there is usually a question or two on every examination that requires such knowledge.

Knowledge Area

Unit II—Assessment and Intervention Planning (Content Area); Biopsychosocial History and Collateral Data (Competency); Common Psychotropic and Nonpsychotropic Prescriptions and Over-the-Counter Medications and Their Side Effects (KSA)

18. D

Rationale

There are **diverse styles of communicating**. Nonverbal gestures and greetings vary across countries, cultures, and religions. What is seen as acceptable for one is not necessarily acceptable for another. Muslims have strict cultural rules about touching. Men and women cannot touch, even casually, in public. You will not see couples, even those who are married, walking down the street holding hands. Muslims not shaking hands with those of the opposite gender is a simple example of a cultural and religious difference that is easy to respect and accommodate.

It is important to point out that Muslims do not distinguish in this matter between Muslim and non-Muslim people, and the issue is the same for Muslim women as it is for men. Islam prohibits nonessential touching and physical contact with a person of the opposite gender, with the exception of certain immediate family members, as a sign of modesty, humility, and chastity. In addition, it is a form of respect toward other persons by acknowledging no one has the right to touch them except for their nearest and dearest.

It is also important to note that this practice is not unique to this cultural group and can be seen in others. When working with a Muslim client, the need for essential touch should be discussed, if applicable, and permission should be granted. For example, if a member of the opposite gender was to faint or experience a seizure, a person may be required to do whatever possible to help, including touching, if appropriate.

However, every Muslim is responsible for his or her own actions, and is free to choose the degree to which he or she implements the various tenets of the religion. For this reason, social workers may meet Muslims who are more than happy to shake the hands of members of the opposite gender; however, the number of Muslims who refrain from doing so is significant and an awareness of the issue is vital when interacting with Muslims, both formally and informally.

Test-Taking Strategies Applied

The question is a recall question about the impact of diversity on styles of communicating. The appropriateness of physical touch is important to understand. In some cultures, individuals rarely touch each other, limiting themselves to handshakes and occasional pats on the shoulder or arm in business relations, or hugs in closer friendships. In other cultures, however, physical touch, such as hugging, is part of many interactions, even those that are casual.

Knowledge Area

Unit I—Human Development, Diversity, and Behavior in the Environment (Content Area); Diversity, Social/Economic Justice, and Oppression (Competency); The Effect of Culture, Race, and Ethnicity on Behaviors, Attitudes, and Identity (KSA)

19. D

Rationale

Social workers should review, with clients, circumstances where confidentiality information may be requested and where **disclosure of confidential information** may be legally required (*NASW Code of Ethics, 2008—1.07 Privacy and Confidentiality*). This discussion should occur as soon as possible in a social worker–client relationship and as needed throughout the course of the relationship.

Test-Taking Strategies Applied

In the case scenario, the client is worried that information disclosed to the social worker "will be used against her." *When words are in quotation marks in questions, they should be considered carefully as they are included for a reason.* They usually relate directly to the KSA being tested or distinguish the correct answer from the other response choices.

Social workers must know the limits of confidentiality and apprise clients of them so that clients can make informed choices. Social workers can release relevant information when clients pose a danger to themselves or others. In the case scenario, there is no threat to safety and the social worker should claim privilege if there is a request for any treatment information. Helping the client to understand that what was revealed to the social worker cannot be used against her is the most appropriate answer.

The question is about confidentiality and its limits, so advising the client to get along with her siblings is a distractor. A lawyer is not needed to explain confidentiality practices of social workers. Lastly, it is evident why she is fearful, so questioning her about it will not produce additional insight or help to calm her fears.

Knowledge Area

Unit IV—Professional Relationships, Values, and Ethics (Content Area); Confidentiality (Competency); Legal and/or Ethical Issues Regarding Confidentiality, Including Electronic Information Security (KSA)

20. B

Rationale

Clients' communication is often covert—with its meaning not readily evident. Social workers must have techniques that explore the **underlying meaning of communication**. Symbolic interactionism is an approach that focuses on interpreting the meanings that clients develop through their interaction with others. The central theme of symbolic interactionism is that human life is lived in the symbolic domain. Symbols are culturally derived social objects having shared meanings that are created and maintained in social interaction. Through language and communication, symbols provide the means by which reality is constructed. Reality is primarily a social product and is dependent on symbolic interactions for its existence. Even the physical environment is relevant to human conduct mainly as it is interpreted through symbolic systems.

Symbolic interactionism is based on three basic premises: (1) Humans act toward things on the basis of the meanings that things have for them; (2) the meanings of things derive from social interaction; and (3) these meanings are dependent on, and modified by, an interpretive process of the people who interact with one another. Meanings depend on a degree of consensual responses between two or more people. If most of those who use it agree, the meaning of a symbol is clear; if consensus is low, the meaning is ambiguous, and communication is problematic. Within a culture, a general consensus prevails on the meanings associated with various words or symbols.

The interpretive process entails the cognitive ability to take the perspective of another. It is a critical process in communication because it enables people to interpret one another's responses, thereby bringing about greater consensus on the meanings of the symbols used. The determination of meanings also depends on negotiation—that is, on mutual adjustments and accommodations of those who are interacting. Defining a situation is not a static process. An initial definition, based on past experiences or cultural expectations, may be revised in the course of interaction.

Self-psychology aims to help clients develop greater senses of self-cohesion by meeting self-object needs.

Operant conditioning explains that behaviors are more or less likely to occur based on their consequences, with reinforcement making them more likely and punishment less likely for reoccurrence.

Object relations helps to understand how lifelong relationship skills are rooted in early attachment with caregivers.

Test-Taking Strategies Applied

The question is a recall question on a theory that helps social workers understand client communication. Knowledge of the theories/ perspectives listed is needed in order to eliminate incorrect answers, with the goal of selecting the correct one. All of the theories/ perspectives listed relate to the KSAs on the examination.

Based on symbolic interactionism, kissing may have had different meanings for the client and the boy. The client clearly saw the action as an indication of affection toward her while the boy did not.

Knowledge Area

Unit I—Human Development, Diversity, and Behavior in the Environment (Content Area); Human Growth and Development (Competency); Communication Theories and Styles (KSA)

21. A

Rationale

Social work is a practical profession aimed at helping people address their problems and matching them with the resources they need to lead healthy and productive lives. Ensuring that community resources reflect problems identified and solutions created by local citizens is essential. This underpinning of this approach can be summarized in two words: social justice. **Social justice** is the view that everyone deserves equal economic, political, and social rights and opportunities. Social workers aim to open the doors of access and opportunity for everyone, particularly those in greatest need.

Central to social justice is the empowerment of clients. Empowerment is the giving of or sharing of power with others. **Community organization** and **social planning** are built on the principles of social justice with members who have complete decision-making power.

Test-Taking Strategies Applied

The correct answer is distinguished from the incorrect ones as it ensures "that services are developed using the principles of social justice." While all of the response choices will be helpful, only advocating for community members to have authority in decision making is consistent with empowerment, a key ingredient in promoting social justice.

Knowledge Area

Unit III—Interventions With Clients/Client Systems (Content Area); Intervention Processes and Techniques for Use With Larger Systems (Competency); Community Organizing and Social Planning Methods (KSA)

22. D

Rationale

Action research is a technique to influence social policy through an interactive inquiry process that balances collaborative problem-solving actions with data-driven collaborative analysis or research. Its aim is to guide change in order to solve an immediate problem. Action research challenges traditional social science by moving beyond reflective knowledge by outside experts through sampling, to an active moment-to-moment theorizing, data collecting, and inquiry occurring in the midst of emergent structure. It is seen as "action science"—rather than "reflective science."

Action research involves actively participating in a change situation, often via an existing organization, while simultaneously conducting research.

Test-Taking Strategies Applied

This question requires social workers to be familiar with specific techniques to influence social policy. While most questions on the examination are broad, requiring social workers to have general information about KSAs, it is likely that successfully answering some questions will require recall of specialized terms. Thus, while studying, social workers should familiarize themselves with key terms used when speaking about these areas.

Knowledge Area

Unit III—Interventions With Clients/Client Systems (Content Area); Intervention Processes and Techniques for Use With Larger Systems (Competency); Techniques to Inform and Influence Organizational and Social Policy (KSA)

23. A

Rationale

These are common abbreviations that appear on medication orders. **Qid** indicates that a medication is to be taken four times a day. **Prn** is used for medications that are to be administered as needed. **Bid** indicates that a medication is to be taken twice daily. **Qh** appears when medications are taken every hour.

Test-Taking Strategies Applied

This is a recall question that relies on social workers understanding common abbreviations used in medication orders. Many of these abbreviations are derived from Latin, with qid coming from the Latin words *quater in die*. Understanding Latin roots may assist in narrowing the choices. Bi means two, tri stands for three, and quad indicates four.

Thus, bid, tid, and qid are medication abbreviations which mean two, three, and four times a day, respectively.

Knowledge Area

Unit II—Assessment and Intervention Planning (Content Area); Biopsychosocial History and Collateral Data (Competency); Common Psychotropic and Nonpsychotropic Prescriptions and Over-the-Counter Medications and Their Side Effects (KSA)

24. B

Rationale

Social workers in managed care settings should be particularly careful about the ways in which they terminate services. If clients' insurance companies refuse to authorize services or an extension of services, social workers should be sure to advise clients of their right to appeal decisions and offer to assist clients with appeal processes. Empowerment of clients, through the provision of education and support, is essential to **advocacy for policies, services, and resources that meet clients' needs**.

Test-Taking Strategies Applied

The question contains a qualifying word—BEST. While prioritizing treatment topics and determining whether the client is able to pay an affordable fee privately may be useful, the social worker has an ethical responsibility to assist the client to use her insurance coverage to the maximum extent possible. Since her existing treatment goals require additional sessions, it would be inappropriate to add more diagnoses or goals in order to justify continued coverage. The social worker should not terminate services as there is still a continued need. The paramount issue is helping the client to understand that she has the right to appeal the decision and provide support and information needed by the client for this appeal.

It is likely that other action by the social worker may be needed if the client's appeal is denied. However, the question focuses on the most suitable action of the social worker now. Care should be taken in any case scenario to address the problem at hand and not choose a response because it may be needed at some point in the future, such as setting an affordable private pay fee for this client.

Knowledge Area

Unit III—Interventions With Clients/Client Systems (Content Area); Intervention Processes and Techniques for Use With Larger Systems (Competency); Theories and Methods of Advocacy for Policies, Services, and Resources to Meet Clients'/Client Systems' Needs (KSA)

25. B

Rationale

Attorney–client interactions were the first to gain the right of **privileged communication**. Over time, other groups of professionals sought legislation to provide them with this right.

It is important for social workers to understand the distinction between confidentiality and privileged communication. Confidentiality refers to the professional norm that information offered by or pertaining to clients will not be shared with third parties. Privilege refers to the disclosure of confidential information in court or during other legal proceedings.

A significant court decision for social workers concerning privileged communications was the landmark case of *Jaffe v. Redmond* (1996) in which the U.S. Supreme Court ruled that the clients of clinical social workers have the right to privileged communication in federal courts. In this case, a police officer sought counseling from a social worker after the officer killed a man involved in a fight. The social worker objected to a court order to disclose clinical notes she made during counseling sessions with the officer, arguing that the psychotherapist–client privilege protected the contents of the conversation. In its decision, the Supreme Court concluded that participants in therapy must be able to predict with some degree of certainty whether particular discussions will be protected.

Disclosure of privileged information may be permissible when a client threatens to commit suicide, has been abused or neglected, is impaired and may pose a threat to the public, and so on. Whether a social worker must disclose privileged information without a client's consent is often a matter of dispute and subject to relevant statutes, regulations, and judicial opinion.

Test-Taking Strategies Applied

The question contains a qualifying word—NOT—that requires social workers to select the response choice which does not "legally" influence a social worker's decision to release privileged information. When NOT is used as a qualifying word, it is often helpful to remove it from the question and eliminate the three response choices that are legal considerations. This approach will leave the one response choice that is NOT a decision-making variable.

Knowledge Area

Unit IV—Professional Relationships, Values, and Ethics (Content Area); Confidentiality (Competency); Legal and/or Ethical Issues Regarding Confidentiality, Including Electronic Information Security (KSA)

26. D

Rationale

Clients use defense mechanisms to manage internal conflicts. **Defense mechanisms** are automatic, involuntary, usually unconscious psychological activities aimed at reducing anxiety.

Displacement involves taking out frustrations, feelings, and impulses on less threatening people or objects. Displaced aggression is a common example of this defense mechanism. Rather than express anger in ways that could lead to negative consequences (such as arguing with a boss or an abuser), anger is expressed toward a person or object that poses no threat (such as a spouse, children, or pet).

Compensation is excelling in one area to make up for deficiencies in another (e.g., a person who stutters becomes an expressive writer).

Incorporation occurs when the psychic representation of a person, or parts of a person, is/are figuratively ingested (e.g., a child models a superhero's behaviors or adopts aspects of his or her personality in order to feel stronger and more confident).

Rationalization happens when controversial behaviors or feelings are justified and explained in seemingly rational or logical manners so that they are made consciously tolerable or even superior (e.g., thinking that cheating on a test is acceptable when the material is known as a good grade would be obtained even without the unethical act).

Test-Taking Strategies Applied

The question contains a qualifying word—MOST. While the child may be exhibiting more than one of the defense mechanisms listed, the behavior specified probably results from directing the anger for his abuser(s) to less threatening targets—namely, his peers. This aggression has manifested in bullying of classmates.

Knowledge Area

Unit I—Human Development, Diversity, and Behavior in the Environment (Content Area); Human Growth and Development (Competency); Psychological Defense Mechanisms and Their Effects on Behavior and Relationships (KSA)

27. B

Rationale

Clients use defense mechanisms to manage internal conflicts. **Defense mechanisms** are automatic, involuntary, usually unconscious psychological activities aimed at reducing anxiety.

Compensation occurs when clients overachieve in one area to compensate for failures in another. For example, clients with poor family lives may direct their energy into excelling above and beyond what is required at work. Compensation can manifest itself in a few different ways. Overcompensation occurs when people overachieve in one area to make up for shortcomings in another aspect of life. Undercompensation, on the other hand, can happen when people deal with such shortcomings by becoming overly dependent on others.

Sublimation is the transformation of unwanted impulses into something less harmful. When faced with the dissonance of uncomfortable thoughts, psychic energy is created. Sublimation channels this energy away from destructive acts and into something that is socially acceptable and/or creatively effective.

Substitution is the replacement of an unattainable or unacceptable goal, emotion, or object by a more attainable or acceptable one.

Conversion results in a physical symptom emerging from a repressed urge, anxiety, or internal conflict.

Test-Taking Strategies Applied

This is a recall question on the defense mechanisms. Knowing the definitions of the defense mechanisms is less important than being able to describe examples in behavioral terms of each. Often questions on defense mechanisms include case scenarios that describe clients' behaviors. Social workers must be able to identify defense mechanisms based on client verbalizations and actions using the situational contexts as clues.

Knowledge Area

Unit I—Human Development, Diversity, and Behavior in the Environment (Content Area); Human Growth and Development (Competency); Psychological Defense Mechanisms and Their Effects on Behavior and Relationships (KSA)

28. C

Rationale

Although most information that social workers obtain when doing assessments comes from interviews or records, **direct observation** can produce a lot of valuable information about interaction patterns. When functioning as observers, social workers can assume many roles, including acting as complete observers when those who are being watched are not aware of the observations. In order to accurately assess problems, social workers often triangulate, gathering relevant information from different sources.

Test-Taking Strategies Applied

The question contains a qualifying word—BEST. While some of the response choices may be helpful, direct observation will provide insight into the relationship between the girl and her classmates. The case scenario calls for the "nature of the problem" to be understood. The client's difficulties center on interactions so only observation will yield information about the relationships present. Observation can help the social worker identify behavioral antecedents and consequences that may be provoking and/or reinforcing behaviors.

Reviewing her academic records will not assist in understanding the relationship tensions, but may shed light on the impact of these conflicts on her performance. It may be useful to determine if she is having behavioral trouble outside of the school setting. However, it is her actions with her peers that are responsible for the decision to separate her in a resource room. Only by resolving the classroom disruption will the social worker be able to keep her with her peers. Interviewing the child about the move provides no insight into the "nature of the problem," just the proposed intervention.

Knowledge Area

Unit III—Interventions With Clients/Client Systems (Content Area); Intervention Processes and Techniques for Use Across Systems (Competency); The Principles of Active Listening and Observation (KSA)

29. D

Rationale

In some situations, social workers may actively encourage members to form subgroups, particularly in groups that are too large and cumbersome for detailed work to be accomplished. For example, subgroup formation is often useful in large task groups such as committees, delegate councils, and some teams. Members are assigned to a particular subgroup to work on a specific task or subtask. The results of the subgroup's work are then brought back to the larger group for consideration and action.

Regardless of whether social workers actively encourage subgroup formation, they occur naturally because not everyone in a group interacts with all members equally. The formation of intense subgroup attraction, however, can be a problem for **group functioning**. Subgroup members may substitute their own goals and methods of attaining them for the goals of the larger group. They can disrupt the group by communicating among themselves while others are speaking.

Subgroup members may fail to listen to members who are not a part of the subgroup. Ultimately, intense and consistent subgroup formation can negatively affect the performance of the group as a whole.

When intense subgroup attraction appears to be interfering with the group as a whole, a number of steps can be taken, including examining whether the group as a whole is sufficiently attractive to members, engaging in exercises that separate subgroup members, and promoting the development of norms that emphasize the importance of members listening to and respecting each other. Terminating or dismissing group members is not a strategy to address the problem; it excludes group participants rather than engages them.

Test-Taking Strategies Applied

The question contains a qualifying word—EXCEPT. Three of the four response choices address the problem of subgroup attraction. Elimination of clients or workers from the larger group does not allow them to get the benefits of participation or make contributions—both essential goals.

Knowledge Area

Unit I—Human Development, Diversity, and Behavior in the Environment (Content Area); Human Growth and Development (Competency); Theories of Group Development and Functioning (KSA)

30. B

Rationale

An **ecomap** helps visualize the social and personal relationships of clients within their environments or ecosystems. With a client at the center, it is a map of everything that may affect him or her including interactions with family, friends, business associations, religious communities, and any other social or educational groups or clubs. Ecomaps were developed in 1975 by Dr. Ann Hartman who is also credited with creating the genogram.

Ecomaps not only document the connections between family members and the outside world, but they also provide a way to visualize the quality of those connections either as positive and nurturing or negative wrought with conflict and stress. Connections can also be considered strong or weak.

An ecomap can be a powerful tool for discovering possible sources of depression and anxiety, as well as uncovering hidden support systems in friends, neighbors, clubs, professional agencies, charities, and churches.

An ecomap is sometimes also referred to as an ecogram.

Test-Taking Strategies Applied

The question contains a qualifying word—BEST. Ecomaps, like genograms, help to understand system dynamics by depicting relationships that clients have with others. They are vital when using a "person-in-environment" perspective to determine opportunities or barriers for change. Ecomaps are not directly related to environmental justice or conservation. They may identify sources of power within systems, but their purpose is broader.

Knowledge Area

Unit I—Human Development, Diversity, and Behavior in the Environment (Content Area); Human Growth and Development (Competency); Systems and Ecological Perspectives and Theories (KSA)

31. D

Rationale

The **effects of discrimination** can be seen on both the micro and macro levels. Exposure to discrimination is linked to anxiety and depression, as well as other mental health and behavioral problems. In addition, clients may experience physical effects such as diabetes, obesity, and high blood pressure. These health problems may be caused by not maintaining healthy behaviors (e.g., physical activity) or engaging in unhealthy ones (e.g., smoking and alcohol or drug abuse).

On a macro level, discrimination also restricts access to resources and systems needed for good health, education, employment, social support, and participation in sports, cultural, and civic activities. Discrimination and intolerance can also create a climate of despondence, apprehension, and fear within a community. The social and economic effects of discrimination on one generation may flow on to affect future generations, which can lead to cycles of poverty and disadvantage for future generations.

Test-Taking Strategies Applied

The question is essentially asking about the desired intervention for a client who has been adversely affected by discrimination. *When clients have been victims of discrimination, social workers must work to empower them.* The correct answer is the only one that is linked to empowerment or eradicating the root cause of the problem. In addition, identifying the need for antidepressants and/or determining the client's current emotional state are assessment tasks that would occur prior to the formulation of treatment planning. The social worker will certainly address the negative impacts of discrimination, but finding ways to support the client in fighting the discrimination is essential.

The correct answer is also the only one which indirectly helps others, who are adversely affected by the discriminatory practices of this employer, not just the individual client. Selecting a response choice that focuses on the root cause of a problem, rather than just addressing its effects, is optimal.

There is no indication that the client is suicidal, so completing a risk assessment is not warranted. Suicide screening is also not a treatment goal in this case scenario.

Knowledge Area

Unit I—Human Development, Diversity, and Behavior in the Environment (Content Area); Diversity, Social/Economic Justice, and Oppression (Competency); The Effects of Discrimination and Stereotypes on Behaviors, Attitudes, and Identity (KSA)

32. C

Rationale

The mission of social work is rooted in a set of **professional core values** which are service, social justice, dignity and worth of the person, importance of human relationships, integrity, and competence. These values guide social workers' conduct via standards, which are statements to the general public about what is expected. Professional standards are outlined in the 2008 *NASW Code of Ethics* and used in guiding decision making, especially when there is a lack of clarity or conflicts arise.

Test-Taking Strategies Applied

The question contains a qualifying word—BEST. Although some of the response choices may assist in determining the extent to which the values are incorporated into agency policies and procedures, employee practices, and client services, reviewing the professional code of ethics is the only way to see the values explicitly stated. In order "to learn about these values," it is most useful for the student to see them and the standards that are derived from them in writing. This foundation is essential before actually using them for decision making.

Knowledge Area

Unit IV—Professional Relationships, Values, and Ethics (Content Area); Professional Values and Ethical Issues (Competency); Professional Values and Principles (e.g., Competence, Social Justice, Integrity, and Dignity and Worth of the Person) (KSA)

33. C

Rationale

Some clients may not be comfortable talking about their sexual history, sex partners, or sexual practices. It is critical that social workers try to put clients at ease and let them know that taking a **sexual history** may be an important part of the assessment process. A history is usually obtained through a face-to-face interview, but can also be gotten from a pencil-and-paper document. A sexual history is a **source of information** that is available to social workers to assist with identifying the root of clients' problems.

Questions included in a sexual history may vary depending upon client issues. However, they should involve collecting information about the "5 Ps": (1) partners (number, gender, risk factors, and length of relationships); (2) practices (risk behaviors, oral/vaginal/anal intercourse, satisfaction with practices, desire/arousal/orgasm); (3) protection from sexually transmitted diseases (STDs; condom use); (4) past history of STDs; and (5) prevention of pregnancy (if desired)/ reproductive history.

If clients are experiencing dissatisfaction or dysfunction, social workers will need to understand the reasons for dissatisfaction and/ or dysfunction. Medical explanations must be ruled out before psychological factors are considered as causes. A systems perspective should be used to understand issues in this area. For example, a medical/ biological condition that decreases satisfaction or causes dysfunction may heavily impact on psychological and social functioning. In addition, a psychological or social issue can lead to a lack of desire, inability to become aroused, or failure to attain orgasm.

Alcohol and/or drug use should also be considered related to concerns about desire, arousal, or orgasm because they can cause decreased interest or abilities in these areas.

Test-Taking Strategies Applied

The question requires selecting an answer that best describes why the social worker's actions in completing a sexual history were flawed. Sexual history information is protected health information, as is all data collected by social workers in the course of treatment. Asking about STDs does not make it any more sensitive. All information obtained during treatment must be kept confidential. A sexual history should be kept with the other client records, not stored separately. Completing sexual histories is within the scope of practice of social workers. It does not have to be done by other professionals. However, social workers need to ensure competence in adequately collecting this data before doing it.

In this case scenario, the social worker did not do a thorough assessment as the sexual history lacked key information.

Knowledge Area

Unit II—Assessment and Intervention Planning (Content Area); Biopsychosocial History and Collateral Data (Competency); The Types of Information Available From Other Sources (e.g., Agency, Employment, Medical, Psychological, Legal, or School Records) (KSA)

34. A

Rationale

Acculturation is defined as a mutual and dynamic process of cultural change that occurs when two or more cultures come into contact. Acculturation requires the mutual accommodation of aspects of each culture (or cultures), although it is acknowledged that nondominant or minority groups often experience a greater change than dominant groups (the majority). However, the aim is change in both the dominant and nondominant groups to achieve interpersonal and intergroup relational outcomes that are the product of both groups' orientations.

Underlying acculturation strategies have two main goals: the desire to preserve heritage and culture and the facilitation of productive interaction between cultural groups. Thus, acculturation must be a process of mutual accommodation. Unfortunately, the role of majority groups is often not acknowledged or is downplayed, leaving the impression that it is the responsibility of nondominant cultures for active integration. *Change in both those in the majority and minority is crucial for achieving true multiculturalism.*

Test-Taking Strategies Applied

The question is a recall question about diversity, social/economic justice, and oppression. Historically, models of acculturation have inappropriately seen the responsibility for change being placed on those in the minority. In addition, they have viewed the goal as a "melting pot" with all societal members adopting the same customs and traditions. This view has been replaced with a more appropriate belief that a pluralistic society is one that respects the differences of its members while having a cooperative agreement to work together toward common goals.

The correct answer is the only one that puts equal responsibility for change on both the minority and majority—a key element in a socially just model of acculturation.

Knowledge Area

Unit I—Human Development, Diversity, and Behavior in the Environment (Content Area); Diversity, Social/Economic Justice, and Oppression (Competency); The Principles of Culturally Competent Social Work Practice (KSA)

35. C

Rationale

Social workers work in a myriad of organizational settings, which may adopt varying management approaches or principles. Classic **scientific management theory** involves creating multiple levels of workers to improve productivity. Employees at the lowest levels find their tasks overseen by supervisors who, in turn, are overseen by managers. At every level, employees are expected to perform tasks according to specific procedures designed to maximize productivity. Rules must be followed exactly.

Classic scientific management theory has several shortcomings. While some components of the theory, such as designing procedures for completing a task and keeping personal issues out of business, help an organization achieve the job at hand, employee feelings and opinions are not taken into account. Thus, the agency may not grow or may experience high levels of employee turnover as employees fail to develop a relationship with the organization and leave in search of a more satisfying job.

Human relations theory focuses more on the individuals in a workplace than the rules, procedures, and processes. Instead of directives coming directly from management, employees and managers interact with one another to help make decisions. The focus of this style is creating fulfilled, productive workers and helping them invest in their companies.

Systems theory in management helps managers look at organizations from a broader perspective. Systems theory has brought a new perspective for managers to interpret patterns and events in their organizations. In the past, managers typically focused on one part of an organization and then moved attention to another. Now, more managers are recognizing the various parts of their organizations, and, in particular, the interrelations of these parts.

Contingency theory is based on the belief that there is no best way to organize, lead, or make decisions in organizations. Instead, the optimal course of action is contingent (dependent) upon internal and external situations. Such a flexible approach ensures that organizations can handle uncertainties in the environment effectively and efficiently.

Test-Taking Strategies Applied

The question contains a qualifying word—MOST. While it is possible that the agency is adhering to some principles from other organizational theories, the characteristics described are hallmarks of a scientific management approach, also known as **Theory X**. It posits that workers will do what is best for themselves and need to be controlled in order to be most efficient. Motivation for enhanced productivity is linked to financial rewards for workers, as money is seen as a salient reinforcer.

Knowledge Area

Unit III—Interventions With Clients/Client Systems (Content Area); Intervention Processes and Techniques for Use With Larger Systems (Competency); Theories of Organizational Development and Structure (KSA)

36. B

Rationale

Major Depressive Disorder is a medical illness that causes persistent feelings of sadness and loss of interest in previously enjoyed activities. Using the fourth edition text revision of the *DSM* (*DSM-IV-TR*), social workers refrained from diagnosing major depression in individuals within the first 2 months following the death of a loved one in what has been referred to as the "bereavement exclusion." By advising social workers not to diagnose depression in recently bereaved individuals, the *DSM-IV-TR* bereavement exclusion suggested that grief somehow protected someone from major depression. For some clients, death of loved ones can precipitate major depression, as can other stressors.

The bereavement exclusion was removed from the *DSM-5*, forcing social workers to have to **differentiate between typical behavior and a diagnosable mental disorder**. While the grieving process is unique to each client, it can contain some of the same features of depression like intense sadness and withdrawal from customary activities. However, grief and depression are also different in important aspects.

Test-Taking Strategies Applied

The question contains a qualifying word—NOT—that requires social workers to select the response choice that is not a difference between grief and depression. When NOT is used as a qualifying word, it is often helpful to remove it from the question and eliminate the three response choices which are true. This approach will leave the one response choice which is NOT a true distinction.

Feelings of worthlessness, suicidal ideas, and impairment of overall function are usually symptoms of depression—NOT grief.

Knowledge Area

Unit II—Assessment and Intervention Planning (Content Area); Assessment Methods and Techniques (Competency); The Use of the Diagnostic and Statistical Manual of the American Psychiatric Association (KSA)

37. B

Rationale

There are different **methods used to facilitate communication**, including using varying types of questions to obtain the information necessary for understanding a client's difficulties and adaptive capabilities. A good approach is to ask questions initially that are somewhat general and then work toward more specific questions that focus on greater detail. This deductive trajectory from the general to the specific is helpful not only in the first few interviews when a social worker conducts a thorough assessment, but also in later interviews when a client is actively engaged in working toward solutions to a problem.

Open-ended questions are quite general and allow clients wide latitude to talk about themselves and their situations. By using minimal prompts and little structure, open-ended questions provoke clients to take the initiative to discuss what they think is important.

Closed-ended questions offer a more limited range of answers and encourage clients to provide more definitive answers to specific topics. *Specific questions are intended to focus the interview in greater detail on important subjects regarding a client's thoughts, feelings, behaviors, or details of a situation or event.* These questions are intended to fill in the gaps of a general narrative about especially important events. The details of a client's problems and experiences may be critical to understanding exactly what has been going on. A directive style introduces more structure into the interview, uses more closed questions that limit response options, and is more purposeful to the task at hand.

Test-Taking Strategies Applied

The correct answer to this question is the one that distinguishes closed-ended from open-ended questions. There is no difference between them with regard to putting clients in charge of the helping process or the ability to learn about the perceptions of clients. Positive regard concerns the ability to view clients as worthy with strengths and potential. It is not directly related to the use of either closed- or open-ended questions.

The major difference between closed- and open-ended questions is the former is directive (structured) while the latter is nondirective (unstructured).

Knowledge Area

Unit III—Interventions With Clients/Client Systems (Content Area); Intervention Processes and Techniques for Use Across Systems (Competency); Verbal and Nonverbal Communication Techniques (KSA)

38. C

Rationale

Agency policy and functioning has a profound influence on service delivery and the ability of social workers to practice ethically and effectively. Social work takes place in a wide variety of settings, including, but not limited to, private practices, public sector organizations (government), schools, hospitals, correctional facilities, and private nonprofit agencies.

Macro-level problem-solving mirrors the steps taken when working with individual clients. The problem-solving process starts with engaging and assessing, respectively, before moving to planning, intervening, evaluating, and finally terminating. *Central to assessment is understanding the problem, including its contributing causes and magnitude.* Driving and restraining forces for change must be understood before alternative solutions are generated.

Test-Taking Strategies Applied

The question contains a qualifying word—NEXT. Its use indicates that the order in which the response choices should occur is critical. Each of the response choices should be evaluated to determine when they occur in the problem-solving process (i.e., whether it is an engaging, assessing, planning, intervening, evaluating, or terminating task). Explaining the rationale for the policy may occur during planning when evaluating whether alternatives are better. Identifying alternatives is also a planning task. Determining the nature and length of the problem is central to assessing which would come "next" after engaging employees by acknowledging their concerns.

Obtaining information from consumers would be useful, but should happen after finding out about the distress of the employees since the social work administrator is currently meeting with them as per the case scenario.

Knowledge Area

Unit III—Interventions With Clients/Client Systems (Content Area); Intervention Processes and Techniques for Use With Larger Systems (Competency); Methods of Service Delivery (KSA)

39. D

Rationale

The term "two-spirited" refers to a person who has both a masculine and a feminine spirit, and is used by some American Indian, Native American, Alaska Native, and/or Indigenous people (also referred to as First Nations people) to describe their **sexual, gender, and/or spiritual identity**. As an umbrella term, it may encompass same-sex attraction and a wide variety of gender variance, including people who might be described in Western culture as gay, lesbian, bisexual, transsexual, transgender, gender queer, cross-dressers, or who have multiple gender identities. Two-spirited can also include relationships that would be considered poly.

Test-Taking Strategies Applied

The question is a recall question about culturally diverse terminology to describe self-image. *A social worker should never make assumptions about wording used by clients.* Instead, clients should be asked about what labels used to identify their self-image mean to them.

While it is unknown precisely what the client in the case scenario means by identifying himself as "two-spirited," the correct answer is the only one which relates to sexual, gender, and/or spiritual identity, which is central to its usage. As "two-spirited" is an umbrella term, the social worker may want to probe into his sexual orientation, gender identity, and/or spirituality if it relates to the presenting problem. A social worker should never elicit information that is not relevant to the problem experience or services needed.

Knowledge Area

Unit I—Human Development, Diversity, and Behavior in the Environment (Content Area); Diversity, Social/Economic Justice, and Oppression (Competency); The Effect of Culture, Race, and Ethnicity on Behaviors, Attitudes, and Identity (KSA)

40. C

Rationale

Sexual Dysfunctions are problems associated with sexual desire or response. Many issues can be classified as Sexual Dysfunctions. For example, for men, problems may include erectile dysfunction and premature or delayed ejaculation. For women, problems may refer to pain during sexual intercourse.

Issues may be caused by psychological factors, physical conditions, or a combination of both. It is essential that a medical examination be the first step in treating Sexual Dysfunctions in order to identify medications or medical conditions that are the causes of the problems. Many of the symptoms can be addressed medically. However, Sexual Dysfunctions can also be due to childhood sexual abuse, depression, anxiety, stressful life events, and/or other psychological issues. Treatment may also be needed to assist with coping with the signs and symptoms; these include, but are not limited to

- Premature or delayed ejaculation in men
- Erectile Disorder (not being able to get or keep an erection)
- Pain during sex
- Lack or loss of sexual desire
- Difficulty having an orgasm
- Vaginal dryness

Test-Taking Strategies Applied

The question contains a qualifying word—FIRST—that is capitalized to stress the importance of the order in which the actions should occur. Whenever social workers are doing assessments, they must determine if client behaviors result from medical or substance use problems before attributing them to mental or emotional issues. The husband's decreased sexual desire may be related to having his children leave the house, but the timing of these events may be coincidental. Often couples are in their 50s when their children leave for college. This age is also when men may experience decreased sexual desire due to lowering of testosterone levels and/or erectile dysfunction. Women can experience physical changes which lead to vaginal dryness, making sexual intercourse painful or more difficult.

It may be useful to pinpoint when the problem started and meet with each spouse separately, but these actions would take place after physical causes have been ruled out. Thus, a physical examination is a priority over the incorrect answers.

Knowledge Area

Unit II—Assessment and Intervention Planning (Content Area); Biopsychosocial History and Collateral Data (Competency); The Indicators of Sexual Dysfunction (KSA)

41. D

Rationale

Social workers should always use evidence-based interventions whenever possible. Available research and clinical expertise should be used as **criteria for selecting intervention modalities**. Evidence-based social work practice combines research knowledge, professional/clinical expertise, social work values, and client preferences/circumstances. It is a dynamic and fluid process whereby social workers seek, interpret, use, and evaluate the best available information in an effort to make the best-practice decisions.

Decisions are based on the use of many sources, ranging from systematic reviews and meta-analyses to less rigorous research designs. Social workers often use "evidence-based practice" to refer to programs that have a proven track record. However, it takes a long time for a program or intervention to be "evidence-based." Thus, most interventions in social work need more empirically supported research in order to accurately apply the term. "Evidence-informed practice" may be more appropriate.

Some questions guide the selection of intervention modalities:

- How will the recommended modality assist with the achievement of the treatment goal and will it help get the outcomes desired?
- How does the recommended treatment modality promote client strengths, capabilities, and interests?
- What are the risks and benefits associated with the recommended modality?
- Is there research or evidence to support the use of this modality for this target problem?
- Is this modality appropriate and tested on those with the same or similar cultural background as the client?
- What training and experience does a social worker have with the recommended modality?

- Is the recommended modality evidence-based or consistent with available research? If not, why?

- Was the recommended modality discussed with and selected by a client?

- Will the use of the recommended modality be assessed periodically? When? How?

Test-Taking Strategies Applied

The question contains a qualifying word—PRIMARY—that indicates that there may be many criteria which go into decision making about selecting intervention modalities. The correct response choice is the one that is paramount in this decision.

At times interventions require modification based on individual client circumstances so consistency is not always achieved, making the first answer incorrect. In addition, not all services are delivered in agency settings or reimbursed by third-party payers, making these choices not primary.

The correct answer always is the one that focuses on the delivery of effective services to assist clients with their problems. Thus, ensuring that interventions are supported by empirical research and consistent with the professional code of ethics is most important in making a selection.

Knowledge Area

Unit II—Assessment and Intervention Planning (Content Area); Intervention Planning (Competency); The Criteria Used in the Selection of Intervention/Treatment Modalities (e.g., Client/Client System Abilities, Culture, Life Stage) (KSA)

42. D

Rationale

Social workers must always respect and promote the right of clients to **self-determination**. When clients are faced with difficult choices, social workers must assist clients to identify and clarify their goals. Social workers may limit clients' self-determination only when clients' actions or potential actions pose a serious foreseeable and imminent risk to themselves or others.

In order for clients to provide **informed consent**, they must be provided with clear and understandable language related to services to be provided, risks, benefits, alternatives, and so on.

Test-Taking Strategies Applied

The case scenario calls for selecting the correct answer based on the standard that it will "best assist the client." Urging the client to get the surgery is not acknowledging his right to self-determination. His refusal does not pose any true safety risk—it simply does not afford him the possibility of enhanced mobility. Speaking to his family would be inappropriate as he is the client; they are not. Providing him with educational materials can be helpful, but outlining only the benefits does not give him all the information needed for informed consent.

The correct answer is the one that does not have the social worker attempting to influence the client's decision. Assisting the client to prioritize his concerns can aid in determining his most salient fears. It may also assist him in determining whether the benefits outweigh the risks and what apprehensions would need to be addressed in order for him to make an alternate choice.

Knowledge Area

Unit IV—Professional Relationships, Values, and Ethics (Content Area); Professional Values and Ethical Issues (Competency); Client/Client System Competence and Self-Determination (e.g., Financial Decisions, Treatment Decisions, Emancipation, Age of Consent, Permanency Planning) (KSA)

43. C

Rationale

The **helping relationship** between a social worker and client is expressed through interaction. This interaction is commonly thought of in terms of verbal communication, which is natural, because the majority of treatment involves talking. However, nonverbal communication is also very important. Body posture, gestures, facial expressions, eye movements, and other reactions often express feelings and attitudes more clearly than do spoken words.

Test-Taking Strategies Applied

The question contains a qualifying word—MOST. While some of the incorrect response choices may be important in practice, the correct answer must be critical to the formation of an "effective helping relationship." Training and experience of a social worker, as well as agency policies, are not directly related to the core of the helping process, namely the relationship between a social worker and a client. Only the correct answer acknowledges the interface between a social worker and a client. The reciprocal nature of the helping process is essential. A social worker is not an advice giver. A therapeutic relationship must be built on trust and respect by both parties that can be achieved only through effective communication.

Knowledge Area

Unit IV—Professional Relationships, Values, and Ethics (Content Area); Professional Development and Use of Self (Competency); The Principles and Techniques for Building and Maintaining a Helping Relationship (KSA)

44. B

Rationale

Echolalia is the repetition of phrases, words, or parts of words. Echolalia may be a sign of **Autism Spectrum Disorder** (ASD). Almost all toddlers go through a stage in which they "parrot" words and phrases that they overhear. Mimicry is an efficient way to experiment with different sounds and practice emerging social language skills. This is a normal and a critical stage in language development. However, these behaviors past early childhood can be considered atypical. Some communication problems that can be used in assisting to make a diagnosis of ASD are pedantic speech or unusually formal language (child speaks like an adult or "little professor"), echolalia (immediate or delayed), "jargon" or gibberish (mature jargoning after developmental age of 24 months), pronoun reversal (e.g., "You" for "I"; not just mixing up gender pronouns), and referring to self by own name (does not use "I"). Other criteria for ASD must also be met in order to make a proper diagnosis.

In *DSM-5*, **Catatonia** may be diagnosed as a specifier for **Depressive Disorders, Bipolar Disorder** (BD), and Psychotic Disorders; as a separate diagnosis in the context of another medical condition; or as an other specified diagnosis. The major characteristic of catatonia is stupor. Stupor is a condition in which a client lacks critical cognitive functioning and is unresponsive to stimuli other than pain. Under *DSM-5*, three of the 12 characteristic symptoms of Catatonia must be present. One of those symptoms is echolalia.

BD and Major Depressive Disorder are not characterized by communication deficits or problems.

Test-Taking Strategies Applied

This is a recall question that relies on social workers knowing concepts and terms associated with communication problems. In order to select the correct answer, the definition of echolalia must be known. The integration of this knowledge and that on the *DSM-5* forms a road map to the correct response choice. Often questions on assessment and intervention planning rely on having a good foundation on child and adult development to know what is typical and what is not.

Knowledge Area

Unit I—Human Development, Diversity, and Behavior in the Environment (Content Area); Human Growth and Development (Competency); Communication Theories and Styles (KSA)

45. B

Rationale

When doing assessment and intervention planning, social workers need to know **basic medical terminology**. Central to this knowledge is understanding how the brain works. The brain is the most complex part of the human body and is the seat of intelligence, interpreter of the senses, initiator of body movement, and controller of behavior. The **cerebrum** fills up most of the skull. It is involved in remembering, problem solving, thinking, and feeling. It also controls movement. The **cerebellum** sits at the back of the head, under the cerebrum. The cerebellum receives information from the sensory systems, the spinal cord, and other parts of the brain and then regulates motor movements. The cerebellum coordinates voluntary movements such as posture, balance, coordination, and speech, resulting in smooth and balanced muscular activity. It is also important for learning motor behaviors. It controls coordination and balance. The **brainstem** sits beneath the cerebrum in front of the cerebellum. It connects the brain to the spinal cord and controls automatic functions such as breathing, digestion, heart rate, and blood pressure.

Test-Taking Strategies Applied

This is a recall question about parts of the brain. While most questions on the examination are broad and do not require knowing this level of detail, social workers must be prepared to know some terms associated with each of the KSAs. As social workers often work with those who have traumatic or acquired brain injuries and the brain is responsible for all thought and movement that is done, one of the few specific questions that may appear on the examination could be in this area. When studying, do not get lost in the details as the bulk of questions will not be this specific. However, it is good to review key terms associated with the KSAs for the few very specific questions that cannot be answered without this knowledge.

Knowledge Area

Unit II—Assessment and Intervention Planning (Content Area);
Biopsychosocial History and Collateral Data (Competency); Basic
Medical Terminology (KSA)

46. D

Rationale

There is common agreement about the **functions of supervision.** They
include administrative, educational, and supportive responsibilities as
follows:

Administrative—the promotion and maintenance of good standards
of work, coordination of practice with policies of administration, and the
assurance of an efficient and smooth-running office

Educational—the educational development of each social worker
in a manner calculated to inspire the full realization of her or his
possibilities of usefulness

Supportive—the maintenance of harmonious working relationships
and the cultivation of positive interactions among colleagues

Test-Taking Strategies Applied

The case scenario asks how documenting attendance at an agency training
would be classified according to supervision function. The question
is asking about the actions of the supervisor—not the social worker.
Administrative functions include, but are not limited to, reviewing
organizational policies and procedures, documenting training experiences,
conducting performance reviews, and/or reporting on client, worker, or
agency activities. While the training may be educational in nature and aims
to support the social worker's activities, the documentation of training
completion in the social worker's personnel file is administrative in nature.

Bureaucratic is not a function of supervision.

Knowledge Area

Unit III—Interventions With Clients/Client Systems (Content Area);
Intervention Processes and Techniques for Use With Larger Systems
(Competency); Educational Components, Techniques, and Methods of
Supervision (KSA)

47. C

Rationale

Role playing is a teaching strategy that offers several advantages. Role
playing in social work practice may be seen between supervisor and

supervisee or social worker and client. In all instances, role playing usually raises interest in a topic as supervisees or clients are not passive recipients in the learning process. In addition, role playing teaches empathy and understanding of different perspectives. In role playing, participation helps embed concepts. Role playing gives clarity to information that may be abstract or difficult to understand.

The use of role playing emphasizes personal concerns, problems, behavior, and active participation. *Role playing improves interpersonal and communication skills and enhances communication.*

Test-Taking Strategies Applied

The question contains a qualifying word—BEST—though it is not capitalized. While several of the incorrect response choices may be useful, the supervisee's primary issue is assertiveness. The goal for the supervisor is to teach the supervisee how to express his positive and negative feelings and stand up for the rights of clients in a way that will not alienate others. Only the correct answer gives the supervisee the opportunity to practice his expressive communication skills. The supervisor explaining the importance of speaking up or clarifying his role will not directly help with the problem. Accompanying the supervisee to future meetings may be supportive, but will not be effective if the supervisee does not feel comfortable and have the needed tools to confidently express his opinions independently in a constructive manner.

Knowledge Area

Unit III—Interventions With Clients/Client Systems (Content Area); Intervention Processes and Techniques for Use Across Systems (Competency); The Techniques of Role Play (KSA)

48. B

Rationale

Social workers need to know **basic medical terminology** even if they are not based in hospitals. This knowledge will help understand health problems experienced by clients and appropriate interventions to address them.

If a client is having ongoing and serious trouble swallowing and can't get enough food or liquids by mouth, a feeding tube may be put directly into the stomach through the abdominal skin. This procedure is called a **percutaneous endoscopic gastrostomy** (PEG). PEG allows nutrition, fluids, and/or medications to be put directly into the stomach, bypassing the mouth and esophagus. Clients who have difficulty swallowing, problems with their appetite, or an inability to take adequate nutrition through the mouth can benefit from this procedure.

Specialized liquid nutrition, as well as fluids, is given through the PEG tube. If the PEG tube is placed because of swallowing difficulty (e.g., after a stroke), there will still be restrictions on oral intake. A few PEG clients may continue to eat or drink after the procedure so it is important for a client to discuss restrictions with his or her physician.

PEG tube placement is one of the most common endoscopic procedures performed today, and more than 100,000 are performed annually in the United States.

Test-Taking Strategies Applied

This question requires knowledge about a common endoscopic procedure, insertion of a PEG tube. "Gastro" is a common English prefix derived from the ancient Greek "gastros" ("stomach"). It is used in many words, including "gastronomy," and can be a clue that the answer is not related to mobility, oxygenation, or waste elimination.

Knowledge Area

Unit II—Assessment and Intervention Planning (Content Area); Biopsychosocial History and Collateral Data (Competency); Basic Medical Terminology (KSA)

49. D

Rationale

Bioethics is the analysis and study of moral, legal, social, and ethical considerations involving the biological and medical sciences. Social workers involved in genetic counseling and reproductive health face difficult ethical issues concerning the use of technology for genetic selection and engineering, in vitro fertilization, surrogate motherhood, and abortion. Social workers in neonatal intensive care units understand the ethical implications of decisions to use technology to sustain the lives of remarkably premature and low-birth-weight infants. Most recently, a handful of social workers associated with health care programs involved in cloning and stem cell research have had to wrestle with a host of widely publicized and daunting bioethical issues. In addition, social workers involved in organ transplantation programs at major medical centers participate in ethical decisions and debates concerning the allocation of scarce hearts, kidneys, and livers, as well as the selection of candidates for artificial organs. Oncology social workers, along with other social workers involved with terminally ill patients, participate in ethical decisions concerning the termination of life support, the limits of aggressive medical treatment, and other end-of-life decisions.

Test-Taking Strategies Applied

The case scenario asked for the answer that would "best assist the client." Social workers should be educational, nonjudgmental, and neutral when the issue of whether to pursue genetic testing is at question and help clients to understand that results not only impact them, but affect their entire family. In terms of presymptomatic testing for Huntington's, most clients at risk of this disease have opted not to undergo testing. Asking clients to think about how their lives will be different by finding out can be useful. There are no right or wrong decisions about testing; it is a highly personal choice. The concept of personal autonomy is one of the guiding principles of biomedical ethics and a major issue when considering genetic testing. Each family member who is at risk of developing an inherited disease has a right to know or not to know his or her genetic risks. Therefore, it is important for clients to understand the impact that testing can have personally and on others in their families.

The incorrect response choices all involve the social worker recommending or discouraging testing. The correct answer assists the client to understand the implication of his decision while not imposing the views of the social worker on the decision.

Knowledge Area

Unit I—Human Development, Diversity, and Behavior in the Environment (Content Area); Human Growth and Development (Competency); Basic Principles of Human Genetics (KSA)

50. A

Rationale

The problem-solving process drives the **methods used to develop an intervention plan**. The steps that precede planning include engagement and assessment, which are both essential to ensuring that a social worker and client have created a therapeutic alliance and collected the information needed to begin planning, the third stage.

In planning, a social worker and client should

1. Define the problem (in a well-defined, clear, and data-driven format)
2. Examine the causes of the problem and how it relates to other positive or negative aspects of a client's life

3. Generate possible solutions that will impact on the problem

4. Identify the driving and restraining forces related to implementation of each of the possible solutions

5. Rate the driving and restraining forces related to consistency and potency

6. Prioritize solutions based on these ratings

7. Develop SMART objectives—Specific, Measurable, Achievable, Relevant, and Time-specific—related to the chosen solutions

8. Create strategies and activities related to the objectives

Test-Taking Strategies Applied

The correct answer is needed "in order to formulate a treatment plan." Social workers should use the problem-solving process when evaluating the response choices, remembering that engaging and assessing are precursors to planning. While some of the answers describe pragmatic actions of a social worker, only one is directly related to assessment.

Insurance companies use medical necessity criteria to make decisions. If appropriate services can be provided in less costly alternative settings, then inpatient hospitalization will not be covered. In this case scenario, the social worker needs to understand the severity of the symptoms and determine an appropriate level of care so he or she can explain to the client the options that will be authorized by her insurance. Just because the client wants inpatient care does not mean that it is needed. Thus, finding out more about the problem is the key to formulating an acceptable treatment plan.

Knowledge Area

Unit II—Assessment and Intervention Planning (Content Area); Intervention Planning (Competency); The Criteria Used in the Selection of Intervention/Treatment Modalities (e.g., Client/Client System Abilities, Culture, Life Stage) (KSA)

51. B

Rationale

Hypomania is a condition similar to mania, but less severe. The symptoms are elevated mood, increased activity, decreased need for sleep, grandiosity, racing thoughts, and so on. Hypomanic episodes differ from mania as they do not cause significant distress or impair client's work or family/social life in an obvious way while manic episodes do. There are never any psychotic features present in hypomanic episodes.

Other symptoms include

1. Inflated self-esteem or grandiosity
2. More talkative than usual or pressure to keep talking
3. Distractibility (e.g., attention too easily drawn to unimportant or irrelevant external stimuli)
4. Increase in goal-directed activity (either socially, at work or school, or sexually) or psychomotor agitation
5. Excessive involvement in pleasurable activities that have a high potential for painful consequences (e.g., the person engages in unrestrained buying sprees, sexual indiscretions, or foolish business investments)

Hypomanic episodes are associated with a change in functioning that is uncharacteristic. This change in functioning and in mood is not subtle—the change is directly noticeable by others (usually friends or family members). Hypomania can be difficult to diagnose because it may masquerade as mere happiness. It is important to diagnose hypomania because, as an expression of Bipolar Disorder, it can cycle into depression and carry an increased risk of suicide.

Test-Taking Strategies Applied

This is a recall question about symptoms associated with mental disorders. Social workers must be familiar with key clinical terms in order to ensure that clients receive correct diagnoses. Social workers should not be quick to label or give clients diagnoses unless all of the required clinical criteria are met. However, ensuring that clients receive the proper diagnoses when symptoms are present is equally important to make certain adequate treatment is received.

Knowledge Area

Unit II—Assessment and Intervention Planning (Content Area); Biopsychosocial History and Collateral Data (Competency); The Indicators of Mental and Emotional Illness Throughout the Lifespan (KSA)

52. A

Rationale

Social workers often find themselves providing services to those who did not choose to receive them and need methods aimed at working with involuntary clients. While there are many interventions that may be helpful, the use of **paradoxical interventions** can assist with the resistance that often accompanies these circumstances. Paradoxical interventions or directives involve prescribing the very symptom that a client wants to resolve. It is a complex concept often equated with reverse psychology. It is asking for something in order to achieve the opposite result. The underlying principle is that clients engage in behaviors for a reason, which is typically to meet a need (rebellion, attention, a cry for help, etc.). In prescribing the symptom, social workers help clients to understand this need and determine how much control (if any) they have over the symptom. By choosing to manifest the symptom, they may recognize they can create it and therefore have the power to stop or change it. It helps clients be in control of their behavior and experiences. Paradoxical interventions are often used with families as part of strategic family therapy.

A **cognitive distortion** is an exaggerated or irrational thought that is believed to perpetuate the effects of psychopathological states. It is the focus of what cognitive behavior and other therapeutic approaches try to change.

A **double bind** is a dilemma in communication in which a client receives two or more conflicting messages whereby a successful response to one message results in a failed response to the other. Thus, a client is automatically wrong regardless of his or her action.

Manifest content is the concrete words or terms in a communication. Thus, a **manifest message** is that which is taken literally without analyzing its hidden or underlying meaning.

Test-Taking Strategies Applied

Questions on the examination often require the integration of knowledge. Social workers have to understand methods to facilitate communication, including both verbal and nonverbal communication techniques. Competency in direct practice requires the ability to apply these strategies to situations involving involuntary clients. Obtaining the correct response requires having knowledge about each of the response choices listed (which relate to one or more of the KSAs tested). The statement by the social worker that is in quotation marks represents the opposite of the desired result. Paradox means contradiction or incongruence—both words describe telling the client that services will not be helpful and not to come back to meet with the social worker.

Knowledge Area

Unit III—Interventions With Clients/Client Systems (Content Area); Intervention Processes and Techniques for Use Across Systems (Competency); Methods to Engage and Work With Involuntary Clients/ Client Systems (KSA)

53. B

Rationale

Often clients have multiple problems. Problem identification must include **methods of involving clients in identifying problems** targeted for intervention. Problems should always be considered using person-in-environment perspectives and strengths-based approaches. It is essential that social workers, through the problem-solving process, view clients as experts in their lives.

Clients should be asked about what they would like to see changed and clients' definitions of problems should be accepted. Clients should be asked about what will be different when their problems are solved. Social workers should listen carefully for, and work hard to respect, the directions in which clients want to go with their lives (their goals) and the words they use to express these directions.

Clients should be asked about the paths that they would like to take to make desired changes. Clients' perceptions should be respected and clients' inner resources (strengths) should be maximized as part of treatment.

Test-Taking Strategies Applied

The question contains a qualifying word—FIRST. In the case scenario, the client's financial troubles may have resulted from her employment instability. However, the cause of her absences is unknown. She may have lost her past jobs due to similar behavior. *The social worker must find out from the client about existing problems.* While the employer wants her to have better attendance, it may not be possible without getting at the root cause of the issues causing the absences. Absences are symptoms of underlying issues—not the problem itself.

According to the steps in the problem-solving process, the social worker must work with the client to assess the situation before acting (interventions represent the incorrect response choices). While her caregiving responsibilities, coupled with financial insecurity, may seem to be pressing, the client may have other areas of concern that require attention.

Knowledge Area

Unit II—Assessment and Intervention Planning (Content Area); Assessment Methods and Techniques (Competency); Methods of Involving Clients/Client Systems in Problem Identification (e.g., Gathering Collateral Information) (KSA)

54. A

Rationale

Assessment is a vital component of the therapeutic process. It begins after engagement and drives planning or the creation of contracts. Social workers must consider biological, psychological, and social factors when identifying the root causes of problems. Diagnostic information should always be shared with clients and used to facilitate the establishment of intervention plans. *Assessment is continual and must incorporate information that is discovered during the entire problem-solving process.*

Test-Taking Strategies Applied

This is a recall question that relies on social workers understanding the process of assessment. While the incorrect response choices may be helpful, they do not directly relate to all of the information contained in the question.

In the case scenario, the client is seeing a social worker for a particular problem, grief, upon which the treatment plan is based. However, the client is experiencing a new issue, a cancer diagnosis, that may result in other, even more immediate, needs. Thus, the social worker "should respond to this disclosure" about his medical condition by assessing its impact to determine whether modifications to existing treatment goals are required.

Adjusting his appointments may be needed, but it does not account for how the diagnosis will impact social work services. The client may need to rely on his natural support network, but the social worker should not be taking charge of this process, especially before an assessment has been made of his needs. Lastly, there is no information in the case scenario about the type or severity of his cancer so reassuring him about the effectiveness of treatment may seem disingenuous to the client. Addressing the impacts of the illness on all areas of well-being—social, emotional, psychological, and so on—will be needed, but can occur only after more information is obtained from the client.

Knowledge Area

Unit II—Assessment and Intervention Planning (Content Area); Assessment Methods and Techniques (Competency); Methods to Assess the Client's/Client System's Strengths, Resources, and Challenges (e.g., Individual, Family, Group, Organization, Community) (KSA)

55. C

Rationale

The traditional definition of race and ethnicity is related to biological and sociological factors, respectively. **Race** refers to physical characteristics, such as skin, hair, or eye color. **Ethnicity** refers to cultural factors, including nationality, regional culture, ancestry, and language. Thus, race is usually judged by appearance while ethnicity is determined based on membership in social and cultural groups. Since ethnicity is about the learned cultural behaviors celebrated throughout regions around the world, it can be altered or mimicked through choice and beliefs. In addition, it is possible to have more than one ethnicity at a given time, but race is considered unchanging or fixed throughout the life course.

Test-Taking Strategies Applied

This is a recall question that requires a social worker to understand the difference and relationship between race and ethnicity.

A client can be discriminated against based on national origin and/ or culture regardless of whether he or she is the dominant (majority) or nondominant (minority) group. Thus, the response choices which state that nondominance or minority status are the bases of the prejudice have to be eliminated.

Knowledge Area

Unit I—Human Development, Diversity, and Behavior in the Environment (Content Area); Human Growth and Development (Competency); Theories of Racial, Ethnic, and Cultural Development Throughout the Lifespan (KSA)

56. C

Rationale

Many ethical standards speak to the **professional boundaries** that social workers should maintain with clients. Social workers must ensure that they do not engage in dual or multiple relationships that may impact on the treatment of clients. Social workers should be alert to and avoid conflicts of interest that interfere with the exercise of professional discretion and impartial judgment. Social workers should avoid potential or real conflicts of interest. Dual relationships can be simultaneous or consecutive.

Test-Taking Strategies Applied

In this case scenario, the student is requesting to engage in a dual relationship with the social worker. According to the 2008 *NASW Code of Ethics,* the social worker should avoid engaging in such a relationship due to potential conflicts. For example, the student may need a professional reference from the social worker in the future. This request presents a problem if the social worker is now providing services as information learned in counseling may positively or negatively influence the social worker's opinion about the former student. There are many other reasons that make the student's request inadvisable.

The student also has interacted with other agency personnel in a professional capacity as a result of her internship. Thus, seeing another social worker in the agency does not mitigate the conflict or existence of a dual relationship. It is best for the student to seek services from another provider. The standards in the 2008 *NASW Code of Ethics* should be used to choose between the correct and incorrect response choices.

Knowledge Area

Unit IV—Professional Relationships, Values, and Ethics (Content Area); Professional Development and Use of Self (Competency); Ethical Issues Related to Dual Relationships (KSA)

57. B

Rationale

Using the *DSM-5,* the diagnostic criteria for **Borderline Personality Disorder** (BPD) requires clients to have five of nine characteristics to be diagnosed. Clients who partially, but incompletely, meet this criteria set may be considered to have borderline personality traits or features. Although not fulfilling criteria for the full disorder, such a formulation may nonetheless be useful in guiding treatment decisions.

BPD is characterized as a pervasive pattern of instability of interpersonal relationships, self-image, and affects, and marked impulsivity beginning by early adulthood and present in a variety of contexts, as indicated by five (or more) of the following:

1. Frantic efforts to avoid real or imagined abandonment
2. A pattern of unstable and intense interpersonal relationships characterized by alternating between extremes of idealization and devaluation
3. Identity disturbance: markedly and persistently unstable self-image or sense of self
4. *Impulsivity* in at least two areas that are potentially self-damaging (e.g., spending, sex, substance abuse, reckless driving, binge eating)

5. *Recurrent suicidal behavior*, gestures, or threats, or self-mutilating behavior

6. *Affective instability* due to a marked reactivity of mood (e.g., intense episodic dysphoria, irritability, or anxiety usually lasting a few hours and only rarely more than a few days)

7. Chronic feelings of emptiness

8. Inappropriate, intense anger or difficulty controlling anger (e.g., frequent displays of temper, constant anger, recurrent physical fights)

9. Transient, stress-related paranoid ideation or severe dissociative symptoms

Test-Taking Strategies Applied

The question contains a qualifying word—EXCEPT. Three of the four response choices include symptoms for BPD in the *DSM-5*. While a client with BPD may have comorbid obsessive tendencies, they are not distinguishing features of this disorder.

Knowledge Area

Unit II—Assessment and Intervention Planning (Content Area); Assessment Methods and Techniques (Competency); The Use of the Diagnostic and Statistical Manual of the American Psychiatric Association (KSA)

58. C

Rationale

Social workers who use **single-subject designs** to evaluate practice find it both a powerful and satisfying research method. One reason for this is that single-subject designs provide feedback quickly about the effects of the treatment conditions. Social workers know relatively soon whether the treatment is working or not working. Day-to-day changes can be observed firsthand, quickly, and in individual clients. If daily changes to the treatment are necessary, they can be made. Seldom do social workers have available scientific evaluation procedures that do this. In contrast to the single-subject approach, a large sample statistical approach may take weeks or months of testing, calculating means, then performing statistical analyses, and so on, and unfortunately, often nothing may be known about the effects of the treatment conditions until the final statistical analysis is complete.

Because the baseline serves as a point from which the treatment effects are judged, *it is important that a stable baseline be established.* There is no set number of days or sessions that define baseline stability. Instead, a criterion of stability must be established with some clients taking a little time to establish stability and others taking much longer. Without stability, it will be impossible to discern if changes in functioning would have occurred naturally without the intervention.

Test-Taking Strategies Applied

This is a recall question that relies on social workers knowing about the use of single-subject designs in practice. Social workers should remember that an intervention phase follows a baseline. It is critical that the target behavior is not increasing, decreasing, or erratic (variable) prior to the introduction of the intervention or social workers will not be able to attribute changes to the treatment rather than continuation of an ongoing trend in the target behavior that would have occurred naturally.

Knowledge Area

Unit II—Assessment and Intervention Planning (Content Area); Assessment Methods and Techniques (Competency); Basic and Applied Research Design and Methods (KSA)

59. D

Rationale

Social workers use **single-subject designs** to determine whether an intervention has had an intended impact. Single-subject designs involve collecting data through repeated, systematic measurement. A client's behavior will be measured before anything is changed to gather a baseline measurement (denoted by an "A") and then an intervention will be introduced to see if change occurs (denoted by a "B"). For example, if a social worker was going to assist a client to stop smoking, then a few weeks may be spent measuring how much the client smokes before an intervention begins. If the intervention had a positive effect and smoking behavior is reduced, the intervention will continue, but if it has no effect or a negative effect, then it will not. A common type of single-subject design is known as a reversal method. In these designs, after a period of intervention, the intervention is removed and a client is returned to a baseline condition. This is desirable as a social worker can see if the new behavioral pattern could continue without the intervention.

One type of reversal method is the ABA design. This method starts with a baseline period followed by an intervention and then returns to baseline. *A problem with reversal designs is that it could be considered unethical to return a client back to a preintervention state (by withdrawing the intervention) if the intervention is working and his or her behavior could be harmful without it.*

Test-Taking Strategies Applied

The question is asking about ethical issues related to reversal designs. Obtaining the correct answer requires knowledge that reversal methods are those in which interventions are withdrawn once introduced. It is optimal to have baseline measurements and social workers should be concerned with making sure that treatments are affordable. However, both these response choices, along with the availability of alternative treatments, are not directly related to reversal methods, making them incorrect.

Knowledge Area

Unit II—Assessment and Intervention Planning (Content Area); Assessment Methods and Techniques (Competency); Basic and Applied Research Design and Methods (KSA)

60. B

Rationale

Short-term interventions or brief therapy focuses on resolving a specific problem within a minimal amount of time to achieve specific goals. Treatments like **dialectic behavioral, task-centered, crisis intervention, cognitive behavioral**, and **solution-focused** are all short-term. Brief treatments are generally aimed at motivating a client to perform a particular action (e.g., to enter treatment, change a behavior, think differently about a situation), whereas long-term therapies are used to address larger concerns (e.g., altering personality characteristics, addressing long-standing problems). Long-term therapies can be very effective for clients with complex mental disorders.

While there are some short-term psychoanalytic models, most are long in duration. **Psychoanalysis** helps clients understand themselves more fully and involves uncovering—and learning to deal more effectively with—unconscious conflicts. It may also assist clients to understand how certain types of adverse childhood experiences interfere with adult functioning.

Test-Taking Strategies Applied

The question contains a qualifying word—MOST. While it is possible to reflect on childhood experiences and unconscious conflicts in any therapeutic approach, these characteristics are the hallmark of psychoanalysis. All of the approaches listed, except the correct one, are also short-term interventions and the social worker "has been helping a client for more than a year."

Knowledge Area

Unit II—Assessment and Intervention Planning (Content Area); Intervention Planning (Competency); Psychotherapies (KSA)

61. B

Rationale

Professional objectivity means that social worker communication should not be burdened with emotional investment. If a client feels judged, he or she will not speak freely. A social worker cannot tell a client what he or she should feel or do. A client will change his or her feelings or actions only when motivated to do so.

In this case scenario, the client's racist language and feelings do not relate to the presenting problem or service goals. Thus, while the comments are disturbing to the social worker, they should not interfere with the delivery of needed services.

The social worker should not modify the client's service plan as the goals in the plan are dictated by assessment findings about current client difficulties. The case scenario clearly states that the discriminatory comments are not related to the firing, which is the presenting problem. Transferring the client is also not appropriate as it does not assist him. The social worker cannot let his or her own emotional reactions to views of the client interfere with treatment. Lastly, there is no justification for exploring the discriminatory attitudes of the client in more depth as they are not germane to the problem or service being provided.

It is important for the social worker to discuss his or her feelings with a supervisor so that they can be resolved in a manner that does not interfere with professional objectivity. The core of the helping process is the relationship between a social worker and client. If the client feels judged by the social worker, he may not be open to assistance.

Test-Taking Strategies Applied

The question requires the maintenance of objectivity—a key professional responsibility—in a challenging situation. When a social worker feels upset or even angry at what is said or done by a client, it is necessary to use supervision and consultation to process these emotional reactions so that they do not adversely interfere with service delivery. This case scenario gets to the essence of an effective helping relationship—unconditional positive regard or being nonjudgmental. A social worker should not make racism a therapeutic issue by exploring it further or incorporating it into the service plan if it is not related to the presenting problem or a concern of the client.

Knowledge Area

Unit IV—Professional Relationships, Values, and Ethics (Content Area); Professional Development and Use of Self (Competency); Professional Objectivity in the Social Worker–Client/Client System Relationship (KSA)

62. D

Rationale

Schizophrenia is characterized by delusions, hallucinations, disorganized speech and behavior, and other symptoms that cause social or occupational dysfunction. For a Schizophrenia diagnosis using the *DSM-5*, symptoms must have been present for 6 months and include at least 1 month of active symptoms. *DSM-5* raises the symptom threshold, requiring that an individual exhibit at least two of the specified symptoms. (In the *DSM's* previous editions, that threshold was one.) Additionally, the diagnostic criteria no longer identify subtypes. Subtypes had been defined by the predominant symptom at the time of evaluation. But, these were not helpful because clients' symptoms often changed from one subtype to another and presented overlapping subtype symptoms, which blurred distinctions among the five subtypes and decreased their validity. Some of the subtypes are now specifiers to help provide further detail in diagnosis. For example, Catatonia (marked by motor immobility and stupor) can be used as a specifier for Schizophrenia Spectrum and Other Psychotic Disorders such as Schizoaffective Disorder. This specifier can also be used with other disorders such as Bipolar Disorder and Major Depressive Disorder.

Test-Taking Strategies Applied

The question contains a qualifying word—NOT—that requires social workers to select the response choice that is NOT required in order to make a diagnosis of Schizophrenia using the *DSM-5*. Since the edition of the manual is mentioned, it provides a clue that the correct response choice may be a change that was made between the *DSM-IV-TR* (the previous edition) and the current one. The elimination of the subtypes for Schizophrenia is a substantive change in the *DSM-5*.

Knowledge Area

Unit II—Assessment and Intervention Planning (Content Area); Assessment Methods and Techniques (Competency); The Use of the Diagnostic and Statistical Manual of the American Psychiatric Association (KSA)

63. B

Rationale

Social workers must know **indicators of substance abuse** and other addictions, as well as signs of withdrawal. When a client describes himself or herself as "**dope sick**," it refers to a severe set of symptoms related to drug withdrawal. *This term most often refers to withdrawal from heroin and other opiate drugs, including prescription narcotics (opioids).* However, less commonly, it may also refer to methamphetamine, cocaine, or other drug withdrawals. When a client is "dope sick," he or she very often feels death is imminent. The duration of use, frequency of use, and other individual factors dictate how severe symptoms will be and how long they will last.

If a client enters a detox program, the symptoms can often be managed and mitigated by monitoring vital statistics, and using other drugs to help with withdrawal symptoms. Opioid withdrawal includes both physical and mental issues—anxiety and depression, severe mood swings, anger, irritability, restlessness, lethargy (feeling extremely tired and sluggish), nausea and vomiting, drug cravings, profuse sweating and/or chills, insomnia, muscle aches and pains, diarrhea, and so on.

Test-Taking Strategies Applied

The question contains a qualifying word—MOST. While "dope sick" can be used to refer to signs of withdrawal from a variety of drugs, it is most commonly associated with opiate and opioid addiction. Opiates are alkaloids derived from the opium poppy. Opium is a strong pain-relieving medication, and a number of drugs, such as morphine, codeine, and heroin, are made from this source. Opioids are synthetic or partly synthetic drugs that are manufactured to work in a similar way to opiates. Their active ingredients are made via chemical synthesis. Some common opioids are methadone, Percocet, Percodan, OxyContin (oxycodone), Lortab (hydrocodone), Demerol (pethidine), Dilaudid (hydromorphone), and Duragesic (fentanyl).

Heroin is the correct response choice as it is the only opiate or opioid listed.

Knowledge Area

Unit II—Assessment and Intervention Planning (Content Area); Biopsychosocial History and Collateral Data (Competency); The Indicators of Addiction and Substance Abuse (KSA)

64. B

Rationale

Clients often need assistance with **advocacy efforts**, including those which protect their rights to confidentiality of all information obtained in the course of professional service. Empowerment of clients is essential in all advocacy efforts. Providing education and support to clients while they try to change policies and/or services helps ensure that clients have the knowledge and assistance needed.

Test-Taking Strategies Applied

The correct answer is the one that will "best assist" the client given the case scenario. The social worker does not know the circumstances surrounding the alleged breach of confidentiality. The credibility of the complaint is best investigated by a regulatory, licensing, and/or credentialing body—not the social worker—by meeting with the former client or questioning the follow-up agency staff. Ceasing referrals would be inappropriate if the breach did not occur or was done to prevent serious, foreseeable, and imminent peril.

Educating the former client about the options available empowers him to make a decision about what action he would like to take and understand the benefits and limitations of each possibility.

Knowledge Area

Unit III—Interventions With Clients/Client Systems (Content Area); Intervention Processes and Techniques for Use With Larger Systems (Competency); Theories and Methods of Advocacy for Policies, Services, and Resources to Meet Clients'/Client Systems' Needs (KSA)

65. C

Rationale

Social workers must ensure that they do not engage in **dual or multiple relationships** that may impact on the treatment of clients. Social workers should be alert to and avoid conflicts of interest that interfere with the exercise of professional discretion and impartial judgment. Social workers should inform clients when a real or potential conflict of interest arises and take reasonable steps to resolve the issue in a manner that makes clients' interests primary and protects clients' interests to the greatest extent possible.

Test-Taking Strategies Applied

This question requires knowledge about the need to avoid conflicts of interests. In the case scenario, the social worker has a personal relationship with the boy that precludes serving him. Offering suggestions about courses of action would not be appropriate as the social worker does not know the root cause of the problem and, therefore, cannot offer advice. Additionally, having the boy meet with the supervisor would not be advisable as it is also a conflict and requires the boy to waste time explaining his situation to someone who will not be treating him. While the case scenario describes the fighting as "destructive," there is no indication that the boy is in danger.

The boy should understand the reasons that the social worker cannot meet with him and freely choose from a listing of multiple appropriate providers. A suggestion by the social worker as to which one may be best may unduly influence the boy's decision.

Knowledge Area

Unit IV—Professional Relationships, Values, and Ethics (Content Area); Professional Development and Use of Self (Competency); Ethical Issues Related to Dual Relationships (KSA)

66. B

Rationale

Institutionalized discrimination or institutional racism is a pattern of giving negative treatment to a group of people based on an attribute, such as race. It leads to inequality, explaining why some people face unequal treatment or occupy unequal status. In hiring, research suggests that people hire people who tend to act and look exactly like themselves. Thus, it is difficult to embrace, celebrate, and hire a racially diverse pool of applicants without diverse leadership from the onset.

Structural and institutional racism is subtle. It is rooted in the operations of organizations, but can be detected. If an organizational structure disproportionately comprises those in the majority, dominant group, there appears to be an institutional racism problem. This discrimination perpetuates itself when those in charge of the hiring are constantly looking for the "right fit," and the "right fit" tends to always look like the rest of those who have already been hired. This bias process leads to homogeneity of those in power.

Test-Taking Strategies Applied

The question contains a qualifying word—FIRST. While many of the incorrect response choices, such as encouraging minority staff to apply for supervisory positions and implementing a human resource program to attract and develop candidates of color, are good ideas, they do not address the apparent root of the problem—institutionalized discrimination.

Without identifying and changing the policies and practices that are preventing minority staff from being promoted and/or hired into leadership positions, the ideas presented in the incorrect response choices will be useless. Discussing the concern with executive staff may be helpful, but only after the social worker has identified the reasons that minority candidates are not applying and/or being selected. Perhaps because they do not see persons of color in executive management, they do not feel that such positions are attainable or are sent the message, consciously or unconsciously, that it is not worth applying as they will not be selected. There also may be formal job requirements that disadvantage minority candidates. These barriers must be identified immediately in order for the social work administrator to begin to address the problem.

Knowledge Area

Unit I—Human Development, Diversity, and Behavior in the Environment (Content Area); Diversity, Social/Economic Justice, and Oppression (Competency); Systemic (Institutionalized) Discrimination (e.g., Racism, Sexism, Ageism) (KSA)

67. C

Rationale

Spirituality and/or religious beliefs are important **considerations in the selection of treatment modalities** as they have a strong influence on client behavior and attitudes. Historically, mental illness was thought to be caused by evil spirits, the "evil eye." In much of the world, it still is. The range of "normal" behavior varies by cultures as well. The "evil eye" is essentially a specific type of magical curse and has its roots in superstition. Any bad event for which there is not an obvious cause might be blamed on a curse. Curses, including the "evil eye," are an answer to why bad things happen to good people.

The best way to deal with the "evil eye" is to avoid it in the first place. The method varies by culture, geographic region, and personal preference. Once a person has been afflicted with the "evil eye," there are a variety of ways to have it removed. Often those who believe they have been harmed by the "evil eye" will seek out shamans, witch doctors, psychics, or other spiritual healers to remove the curses—often for a fee. In working with these populations, social workers should be aware of common folk beliefs and practices.

Test-Taking Strategies Applied

This question tests social workers' knowledge about cultural diversity. In social work, cultural diversity has primarily been associated with race and ethnicity, but it has a broader meaning that includes the sociocultural experiences of people of different genders, social classes, religious and spiritual beliefs, sexual orientations, ages, and physical and mental abilities. Understanding the religious and spiritual beliefs of clients is essential. Cultural competence in social work practice implies a heightened consciousness of how clients experience their uniqueness and deal with their differences and similarities within a larger social context.

Knowledge Area

Unit II—Assessment and Intervention Planning (Content Area); Intervention Planning (Competency); The Criteria Used in the Selection of Intervention/Treatment Modalities (e.g., Client/Client System Abilities, Culture, Life Stage) (KSA)

68. A

Rationale

Unconditional positive regard was used by humanistic psychologist Carl Rogers in client-centered therapy. Practicing unconditional positive regard means *accepting and respecting clients without judgment or evaluation*. It refers to acceptance of others whether they are liked or not. Unconditional positive regard can be misunderstood as being nice, pleasant, or agreeable with others; however, unconditional positive regard is not an action toward others. Rather, it is a feeling or mindset.

Test-Taking Strategies Applied

The question contains a qualifying word—BEST. While some of the response choices may be related to positive regard, unconditional acceptance is central to this construct, making it the correct answer.

Knowledge Area

Unit III—Interventions With Clients/Client Systems (Content Area); Intervention Processes and Techniques for Use Across Systems (Competency); Verbal and Nonverbal Communication Techniques (KSA)

69. B

Rationale

Social workers should provide clients with reasonable **access to records**. Social workers who are concerned that clients' access to their records could cause serious misunderstanding or harm should provide assistance in interpreting the records and consultation regarding the records. Social workers should limit clients' access to their records, or portions of their records, only in exceptional circumstances when there is compelling evidence that such access would cause serious harm. Both clients' requests and the rationale for withholding some or all of the record should be documented in clients' files.

Test-Taking Strategies Applied

This is a recall question that relies on social workers understanding the ethical mandate to provide clients access to records except when there is the possibility of serious misunderstanding or harm to clients if such information is released. In practice, social workers often treat records as belonging to employing agencies or themselves if in private practice. Social workers should view client records as the property of clients. Records are created and safeguarded for clients' benefit so that the most effective and efficient services can be delivered.

In this case scenario, the client has the right to access her file and should not be coerced into meeting with the social worker again to do so. The record cannot be withheld because the client terminated abruptly. The client should not have to contact the insurance company to receive the information. In addition, the insurance company may not have copies of all documents in the file that have been requested.

Knowledge Area

Unit IV—Professional Relationships, Values, and Ethics (Content Area); Confidentiality (Competency); The Use of Client/Client System Records (KSA)

70. A

Rationale

Mandated reporters are individuals required by law to report suspicions of child abuse or neglect. Since social workers work with children and families in a variety of settings and roles, it makes sense that the law in all states requires social workers to report their suspicions of child abuse and neglect. Although some social work settings—such as schools, hospitals, and mental health clinics—are more likely than others, like nursing homes, to yield suspicions of child maltreatment, all social workers regardless of setting are mandated reporters of suspected child abuse and neglect.

Social workers should report suspected child abuse or neglect even when they believe that it has already been investigated. Victims may be fearful about making their perpetrators angry and may be intentionally misinforming social workers about child protective services' involvement. *Reports should also not be delayed for any reason, such as consulting with a supervisor.* Documenting in clients' files may be useful, but it does not replace or fulfill the duty to report suspected abuse.

Test-Taking Strategies Applied

This is a recall question that relies on social workers understanding abuse and neglect concepts. Central to this knowledge base is the recognition that social workers are mandatory reporters who must be aware of the signs of abuse and report without delay. Proving that abuse has occurred is not the responsibility of a social worker. Child protective services must gather information and determine whether abuse or neglect is occurring. *All reasonable suspicions must be immediately reported by social workers to child protective services via abuse hotlines, regardless of agency protocol or policy as to how such reports should occur.*

Knowledge Area

Unit I—Human Development, Diversity, and Behavior in the Environment (Content Area); Concepts of Abuse and Neglect (Competency); Indicators and Dynamics of Abuse and Neglect Throughout the Lifespan (KSA)

71. A

Rationale

Trauma bonding is when a client wants to go back to or stays with a person who has caused him or her pain, with the irrational thinking that the person who caused the pain can take it away. Trauma bonding is similar to Stockholm syndrome, in which a victim sympathizes with an abuser. Exploitive relationships can create trauma bonds—chains that link a client to someone who is dangerous to him or her. They occur in situations of incredible intensity or importance where there is an exploitation of trust or power. Trauma bonds are characterized by betrayal that is so purposeful and self-serving it moves to the realm of trauma. Trauma bonds create chains of trust that link a client to someone who is exploitive, dangerous, abusive, and/or toxic. A client in a trauma bond feels very confused about his or her relationship, yet is unable to break free from it. Trauma bond relationships are manipulative and exploitive. Sometimes relationships that start out as intimate and lifelong can move into trauma bonds.

Test-Taking Strategies Applied

This is a recall question that relies on social workers to understand the psychological impact of stress, trauma, and violence. While the incorrect response choices may be true statements, they are not directly related to trauma bonding. Trauma bonding is loyalty to a person who is destructive. While the idea of bonding tends to bring up connotations of something good and beneficial, trauma bonds are unhealthy. They explain why victims of intimate partner abuse stay with their perpetrators.

Knowledge Area

Unit I—Human Development, Diversity, and Behavior in the Environment (Content Area); Human Growth and Development (Competency); The Impact of Stress, Trauma, and Violence (KSA)

72. A

Rationale

Religion provides people with meaning to their lives and helps guide them in their everyday moral choices.

Religion has connected the races and societies of the world. It has given meaning to lives that may seem otherwise hopeless. Religion has provided for a universal language and culture among those who believe in a higher power. The spirit or being who is worshiped and praised may not be the same, but the practices are usually similar and serve the same purpose—to give direction, insight, courage, and a divine connection.

Spirituality and/or religious beliefs have a profound impact on behaviors and attitudes. Thus, social workers must find out about these beliefs and assess their impact in contributing to and/or solving presenting problems.

Test-Taking Strategies Applied

The question contains a qualifying word—NEXT. The order in which the response choices are to occur is critical. When a question asks about the sequencing of actions by a social worker, it is helpful to recall the stage of the problem-solving process. This case scenario is occurring "upon intake," indicating that the social worker is meeting with the client on or close to the first session. Thus, the social worker is still engaging or building a therapeutic alliance with the client. Finding out more about the client's self-image and helping her to analyze her decision more carefully may be helpful, but these are incorrect responses as dealing with her feelings must occur first.

Universalization is a supportive intervention used to reassure and encourage clients. It places a client's experience in the context of other individuals who are experiencing the same or similar challenges, and seeks to help a client grasp that his or her feelings and experiences are not uncommon given the circumstances. Universalization "normalizes" a client's experience in an attempt to help avert natural feelings of "being alone," or, in this case scenario, help the client to see that she is not being punished or a bad person for having these feelings.

The woman is the client, so having the husband come to the next session is not appropriate as the social worker is not engaged in couples counseling.

Knowledge Area

Unit I—Human Development, Diversity, and Behavior in the Environment (Content Area); Diversity, Social/Economic Justice, and Oppression (Competency); The Effect of Culture, Race, and Ethnicity on Behaviors, Attitudes, and Identity (KSA)

73. A

Rationale

Problems can arise when a client is not clear on a **social worker's role**. Initial clarification should be made during engagement and should be discussed during the therapeutic process if the role of a social worker changes. Role is a behavior prescribed for an individual occupying a designated status.

Social role theory has some important terms that relate to role issues.

Role ambiguity is a lack of role clarity.

Role reversal is when two or more individuals switch roles.

Role conflict is an incompatibility with role expectations.

Role complementarity occurs when a role is carried out in an expected way.

People generally like to give advice. A danger is that clients may expect social workers to fulfill this inappropriate role. Social workers must correct role ambiguity so clients see them as consultants, advocates, case managers, catalysts, mediators, brokers, and so on—not advice givers.

Test-Taking Strategies Applied

Material in quotation marks deserves particular attention and usually relates to the answer. In this question, the client wants "to be told how to fix the problem." Based on this statement, the client is clearly unaware of a social worker's role in the problem-solving process. Role ambiguity exists and clarity is needed.

The question also contains a qualifying word—BEST. There is no role reversal as the client statement refers to only one role—the social worker's. There is also no role conflict as the performance of the social worker is not inconsistent with expectations—it is the expectation itself that is ambiguous. Lastly, role complementarity is not the optimal response choice as it relates to the fulfillment of role expectations. The social worker would need to be an advice giver in order for this answer to be correct.

Knowledge Area

Unit I—Human Development, Diversity, and Behavior in the Environment (Content Area); Human Growth and Development (Competency); Role Theories (KSA)

74. D

Rationale

Static risk factors are those that cannot be changed—characteristics of the offense (such as use of force), history of antisocial behavior (sexual and otherwise), age at first offense, gender of victims, and prior criminal history. Static risk variables are relatively easy to identify as they can be gathered from archival data, such as existing records.

Though many assessments are based on static, historical risk factors, they have been criticized for neglecting **dynamic (changeable) risk factors**. After all, if a client's risk is completely determined by historical, unchangeable factors, there is no reason to provide rehabilitative treatment. Psychotherapy cannot change a client's history; it can only affect variables that are amenable to change. Although age is considered a dynamic risk factor, the most useful dynamic risk factors are those amenable to deliberate interventions (e.g., substance abuse, unemployment).

Test-Taking Strategies Applied

This is a recall question that relies on social workers understanding the difference between static and dynamic risk factors. All of the response choices are risk factors, but only the correct one is dynamic. The remaining answers are static as they cannot be changed. Social workers should focus their efforts on interventions aimed at reducing or eliminating dynamic risk factors.

Knowledge Area

Unit I—Human Development, Diversity, and Behavior in the Environment (Content Area); Concepts of Abuse and Neglect (Competency); The Characteristics of Perpetrators of Abuse, Neglect, and Exploitation (KSA)

75. A

Rationale

The 2008 *NASW Code of Ethics* includes numerous standards that relate to **professional boundaries**. First, social workers should not take unfair advantage of any professional relationship or exploit others to further their personal, religious, political, or business interests (*NASW Code of*

Ethics, 2008—1.06 Conflicts of Interest). They should also be alert to and avoid conflicts of interest that interfere with the exercise of professional discretion and impartial judgment. As in relationships with clients, social workers should not engage in dual or multiple relationships with colleagues in which there is a risk of exploitation or potential harm.

Test-Taking Strategies Applied

As the provided response choices to the case scenario are asking whether actions are ethical or unethical, the question requires reliance on the professional code of ethics. Choosing the correct answer relies on applying several ethical standards. While the social worker did not directly gain financially from the client information, it was used for a personal interest, assisting a colleague, which is unethical. It is easy to see how using information obtained from this client can lead to many problems. For example, what if the colleague wants additional information about the timing of the new corporate center opening? The social worker may feel pressure to use client sessions to obtain additional information to assist the colleague rather than focus on client treatment. There also can be issues if the information provided by the social worker does not lead to financial gain. Feelings of resentment by the colleague toward the social worker or by the social worker toward the client can result. Contrarily, if the colleague's investment is prosperous, the colleague may reward the social worker in some way. In this instance, the social worker is indirectly benefiting from the client information.

Knowledge Area

Unit IV—Professional Relationships, Values, and Ethics (Content Area); Professional Development and Use of Self (Competency); Ethical Issues Related to Dual Relationships (KSA)

76. D

Rationale

Empathy is defined as the act of perceiving, understanding, experiencing, and responding to the emotional state and ideas of another person. It is understanding, being aware of, being sensitive to, and vicariously experiencing the feelings, thoughts, and experience of another of either the past or present without having the feelings, thoughts, and experience fully communicated in an objectively explicit manner. Empathy is sensing others' feelings and perspectives.

Empathy is not the same as sympathy. Sympathy is a feeling or an expression of pity or sorrow for the distress of another; an expression of compassion or commiseration. Sympathy can sometimes be perceived as denoting a paternalistic attitude, thereby being disempowering. Clients do not need sympathy or sorrow, but instead *someone to listen to them and validate their emotions* in a caring manner.

Test-Taking Strategies Applied

The question contains a qualifying word—BEST. While some of the response choices may be helpful, they do not "start where the client is" by addressing her feelings. Empathy is not pity. Also, helping the client prioritize her problems does not directly show sensitivity to her emotions, which is the most appropriate response. Trying to cheer the client up by suggesting that her job loss may be positive is not helpful as she is clearly distraught by this and other events. The social worker must address her feelings of being overwhelmed in order to be empathic.

Knowledge Area

Unit IV—Professional Relationships, Values, and Ethics (Content Area); Professional Development and Use of Self (Competency); The Concept of Acceptance and Empathy in the Social Worker–Client/Client System Relationship (KSA)

77. B

Rationale

In systems theory, **entropy** has been used to describe a force or tendency that is present in all systems. All systems tend to "run down," and to progress to a stage of reduced coherence and eventually completely random order. They tend to consume all the energy that they have available and eventually stop functioning or "fall apart." Families can be considered as systems. If there is an insufficient amount of social energy of the appropriate kind (some call this love) exchanged, there is likely to be some sort of breakdown in their ordered relationship, and the bond between them could weaken. Communities are also systems. Oppression, injustice, violence, malnutrition, and poverty all prevent people from working together in harmony, thereby causing entropy.

The reverse tendency, which has been called **negative entropy**, maintains or increases the order or harmony within systems. Examples of energy or influence that can act as negative entropy are food, affection, education, medicine, or anything else that helps sustain or improve well-being.

Test-Taking Strategies Applied

This is a recall question that relies on social workers understanding critical systems theory terms. When studying, it is critical to know the meaning of terms that are associated with social work theories, models, and perspectives. Questions such as this one may not even specify to which theory, model, or perspective the nomenclature responds.

The meaning of negative entropy is counterintuitive as it is positive for a system. "Negative" in this context means the opposite of entropy, which is the loss of energy. Thus, negative entropy is "good" for a system and entropy is "bad."

Knowledge Area

Unit I—Human Development, Diversity, and Behavior in the Environment (Content Area); Human Growth and Development (Competency); Systems and Ecological Perspectives and Theories (KSA)

78. C

Rationale

Values are linked to both behaviors and attitudes. For example, extrinsic values—such as wealth or preservation of public image—tend to influence levels of personal well-being. In general, the esteem of others or pursuit of material goods seem to drive people toward their pursuit, though more inherently rewarding motivations and self-direction values seem to provide more self-satisfaction.

It is common to see people segmented into distinct groups or dichotomies based on their values. People who hold strong traditional values are more likely to observe national holidays and customs. Stronger achievement values are associated with stress-related behaviors (such as taking on too many commitments).

Aspects of our society may constrain people from expressing the intrinsic values they hold. Education, the media, and social pressures are likely to influence the kinds of values seen as relevant to particular situations. Given the relationship between values and actions, it is important for a social worker to look at what influences values and how they develop and change over time.

Test-Taking Strategies Applied

The correct response must be chosen as it is the basis of being able "to effectively serve the client." Some of the incorrect answers provide tangible actions or interventions that may be useful. However, these interventions are not tied to the acknowledgment that a client's values will drive his or her attitudes and behaviors. Social workers must acknowledge and respect client values, understanding that they may be different from their own. *All individuals, including social workers and clients, tend to use their own social, economic, religious, and cultural background as the norm. Social workers must acknowledge the differences in values that they have from clients in order to be effective partners in the change process.*

In the case scenario, it is evident that the client's values are driving her decisions. Only through understanding and acknowledging these value-based choices can the social worker help her.

Knowledge Area

Unit I—Human Development, Diversity, and Behavior in the Environment (Content Area); Diversity, Social/Economic Justice, and Oppression (Competency); The Effect of Culture, Race, and Ethnicity on Behaviors, Attitudes, and Identity (KSA)

79. D

Rationale

Family theories provide theoretical and therapeutic bases for family-related situations. A family systems approach argues that in order to understand a family system, a social worker must look at the family as a whole, rather than focusing on its members.

In this case scenario, there are many problems mentioned that may or may not stem from the same underlying issue(s). The social worker can "best assist" by determining more specifically the expectations of the family members with regard to treatment outcomes. If all members are not focused on achieving the same results, it will be less likely that change will occur. It is unclear in the case scenario if they all view the problem, and desired outcomes, consistently.

Modeling good communication would be helpful, but does not address the underlying issues that need to be identified and prioritized in order for the intervention to be effective.

Test-Taking Strategies Applied

In case scenarios, it is critical to identify the client. In this scenario, it is the family as a whole, so two of the four response choices can be easily eliminated as they involve intervening with the son or parents separately. Often it is possible to help narrow down the number of possible correct response choices by ensuring that attention is being directed at the identified client.

Knowledge Area

Unit III—Interventions With Clients/Client Systems (Content Area); Intervention Processes and Techniques for Use Across Systems (Competency); Family Therapy Models, Interventions, and Approaches (KSA)

80. B

Rationale

There are three types of recognized **Personality Disorders**: odd-eccentric, dramatic, and anxious-fearful. Cluster A Personality Disorders are characterized by odd, eccentric thinking or behavior. They include Paranoid Personality Disorder, Schizoid Personality Disorder, and Schizotypal Personality Disorder. Cluster B Personality Disorders are characterized by dramatic, overly emotional, or unpredictable thinking or behavior. They include Antisocial Personality Disorder, Borderline Personality Disorder, Histrionic Personality Disorder, and Narcissistic Personality Disorder. Cluster C Personality Disorders are characterized by anxious, fearful thinking or behavior. They include Avoidant Personality Disorder, Dependent Personality Disorder, and Obsessive-Compulsive Personality Disorder.

Histrionic Personality Disorder is characterized by

- Constantly seeking attention
- Excessively emotional, dramatic, or sexually provocative actions to gain attention
- Speaking dramatically with strong opinions, but few facts or details to back them up
- Being easily influenced by others
- Having shallow, rapidly changing emotions
- Showing excessive concern with physical appearance
- Thinking relationships with others are closer than they really are

Test-Taking Strategies Applied

The question contains a qualifying word—MOST. While clients with other Personality Disorders may engage in attention-seeking behaviors, it is a hallmark of Histrionic Personality Disorder. Narcissistic Personality Disorder is within the same cluster as Histrionic Personality Disorder. It is based on the belief of self-importance and fantasies about power, success, and attractiveness. Clients with Narcissistic Personality Disorder fail to recognize others' needs and feelings. Thus, while there may be some attention-seeking with this disorder, it is based on receiving praise and admiration. Clients with Narcissistic Personality Disorder do not feel the need to seek attention as they feel that they already are the center of it.

Knowledge Area

Unit II—Assessment and Intervention Planning (Content Area); Assessment Methods and Techniques (Competency); The Use of the Diagnostic and Statistical Manual of the American Psychiatric Association (KSA)

81. A

Rationale

The **problem-solving approach** is based on the belief that an inability to cope with a problem is due to some lack of motivation, capacity, or opportunity to solve problems in an appropriate way. Clients' problem-solving capacities or resources are maladaptive or impaired.

The goal of the problem-solving process is to enhance client mental, emotional, and action capacities for coping with problems and/or making accessible the opportunities and resources necessary to generate solutions to problems.

A social worker engages in the problem-solving process via the following steps—engaging, assessing, planning, intervening, evaluating, and terminating.

Test-Taking Strategies Applied

The question contains a qualifying word—FIRST. This question is seeking the initial step that the social worker should take "in order to discuss the available options" with the client. Discussing options for treatment or intervention is the basis of the planning step in the problem-solving approach. Thus, the question is asking which of the response choices would occur before planning with the client. Two of the response choices—discussing the grief and helping the client contact the parents—are interventions that occur after planning, not before. The remaining two answers are tied to assessment, which precedes planning, but learning about the family history and relationships will be more helpful than simply finding out about the last contact when designing an appropriate intervention, making it the correct response choice.

Knowledge Area

Unit III—Interventions With Clients/Client Systems (Content Area); Intervention Processes and Techniques for Use Across Systems (Competency); Problem-Solving Models and Approaches (e.g., Brief, Solution-Focused Methods or Techniques) (KSA)

82. D

Rationale

The participation of clients in the process of identifying what is important to them now and in the future, and acting upon these priorities, is paramount. **Clients' participation in the intervention process** will reduce resistance, increase motivation to change, and ensure sustainability of progress made. In order to involve clients, social workers must continually listen to, learn about, and facilitate opportunities with clients whom they are serving. Methods should be used to enhance client involvement during intervention planning in each aspect of constructing a contract.

The goals of intervention and means used to achieve these goals are incorporated in a contractual agreement between a client and social worker. The contract (also called an intervention or service plan) may be informal or written. The contract specifies problem(s) to be worked on; the goals to reduce the problem(s); client and social worker roles in the process; the interventions or techniques to be employed; the means of monitoring progress; stipulations for renegotiating the contract; and the time, place, fee, and frequency of meetings.

Test-Taking Strategies Applied

Each of the response choices is linked to an important element of a contract between a client and social worker. The questions in quotation marks help the client to articulate goals that are concrete and observable, as well as set criteria for what real change will look like—when the problem no longer exists. Responses to the questions will not help to clarify roles, identify ways to solve the problem, or develop an evaluation strategy, making these answers incorrect.

Asking clients to think about how their lives would be different if their problems were gone is often referred to as "the miracle question."

Knowledge Area

Unit II—Assessment and Intervention Planning (Content Area); Intervention Planning (Competency); Methods to Involve Clients/Client Systems in Intervention Planning (KSA)

83. B

Rationale

Cognitive distortions, which were first theorized by Aaron Beck, are simply ways that the mind convinces clients of something that is not really true. These inaccurate thoughts are usually used to reinforce negative thinking or emotions—telling clients things that sound rational and accurate, but really serve only to keep them feeling bad about themselves. For instance, a client might tell himself or herself, "I always fail when I try to do something new; I therefore fail at everything I try." This is an example of "black-or-white" (or polarized) thinking. The client is only seeing things in absolutes—that if he or she fails at one thing, he or she must fail at all things. Cognitive distortions are at the core of what many social workers using **cognitive behavioral techniques** try to help a client learn to change. By learning to correctly identify these negative thought patterns, a client can then answer the negative thinking back, and refute it. By refuting the negative thinking over and over again, it will slowly diminish over time and be automatically replaced by more rational, balanced thinking. There are many cognitive distortions.

Jumping to conclusions is when clients know how others feel and why they act as they do without being told. For example, a client may conclude that someone is reacting negatively toward him or her, but doesn't actually bother to find out if it is correct. Another example is a client may anticipate that things will turn out badly, and will feel convinced that the prediction is already an established fact.

In **polarized thinking**, things are either "black or white." It is either perfection or failure—there is no middle ground. Clients place people or situations in "either/or" categories, with no shades of gray or allowing for the complexity of most people and situations. If a client's performance falls short of perfect, it is seen as total failure.

Catastrophizing is when clients expect disaster to strike no matter what. This is also referred to as "magnifying or minimizing." Clients hear about a problem and use "what if" questions (e.g., "What if tragedy strikes?" "What if it happens to me?"). For example, a client might exaggerate the importance of insignificant events (such as a mistake or someone else's achievement), or inappropriately shrink the magnitude of significant events until they appear tiny (e.g., a client's own desirable qualities or someone else's imperfections).

Blaming is holding other people responsible for pain or blaming oneself for every problem.

Test-Taking Strategies Applied

The question contains a qualifying word—MOST. While the client may be experiencing other cognitive distortions, the "black-or-white," "all-or-nothing" thinking is the hallmark of polarized thinking.

Knowledge Area

Unit III—Interventions With Clients/Client Systems (Content Area); Intervention Processes and Techniques for Use Across Systems (Competency); Cognitive and Behavioral Interventions (KSA)

84. C

Rationale

The concept of **mental health parity** generally refers to legal provisions that further the aim of achieving coverage in health insurance plans for the *treatment of mental health conditions that is equivalent to the coverage provided for physical conditions*. Just as there are many types of physical illness, mental illness is varied and can affect people at all stages of life. In fact, nearly all people will be affected by mental health or Substance Use Disorders themselves or in their families at some point during their life courses. Mental health parity acknowledges that mental illness is treatable and most who experience it recover and live happy, productive lives. However, treatment must be available to achieve optimum behavioral health. Physical health and mental health cannot be viewed as separate and distinct. One is not possible without the other.

Almost all states have passed some form of mental health parity legislation; however, most of these laws are limited in scope. Only a few states have parity requirements that apply to all mental health and Substance Abuse Disorders. Federal legislation, the Mental Health Parity and Addiction Equity Act of 2008 (MHPAEA), requires group health plans and health insurance issuers to ensure that financial requirements (e.g., co-pays, deductibles) and treatment limitations (e.g., visit limits) applicable to mental health and substance use treatment benefits are no more restrictive than the predominant requirements or limitations applied to substantially all medical/surgical benefits.

Test-Taking Strategies Applied

The question contains a qualifying word—BEST. Some of the incorrect response choices may be true, but they do not directly relate to the reason for "parity." Mental health treatment should be done by those with specialized education and experience who are compensated commensurate with other health care professionals. Mental health screenings are also critically important for detecting problems. However, the premise of Mental health parity is the equal treatment of Mental health and health conditions. This belief is supported by viewing both as interrelated. If Mental health issues are not addressed, clients will experience greater physical illness, so there are financial and physical benefits from enhancing access and payment for the treatment of mental disorders.

Knowledge Area

Unit III—Interventions With Clients/Client Systems (Content Area); Intervention Processes and Techniques for Use With Larger Systems (Competency); The Effects of Policies, Procedures, Regulations, and Legislation on Social Work Practice and Service Delivery (KSA)

85. C

Rationale

Clients may have a hard time achieving their goals if barriers exist within their larger environment (such as in work or school) or in their communities. In addition, if organizational and/or community factors have contributed to client distress, they must be changed to prevent them from affecting others in the same way. Social workers must not only assist with individual problems, but also must make **system-level changes** to achieve broader outcomes.

The problem-solving process can be used with organizations and communities. With these larger units of intervention, it includes

1. Acknowledging the problem
2. Analyzing/defining the problem
3. Generating possible solutions—"brainstorming"
4. Evaluating each option
5. Implementing the option of choice
6. Evaluating the outcome

Thus, a social worker uses the same process of engagement, assessment, planning, intervention, evaluation, and termination in planning interventions with organizations and communities.

Test-Taking Strategies Applied

The question contains a qualifying word—BEST. While some of the incorrect response choices would be acceptable, the correct answer must be linked to the comment by the agency administrator in quotation marks. The case scenario specifies that the social worker just started, not allowing proper time to assess the reasons for the staff turnover. Thus, the social worker should explain the shortcomings of designing an intervention before his or her assessment is complete.

A common mistake when planning interventions with organizations and communities is to move too quickly toward selecting and planning an intervention after spending too little time clarifying the problem or concern and exploring possible options on how to improve the situation.

Knowledge Area

Unit III—Interventions With Clients/Client Systems (Content Area); Intervention Processes and Techniques for Use With Larger Systems (Competency); Theories and Methods of Advocacy for Policies, Services, and Resources to Meet Clients'/Client Systems' Needs (KSA)

86. D

Rationale

Structural family therapy, developed by Salvador Minuchin, is a strengths-based, outcome-oriented treatment modality based on ecosystemic principles. The social worker focuses on what is taking place among family members, rather than on individual psyches. Family structure consists of recurrent patterns of interaction that its members develop over time as they accommodate to each other. A well-functioning family is not defined by the absence of stress or conflict, but by how effectively it handles them as it responds to the developing needs of its members and the changing conditions in its environment. The job of the social worker is to locate and mobilize underutilized strengths, helping the family outgrow constraining patterns of interaction that impede the actualization of its own resources.

Families are organized into subsystems with boundaries regulating the contact family members have with each other. *Enactment, in which family members are encouraged to deal directly with each other in sessions, permits the social worker to observe and modify their interactions.* Enactments are seen as in-session dialogues.

Behavioral family therapy approaches center on reinforcing desired behavior to improve communication within a family, rather than focusing on negative acts. This method operates on the theory that actions are learned responses acquired from past experiences. Social workers using this type of counseling encourage families to focus on the present and not dwell on the past. Families might learn ways to use positive reinforcement to achieve conflict resolution.

A **Bowenian**-trained social worker is interested in focusing on the intergenerational transmission process. Improvement in overall functioning will ultimately reduce a family member's symptomology. Eight major theoretical constructs are essential to understanding Bowen's approach—differentiation, emotional system, multigenerational transmission, emotional triangle, nuclear family, projection process, sibling position, and societal regression.

Strategic family therapy is active, directive, and task-centered. It is more interested in creating change in behavior than change in understanding.

Test-Taking Strategies Applied

The question contains a qualifying word—MOST. While a social worker may ask clients to role play or demonstrate interactions, it is very closely associated with structural family therapy. Knowledge about techniques to work with families is critical as all clients are part of family systems. Thus, social workers must be familiar with approaches that optimize functioning of the family and the well-being of its members.

Knowledge Area

Unit III—Interventions With Clients/Client Systems (Content Area); Intervention Processes and Techniques for Use Across Systems (Competency); Family Therapy Models, Interventions, and Approaches (KSA)

87. B

Rationale

Social workers must understand the indicators of psychosocial stress in order to provide effective treatment when there is a perceived threat to health or safety. The aim of **crisis intervention** should be the humane, competent, and compassionate care of all affected. The goal should be to prevent adverse health outcomes and to enhance the well-being of individuals and communities. In particular, it is vital to use all appropriate endeavors to prevent the development of chronic and disabling problems, such as Posttraumatic Stress Disorder, depression, alcohol/substance abuse, and relationship difficulties. A number of factors help to facilitate positive outcomes and prevention when clients encounter traumatic or other threatening situations.

First, it is crucial to recognize clients' strengths as well as the suffering they have experienced. While survivors' suffering must be acknowledged, and compassion and empathy conveyed to them, it is also important that those who care for them believe in and support their capacity to master this experience.

Second, information and education to help clients understand what has happened should be an integral part of the support and care systems.

Third, many clients need to tell the story of their experience, to give testimony both to externalize it and obtain emotional release, and to gain understanding and support from others. Supportive networks are critical and should be retained, reinforced, and rebuilt. These networks help people in the ongoing recovery process, both through the exchange of resources and practical assistance and through the emotional support they provide to deal with the disaster and its aftermath.

Test-Taking Strategies Applied

The question contains a qualifying word—NOT—that requires social workers to select the response choice that is not a focus of crisis intervention. When NOT is used as a qualifying word, it is often helpful to remove it from the question and eliminate the three response choices that are appropriate foci. This approach will leave the one response choice that is NOT an aim. Implementing strategies to prevent further reoccurrences are important, but done after the immediate effects of the crisis have been addressed. Thus, this response choice is correct as it is not critical right away.

Knowledge Area

Unit III—Interventions With Clients/Client Systems (Content Area); Intervention Processes and Techniques for Use Across Systems (Competency); Crisis Intervention and Treatment Approaches (KSA)

88. B

Rationale

Understanding a client's **family history** is an important part of the assessment process. A client is part of a larger family system. Thus, *gaining a better understanding of the experiences of other family members may prove useful in understanding influences on a client throughout his or her life course.*

There are no set questions that must be included in a family history; often, they relate to the problem or issue experienced by a client at the time. However, they may include identifying family members':

- Ethnic backgrounds (including immigration) and traditions
- Biological ties (adoption, blended family structures, foster children)
- Occupations and educational levels
- Unusual life events or achievements
- Psychological and social histories, as well as current well-being
- Past and present substance use behaviors
- Relationships with other family members
- Roles within the immediate and larger family unit

- Losses such as those from death, divorce, or physical separation
- Past and present significant problems, including those due to medical, financial, and other issues
- Values related to economic status, educational attainment, and employment
- Coping skills or defense mechanisms

Finding out which adults and/or children get the most attention or recognition and which get the least may also be useful.

Test-Taking Strategies Applied

The question contains a qualifying word—MOST. While there is more than one valid reason for completing a family history, the correct answer is most useful "during an assessment." Assisting the client to understand how problems repeat themselves is an intervention, causing it to be eliminated.

Assessment aims to learn more about a problem or issue. While past traumas may be revealed in a family history, this response choice is incorrect due to its narrow focus. Additionally, while information obtained from a family history may reveal informal supports that can be leveraged, such identification is not the main justification for its completion. Assessment aims to gather data to assist in understanding a problem. Since a client's situation is greatly influenced by his or her family, learning more about those in the larger system may illuminate how problems emerged or have been sustained.

Knowledge Area

Unit II—Assessment and Intervention Planning (Content Area); Biopsychosocial History and Collateral Data (Competency); The Types of Information Available From Other Sources (e.g., Agency, Employment, Medical, Psychological, Legal, or School Records) (KSA)

89. D

Rationale

"Self-actualization" represents a concept derived from humanistic theory by Abraham Maslow. Self-actualization represents growth of an individual toward fulfillment of the highest needs; those for meaning in life. It focuses on the achievement of one's full potential through creativity, independence, spontaneity, and a grasp of the real world.

Maslow created a psychological hierarchy of needs that reflects a linear pattern of growth depicted in a direct pyramidal order of ascension—toward **self-actualization**. Maslow identified some of the key characteristics of self-actualized people:

- Acceptance and realism: Self-actualized people have realistic perceptions of themselves, others, and the world around them.

- Problem-centering: Self-actualized individuals are concerned with solving problems outside of themselves, including helping others, and finding solutions to problems in the external world. These people are often motivated by a sense of personal responsibility and ethics.

- Spontaneity: Self-actualized people are spontaneous in their internal thoughts and outward behavior. While they can conform to rules and social expectations, they also tend to be open and unconventional.

- Autonomy and solitude: Self-actualized people need independence and privacy. While they enjoy the company of others, these individuals need time to focus on developing their own individual potential.

- Continued freshness of appreciation: Self-actualized people tend to view the world with a continual sense of appreciation, wonder, and awe. Even simple experiences continue to be a source of inspiration and pleasure.

Test-Taking Strategies Applied

The question contains a qualifying word—BEST. While a self-actualized person may engage in some of the actions listed in the incorrect response choices, the most suitable definition of self-actualization is growth toward reaching one's full potential. Knowledge of Maslow's work, including the hierarchy of needs, will assist in identifying the correct answer from the incorrect ones.

Knowledge Area

Unit I—Human Development, Diversity, and Behavior in the Environment (Content Area); Human Growth and Development (Competency); Basic Human Needs (KSA)

90. A

Rationale

Social workers respect and promote the **rights of clients to self-determination** and assist clients in their efforts to identify and clarify their goals. Social workers may limit clients' right to self-determination only when, in their professional judgment, clients' actions or potential actions pose serious, foreseeable, and imminent risk to themselves or others (*NASW Code of Ethics, 2008—1.02 Self-Determination*).

Test-Taking Strategies Applied

The question contains a qualifying word—FIRST. It is essential that social workers recognize that clients have the right to make their own decisions, even when they are thought to be unwise.

In the case scenario, the social worker can assist the client in analyzing the decision further, but must do this work with the understanding that every client has the right to self-determination. Acknowledging this right must be at the core of every professional relationship.

Respecting the dignity and worth of the person means supporting the client as needed through the decision-making process and not passing judgment. The client may choose to move in with friends even when there appear to be negative consequences associated with this decision. The social worker should not interject his or her opinion or try to influence the client's decision toward what the social worker thinks is best.

Knowledge Area

Unit IV—Professional Relationships, Values, and Ethics (Content Area); Professional Values and Ethical Issues (Competency); Client/Client System Competence and Self-Determination (e.g., Financial Decisions, Treatment Decisions, Emancipation, Age of Consent, Permanency Planning) (KSA)

91. C

Rationale

Psychodynamic theories explain the origin of the personality. Freud proposed that personalities have three components—the id, ego, and superego. The ego is the component that manages the conflict between the id and the constraints of the real world. **Ego-syntonic** refers to instincts or ideas that are acceptable to the self and are compatible with one's values and ways of thinking. They are consistent with one's fundamental personality and beliefs. **Ego-dystonic** refers to thoughts, impulses, and behaviors that are felt to be repugnant, distressing, unacceptable, or inconsistent with one's self-concept.

For a person who is a thief, stealing would be considered ego-syntonic, meaning that it comes naturally; there is unlikely to be any conflict about the act of stealing, and there is little or no guilt, as a result. For most people, stealing would be ego-dystonic.

One of the problems in working with certain psychiatric disorders in a therapeutic setting is the extent to which the disorder is experienced by the client as ego-syntonic or ego-dystonic. Social workers who work with certain eating disorders encounter the problem of clients who believe that their eating behavior is perfectly normal (e.g., ego-syntonic). Anorexia Nervosa is just such an example. This is an eating disorder that is characterized by extremely low body weight and body image distortion with an obsessive fear of gaining weight. Clients who have this condition typically have poor insight and often refuse to accept that their weight is dangerously low even when it could be deadly. In other words, their body and their eating behavior is "normal," or ego-syntonic, in that they feel that there is nothing the matter with how they eat and live.

The task for social workers involved in treating this disorder is, essentially, to make something that is ego-syntonic for the client something that is ego-dystonic instead, so that there might be some leverage in bringing about meaningful and necessary emotional, physical, and behavioral change.

Clients who experience the behaviors associated with the eating disorder as problematic and incongruent with how they see themselves view their eating disorder as ego-dystonic; this view is typically endorsed in Bulimia Nervosa and Binge Eating Disorder. As a result, clients often want help because they are frustrated with unsuccessful weight loss attempts and are ashamed of their binge eating/purging behaviors. This desire for help leads to an improved therapeutic alliance and motivation to change.

In contrast, clients with eating disorders who experience their behaviors as congruent with their personality and have a certain amount of pride in the ability to diet and exercise to extremes view the eating disorder as ego-syntonic. This ego-syntonic view is most often seen in Anorexia Nervosa. In most cases, when the eating disorder is experienced as ego-syntonic, there will be little or no motivation to change the behaviors, which results in high levels of treatment resistance that increase with time.

Ego alien is another term used to refer to ego-dystonic behavior.

Egocentric is having little or no regard for others' interests, beliefs, or attitudes (e.g., being self-centered).

Test-Taking Strategies Applied

This is a recall question that relies on social workers understanding the components of the personality. The ego's job is to determine the best course of action based on information from the id, reality, and the superego. When the ego is comfortable with its conclusions and behaviors, a client is ego-syntonic.

Knowledge Area

Unit I—Human Development, Diversity, and Behavior in the Environment (Content Area); Human Growth and Development (Competency); Psychoanalytic and Psychodynamic Approaches (KSA)

92. C

Rationale

Exploitation is treating someone badly in order to benefit from his or her resources or work. It is when someone uses a situation to gain unfair advantage. Exploitation is more common when there is a power differential between parties due to social status, abilities, income, education, job position, and so on.

There is no one explanation of why prejudice exists, but several approaches taken together offer insight.

Exploitation theory is based on using others unfairly for economic advantage. When an individual who is a minority is hired at a lower wage, it perpetuates the power differential between those in the majority and those in the minority, as well as unfairly exploits based on an individual attribute or characteristic.

Scapegoating theory explains putting blame on others for one's own failings, such as an unsuccessful applicant assuming that an individual who is a minority got "his or her" job.

Authoritarian personality theory posits that child-rearing can lead to developing intolerance as an adult. This rigid personality type dislikes people who are different.

Normative theory explains prejudice through peer and social influences that encourage tolerance or intolerance.

Test-Taking Strategies Applied

Social workers need to be aware that abuse, neglect, and exploitation can occur on both micro and macro levels. This question views discrimination as exploitation that occurs globally. As social workers are mandated to work to correct discriminatory practices, they should continually monitor to ensure that everyone has the same access to social rewards and is treated equally.

A clue to selecting the correct answer is that the case scenario concerns disparate economic treatment of those in the majority and those in the minority. This is a form of exploitation.

Knowledge Area

Unit I—Human Development, Diversity, and Behavior in the Environment (Content Area); Concepts of Abuse and Neglect

(Competency); The Indicators, Dynamics, and Impact of Exploitation Across the Lifespan (e.g., Financial, Immigration Status, Sexual Trafficking) (KSA)

93. A

Rationale

The APA developed the original *Diagnostic and Statistical Manual of Mental Disorders* (*DSM®*) in 1952 to create a uniform way to define mental health disorders. The APA first introduced the multiaxial system in the third edition (*DSM-III*, published in 1980), which suggested, but did not require, that social workers report diagnostic information on five distinct axes. This tradition continued with only modest changes in the *DSM-IV* (1994) and *DSM-IV-TR* (2000).

Axis I listed the primary or principal diagnoses that needed immediate attention; this included recording of clinical disorders as well as "Other Conditions That May Be a Focus of Clinical Attention" (e.g., life stressors, impairments in functioning). Axis II contained pervasive psychological issues such as Personality Disorders, personality traits, and Mental Retardation (now Intellectual Disability Disorder) that shaped responses to Axis I disorders. Axis III was intended to cue reporting of medical or neurological problems that were relevant to the individual's current or past psychiatric problems. Axis IV required social workers to indicate which of nine categories of psychosocial or environmental stressors influenced client conceptualization or care (e.g., recent divorce, death of partner, job loss). Finally, Axis V included the opportunity to provide a Global Assessment of Functioning (GAF) rating, a number up to 100 intended to indicate overall level of distress or impairment.

Concerns of the multiaxial system included the degree to which Axes I and II were mutually exclusive and distinct; lack of clear boundaries between medical and mental health disorders; inconsistent use of Axis IV for clinical and research purposes; and poor psychometric properties and clinical utility of the GAF.

As Axes I, II, and III have been eliminated, social workers can simply list any disorders or conditions previously coded on these three axes together and in order of clinical priority or focus. Because many billing systems already used this system, this does not result in meaningful changes in terms of third-party billing. This change removes the distinction of previous clinical disorders, Personality Disorders, and Intellectual Disability Disorders.

Social workers previously listed psychosocial and contextual factors that affect clients and are relevant to conceptualization on Axis IV. This included notation regarding concerns in nine key areas: primary support group, social environment, education, occupation, housing, economic, access to health care, legal system/crime, and other. Beginning with the *DSM-5*, social workers are advised to make a separate notation regarding contextual information, rather than including it in axial notation. However, there is not guidance regarding how or where to do so.

Initially developed as the Health-Sickness Rating Scale, the GAF was introduced as Axis V. Over time, this single number scale came to be used to assist in payers' determinations of medical necessity for treatment and in determining eligibility for disability compensation. The discontinued use of the GAF in the *DSM-5* suggests that social workers use the *World Health Organization Disability Assessment Schedule 2.0 (WHODAS 2.0)* as a measure of disability. The GAF scale was removed from the *DSM-5* because of perceived lack of reliability and poor clinical utility.

Test-Taking Strategies Applied

This is a recall question that relies on social workers not only understanding the diagnostic criteria changes that occurred from the *DSM-IV-TR* to the *DSM-5*, but also the format changes. Social workers must be aware of these revisions to ensure that they are appropriately diagnosing clients.

Knowledge Area

Unit II—Assessment and Intervention Planning (Content Area); Assessment Methods and Techniques (Competency); The Use of the Diagnostic and Statistical Manual of the American Psychiatric Association (KSA)

94. D

Rationale

Personality Disorders are defined as deeply ingrained and enduring attitude and behavioral patterns that deviate markedly from the culturally expected range. They are not secondary to other mental illnesses or attributable to gross brain damage or disease, although they may precede and coexist with other disorders. Disorders of personality tend to appear in late childhood or adolescence and continue to manifest into adulthood. However, while most Personality Disorders can be diagnosed prior to adulthood, few are, as there is a belief that adolescent personality problems are transient. There are also concerns about the negative effects of labeling. Thus, the diagnosis of Personality Disorders is likely to occur during adulthood.

There is also evidence that the symptoms of Personality Disorder do not remain stagnant, but actually change in magnitude and scope over time.

Test-Taking Strategies Applied

The question contains a qualifying word—MOST. While the behaviors associated with Personality Disorders may be evident prior to age 18, clients are not likely to be diagnosed until adulthood as the behaviors need to be long-standing and inflexible.

Knowledge Area

Unit II—Assessment and Intervention Planning (Content Area); Assessment Methods and Techniques (Competency); The Use of the Diagnostic and Statistical Manual of the American Psychiatric Association (KSA)

95. D

Rationale

Couples intervention/treatment is not a viable therapeutic tool for use in violent relationships. Violent relationships are those in which physical or sexual assaults occur, threats of violence occur, and/or partners live in environments of fear caused by their partners. Couples counseling is inappropriate even when both parties request it and/or want to maintain their relationship. Treating a couple together before violence is addressed and stopped can endanger victims, lend credibility to the misunderstanding that partners are responsible for violence inflicted upon them, minimize the attention on the violence by focusing on couple interactions, and increase the isolation of victims by reinforcing fears about speaking freely.

Ending violence in relationships is primary and dependent solely on batterers' motivation and commitment to do so.

Test-Taking Strategies Applied

This is a recall question about the goals and appropriateness of couples treatment. Couples counseling is beneficial to work on relationship problems. Battering is a violent act, not a relationship problem. It is a behavior that is solely the responsibility of the violent person. This is true regardless of the alleged provocation, since the behavior of one individual cannot compel violence by another. Violent behavior must be addressed and stopped before couples counseling takes place.

Knowledge Area

Unit IV—Professional Relationships, Values, and Ethics (Content Area); Professional Development and Use of Self (Competency); The Impact of Domestic, Intimate Partner, and Other Violence on the Helping Relationship (KSA)

96. A

Rationale

Often social workers who want to **influence social policy** need to address resistance to change. Forming strong ties to potentially influential people who are ambivalent about a change can be helpful as there is the opportunity to coopt them. This cooptation increases the probability that the change will occur. In addition, creating strong ties to potentially influential individuals who disapprove of a change outright can also be effective. Often when they are asked to be part of coming up with an acceptable solution, resistance is reduced as they are less likely to disagree with something that they have been part of creating.

Cooptation is the process by which a group subsumes or assimilates another (usually smaller or weaker) with the goal of gaining support by adopting views or ideals of the group(s) subsumed.

Test-Taking Strategies Applied

This is a recall question that relies on social workers understanding methods to reduce resistance when engaging in macro-level practice. If the correct answer is a term that is not familiar, it may be useful to start with evaluating the others given the case scenario presented. Advocacy, planning, and mobilization may be used by a social worker in policy-making, but none directly involve reducing resistance by including opponents in possible solutions, which is the essence of cooptation.

Knowledge Area

Unit III—Interventions With Clients/Client Systems (Content Area); Intervention Processes and Techniques for Use With Larger Systems (Competency); Techniques to Inform and Influence Organizational and Social Policy (KSA)

97. C

Rationale

There are important steps in helping clients with the **utilization of available community resources**. Sometimes, they may need to be referred for services. When making referrals, social workers must engage in the following steps.

Step 1: Identify the Need or Purpose for the Referral

Social workers often find that client needs require specialized knowledge or cannot be met by their agencies.

Step 2: Research Resources

When making a referral, it is critical that social workers refer to competent providers, those with expertise in the problems that clients are experiencing. *In addition, if clients are already receiving services from agencies, it may be advisable to see if there are available services provided by these agencies in order to avoid additional coordination and fragmentation for clients.*

Step 3: Discuss and Select Options

Clients' rights to self-determination should be paramount.

Step 4: Plan for Initial Contact

Social workers may want to work with a client to prepare for the initial meeting. Preparation may include helping clients to understand what to expect.

Step 5: Make Initial Contact

Social workers may be asked to assist with providing transportation and/or support for clients to access new providers.

Step 6: Follow-Up to See If Need Was Met

Social workers should always follow-up to ensure that there was not a break in service and that new providers are meeting clients' needs.

Test-Taking Strategies Applied

The question contains a qualifying word—NEXT. Its use indicates that the order in which the response choices should occur is critical. Social workers must know the process used to refer clients for services.

In this case scenario, the need for the referral, the first step in the process, has already been established. The next step is to research resources, including determining the existing relationships that the client has with service providers. There are many types of nutrition assistance programs, so the social worker will subsequently need to discuss service options with the client who will ultimately come to a decision about the optimal type of service and provider. Only after these steps have occurred will the social worker contact the agency and assist with preparing for the initial intake.

There is no reason to believe that the client is not aware of the importance of healthy eating, making education irrelevant.

Knowledge Area

Unit III—Interventions With Clients/Client Systems (Content Area); Intervention Processes and Techniques for Use With Larger Systems (Competency); Methods to Assess the Availability of Community Resources (KSA)

98. A

Rationale

Psychopharmacology is the prescription of psychotropic medications to affect brain chemicals associated with mood and behavior. Psychotropic drugs are prescribed to treat a variety of mental health problems, including Bipolar Disorder (BD) and Schizophrenia. Usually psychotropic medications are prescribed by psychiatrists, though other physicians and professionals may be able to prescribe them in certain jurisdictions. Doctors often treat the manic symptoms associated with BD with one set of drugs and use other drugs to treat depression. Certain drugs are also used for "maintenance" of a steady mood over time. A number of medications are used to treat BD. The types of medications prescribed are based on particular symptoms and can include combinations of **mood stabilizers** (such as lithium), **antipsychotics**, **antidepressants**, and **antianxiety medications**.

Test-Taking Strategies Applied

The question contains a qualifying word—MOST. While clients may benefit from all treatment interventions, clients with BD need medication, often for their lifetimes. Drug treatment is viewed as primary, or essential, with ongoing psychotherapy as an ancillary treatment to discuss feelings, thoughts, and behaviors that cause problems.

Knowledge Area

Unit II—Assessment and Intervention Planning (Content Area); Biopsychosocial History and Collateral Data (Competency); Common Psychotropic and Nonpsychotropic Prescriptions and Over-the-Counter Medications and Their Side Effects (KSA)

99. C

Rationale

Indicators of substance abuse require social workers to understand the ways in which substances produce physiological and psychological changes in the body. The half-life of a drug is the time it takes for the amount currently in the body to be reduced by half. It does not matter what the current amount is—the time it takes for it to be reduced by half will always be the same for a particular drug. For most drugs, the half-life cannot be measured accurately and can only be a rough estimate as it varies from client to client.

But, half-life is still a helpful concept, because if a drug has a short half-life (24 hours or less) it means that it is more difficult to come off of it. If a drug has a long half-life, withdrawal is naturally slower and usually easier to tolerate. Drugs with a short half-life are designed for fast action. They are made to hit the body quickly, so they can provide relief with speed. Long-acting drugs tend to maintain their effects for a longer period of time, though the first dose takes longer to take effect.

Due to their quick effect, drugs with short half-lives tend to be popular with people who have addictions. They tend to deliver huge changes in a very short time period. For drug users who want a big high in a hurry, these medications are tailor-made.

Withdrawal symptoms come quickly, drawing clients back into addiction. Withdrawal discomfort contributes substantially to the risk of relapse. Clients who feel ill immediately are desperate for relief, and they might get that release by going back to drugs.

If withdrawal discomfort can lead right back to drug use, it is imperative that an addiction treatment program soothe discomfort. Often, the best way to provide relief is to provide clients accustomed to short half-life drugs with medications in the same class that have a longer half-life.

For example, alcohol is a sedating drug with a very short half-life. Chronic users who attempt to withdraw may experience a variety of life-threatening symptoms, including seizures. Switching to a long half-life, sedating drug can help the brain to adjust to the lack of drugs without plunging a client into a state of medical emergency.

Test-Taking Strategies Applied

The question requires recall knowledge about the meaning of "half-life." All detoxification can cause life-threatening symptoms. Hence, there is a need to carefully monitor clients for health and safety before dealing with the underlying causes of the addiction and strategies for reducing the likelihood of relapse. Often psychopharmacological interventions are used to reduce the discomfort of withdrawal. However, these answers do not directly relate to the relationship between the "very short half-life" of the medication and withdrawal symptoms that is the focus of the question.

Detoxification of drugs with a longer half-life may be less difficult as the symptoms may be more gradual or appear after the client has had the opportunity to be abstinent for a period of time.

Knowledge Area

Unit II—Assessment and Intervention Planning (Content Area); Biopsychosocial History and Collateral Data (Competency); The Indicators of Addiction and Substance Abuse (KSA)

100. C

Rationale

A **humanistic approach** studies the whole client and the uniqueness of each individual. Sometimes the humanistic approach is called phenomenological. This means that personality is studied from the point of view of a client's subjective experience.

Humanism rejected the assumptions of the behaviorist perspective that is characterized as deterministic, focused on reinforcement of stimulus–response behavior, and heavily dependent on animal research.

Humanistic psychology also rejected the psychodynamic approach because it, too, is deterministic, with unconscious irrational and instinctive forces determining human thought and behavior. Both behaviorism and psychoanalysis are regarded as dehumanizing by humanists.

A humanistic approach begins with the existential assumption that clients have free will. A further assumption is that clients are basically good and have an innate need to make themselves and the world better. The humanistic approach emphasizes the personal worth of a client, the centrality of human values, and the creative, active nature of human beings. The approach is optimistic and focuses on human capacity to overcome hardship, pain, and despair.

Humanists argue that objective reality is less important than a client's subjective perception and understanding of the world. Thus, little value is placed on scientific research like experiments. Humanism also rejects the study of animals because it does not consider the unique properties of human beings.

Humanism views human beings as fundamentally different from other animals, mainly because humans are conscious beings capable of thought, reason, and language.

Test-Taking Strategies Applied

This is a recall question that relies on social workers knowing the names of varying perspectives, especially those that are based on the strengths perspective. A humanistic approach views clients as having the knowledge that is important in defining and solving their problems. Clients are experts about their own lives and situations. They are resilient and survive and thrive despite difficulties.

Knowledge Area

Unit I—Human Development, Diversity, and Behavior in the Environment (Content Area); Human Growth and Development (Competency); Strengths-Based and Resilience Theories (KSA)

101. D

Rationale

The primary mission of the social work profession is to enhance well-being and help meet the basic human needs of all, with particular attention to the empowerment of those who are vulnerable, oppressed, and living in poverty. A historic and defining feature of social work is the profession's focus on individual well-being in a social context. Fundamental to social work is the examination of environmental forces that create, contribute to, and address social problems.

Social work is rooted in a set of **core values**. These core values, embraced by social workers throughout the profession's history, are the foundation of social work's unique purpose and perspective. They are explicitly stated in the 2008 *NASW Code of Ethics* as service, social justice, dignity and worth of the person, importance of human relationships, integrity, and competence. This constellation of core values reflects what is unique to the social work profession. Core values, and the principles that flow from them, must be balanced within the context and complexity of the human experience.

Professional capacity is not a social work core value.

Test-Taking Strategies Applied

The question contains a qualifying word—NOT—that requires social workers to select the response choice which is not a core value in the professional code of ethics. When NOT is used as a qualifying word, it is often helpful to remove it from the question and eliminate the three response choices that are core values. This approach will leave the one response choice which is NOT listed in the 2008 *NASW Code of Ethics* as a basic value upon which the mission of the social work profession is rooted.

Knowledge Area

Unit IV—Professional Relationships, Values, and Ethics (Content Area); Professional Values and Ethical Issues (Competency); Professional Values and Principles (e.g., Competence, Social Justice, Integrity, and Dignity and Worth of the Person) (KSA)

102. C

Rationale

The influence of **cultural diversity** on the social worker–client relationship is profound and can influence all steps in the problem-solving process. *A social worker's self-awareness about his or her own attitudes, values, and beliefs about cultural differences and a willingness to acknowledge cultural differences are critical factors in working with diverse populations.* A social worker is responsible for bringing up and addressing issues of cultural difference with a client and is also ethically responsible for being culturally competent by obtaining appropriate knowledge, skills, and abilities for working with diverse clients.

The relationship between a social worker and client is expressed through interaction. This interaction is commonly thought of in terms of **verbal communication**, which is natural, because the greater part of treatment consists of talking. However, **nonverbal behavior** is also very important. Body posture, gestures, facial expressions, eye movements, and other reactions often express feelings and attitudes more clearly than do spoken words. It is often for these reasons that a social worker must be aware of his or her own feelings, attitudes, and responses, as well as those of a client if he or she is to understand what is taking place and be of assistance.

Test-Taking Strategies Applied

The question contains a qualifying word—MOST—that is capitalized to emphasize its importance in distinguishing the correct answer from the incorrect ones. It is important for social workers to understand clients' customs and traditions, especially if they are very different from their own. However, social workers' self-awareness is a necessity in helping clients, especially when they come from diverse backgrounds. Race and culture can impact attitudes, behaviors, communication, and so on. These factors will greatly impact all steps in the problem-solving process and failing to understand these differences can greatly inhibit therapeutic alliances.

Ensuring that clients feel comfortable and using thorough assessments to drive treatment planning are critical regardless of racial or other differences, making them incorrect answers. They do not address the fundamental point of the question, namely the impact of social worker–client diversity on service delivery.

Knowledge Area

Unit I—Human Development, Diversity, and Behavior in the Environment (Content Area); Diversity, Social/Economic Justice, and Oppression (Competency); The Principles of Culturally Competent Social Work Practice (KSA)

103. B

Rationale

Psychodynamic theories explain the origin of the personality. Freud proposed that personalities have three components—the id, the ego, and the superego. The id is the only component of personality that is present from birth. This aspect of personality is entirely unconscious and includes the instinctive and primitive behaviors. The id is driven by the pleasure principle, which strives for immediate gratification of all desires, wants, and needs. However, immediately satisfying these needs is not always realistic or even possible. The ego is the component of personality that is responsible for dealing with reality. According to Freud, the ego develops from the id and ensures that the impulses of the id can be expressed in a manner acceptable in the real world. The last component of personality to develop is the superego. The superego is the aspect of personality that holds all of our internalized moral standards and ideals that we acquire from both parents and society—our sense of right and wrong. *According to Freud, the superego begins to emerge at around age 5.*

Test-Taking Strategies Applied

This is a recall question that relies on social workers being familiar with psychodynamic theories and personality components. Knowing that the superego is the cause of guilt when going against societal rules will greatly assist in eliminating incorrect response choices. Six months is far too young for understanding the difference between "right and wrong." By age 11, children have entered the formal operations stage of cognitive development and can abstractly think at higher levels. They are assuming adult roles. Thus, the superego is firmly in place—not emerging—at 16 years of age. The elimination of these incorrect response choices leaves only two possible answers.

The question asks about when the superego "begins to emerge." This wording is important and may assist in identifying the correct answer. Children enter school usually at about this age and are moving from concrete thinking to the beginnings of abstract thought. Cause-and-effect relationships are just starting to become clear, which are essential for judging actions against societal norms.

Knowledge Area

Unit I—Human Development, Diversity, and Behavior in the Environment (Content Area); Human Growth and Development (Competency); Psychoanalytic and Psychodynamic Approaches (KSA)

104. C

Rationale

Object permanence is the understanding that objects continue to exist even when they cannot be observed (seen, heard, touched, smelled, or sensed in any way). Object permanence occurs during the first of Piaget's four stages, the sensorimotor stage.

Piaget assumed that a child could search for a hidden toy only if she or he had a mental representation of it. Piaget found that infants searched for hidden toys when they were around 8 months old.

Object permanence typically starts to develop between 4 and 7 months of age and involves a baby's understanding that when things disappear, they are not gone forever. Before a baby understands this concept, things that leave his or her view are gone, completely gone. Developing object permanence is an important milestone. It is a precursor to symbolic understanding (which a baby needs to develop language, pretend play, and exploration) and helps children work through separation anxiety.

Test-Taking Strategies Applied

The question contains a qualifying word—BEST. While some of the response choices may have concepts related to cognitive theory, the correct response choice most aptly describes this important cognitive milestone in the first year of life.

Knowledge Area

Unit I—Human Development, Diversity, and Behavior in the Environment (Content Area); Human Growth and Development (Competency); Theories of Human Development Throughout the Lifespan (e.g., Physical, Social, Emotional, Cognitive, Behavioral) (KSA)

105. C

Rationale

Classical conditioning is based on the premise that learning occurs as a result of pairing a previously neutral (conditioned) stimulus with an unconditioned (involuntary) stimulus so that the conditioned stimulus eventually elicits the response typically elicited by the unconditioned stimulus.

In this case scenario, the hospital is the neutral (conditioned) stimulus that causes the same response—nausea (unconditioned when occurs from chemotherapy and conditioned when occurs from visiting the hospital). This reaction originally resulted from the receipt of chemotherapy (unconditioned stimulus) that naturally makes one nauseous.

Test-Taking Strategies Applied

This is a recall question that relies on social workers understanding behavioral theories, including classical conditioning. Pavlov conducted an important "experiment" with a dog in which he showed the dog a bone (an unconditioned stimulus), causing the dog to salivate (unconditioned response). The dog did not learn to salivate when the bone was presented—the response just occurred naturally. He then rang a bell every time the bone was revealed to the dog. The bell is an innate object (conditioned stimulus) when continually paired with the bone (unconditioned stimulus) that elicited salivation (conditioned response) even when the bone was not shown.

Knowledge Area

Unit I—Human Development, Diversity, and Behavior in the Environment (Content Area); Human Growth and Development (Competency); Theories of Human Development Throughout the Lifespan (e.g., Physical, Social, Emotional, Cognitive, Behavioral) (KSA)

106. C

Rationale

Continuity of care ensures coordination within an organization or across different agencies or settings to reduce duplicate services, address gaps in existing services, and ensure consistent and continuous services for clients as they transition in care or are discharged.

Social workers must make sure that goals achieved as a result of interventions are sustained. Treatment plans should be reviewed during interventions, at termination, and, if possible, following termination of services to make adjustments, ensure progress, and determine the sustainability of change after treatment.

Test-Taking Strategies Applied

The question contains a qualifying word—PRIMARY—that indicates that the discharge plan may address more than one objective. The case scenario states that "the client will need ongoing services to maintain his current functioning." Thus, the correct response choice is the one that will ensure that these services are delivered.

Discharge plans should document reasons for the hospitalization and services delivered, as well as address a client's ongoing educational, psychological, and emotional needs. However, only the correct answer focuses on continuity of care that is essential to ensure that services received in the hospital continue in the community. This focus is needed to maximize development and functioning.

Knowledge Area

Unit II—Assessment and Intervention Planning (Content Area); Intervention Planning (Competency); The Criteria Used in the Selection of Intervention/Treatment Modalities (e.g., Client/Client System Abilities, Culture, Life Stage) (KSA)

107. A

Rationale

The **mental status exam** (MSE) is the psychological equivalent of a physical exam that describes the mental state and behaviors of a client. It includes both objective observations of social workers and subjective descriptions given by clients. There are many methods for gathering the information. The MSE provides information for diagnosis and assessment, as well as evaluation of treatment. It is a snapshot in time. To properly complete an MSE, information about clients' histories is needed including education, culture, and social factors. It is important to ascertain what is typical (baseline) for clients.

Components of an MSE include appearance, behavior, speech, mood, affect, thought process, thought content, cognition, and insight/judgment. Appearance describes what is seen (build, posture, dress, grooming, prominent physical features, etc.). Speech includes rate (increased/pressured, decreased/monosyllabic, latency), rhythm (articulation, prosody, dysarthria, monotone, slurred), and volume (loud, soft, mute), all of which can be observed. Affect notes the emotional states exhibited, including euthymic (normal mood), dysphoric (depressed, irritable, angry), and euphoric (elevated, elated).

Mood is probably the least likely to be assessed solely through observation as it is the prevalent emotional state clients report feeling. Often it is recorded in quotes since it is what clients indicate (such as "fantastic," "elated," "depressed," "anxious," "sad," or "angry"). Social workers may need to ask clients about their moods in order to get this information as it is usually not revealed without solicitation.

Test-Taking Strategies Applied

The question contains a qualifying word—LEAST. While many of the components of an MSE are based on both observation and inquiry, some, such as appearance and speech, are easily noted. Affect is also likely observed as it includes the appropriateness of clients' reactions to the situation, the range and stability of emotions evident, and the attitude of clients toward services. Thus, elimination of these three incorrect response choices leads to the correct answer, which will probably be revealed only as a result of questioning by social workers.

Knowledge Area

Unit II—Assessment and Intervention Planning (Content Area); Biopsychosocial History and Collateral Data (Competency); The Components and Function of the Mental Status Examination (KSA)

108. B

Rationale

Social workers often have to apply **organizational theories** when engaged in management and administrative roles. The **human relations theory** of management began development in the early 1920s during the Industrial Revolution. At that time, productivity was the focus of business. The Hawthorne studies proved the importance of people for productivity—not machines.

The human relations theory is based on a belief that people desire to be part of a supportive team that facilitates development and growth. Therefore, if employees receive special attention and are encouraged to participate, they perceive their work has significance and they are motivated to be more productive, resulting in high-quality work.

According to the human relations theory, the factor most influencing productivity is relationships. In the Hawthorne studies, the researchers realized that productivity increased due to relationships and being part of a supportive group where each employee's work had a significant effect on the team output. Researchers also noticed that the increased attention the workers received increased motivation and productivity, which resulted in what is called the Hawthorne effect.

Test-Taking Strategies Applied

The question is testing knowledge about management theories. Management theories are implemented to help increase organizational productivity and service quality. Not many social work managers use a single theory or concept when implementing strategies in the workplace; they commonly use a combination of a number of theories, depending on the workplace, purpose, and workforce. Human relations theory is also known as **Theory Y** and its basic premise is to maximize productivity of employees by making them feel valued; employees are seen as significant contributors to the success of an organization.

Knowledge Area

Unit III—Interventions With Clients/Client Systems (Content Area); Intervention Processes and Techniques for Use With Larger Systems (Competency); Theories of Organizational Development and Structure (KSA)

109. C

Rationale

Follow-up in social work practice can take many forms, but is essential to ensure that clients have been able to sustain progress made in treatment. Clients are at risk for developing problems after services have ended and should receive regular assessments after discharge to determine whether services are needed or discharge plans are being implemented as planned.

Test-Taking Strategies Applied

The question requires integration of knowledge related to several KSAs. Social workers must realize that the problem-solving process—engaging, assessing, planning, intervening, evaluating, and terminating—is fluid. In the case scenario, the client has successfully terminated due to resolution of one problem, but is experiencing another. This situation calls for an assessment of the new situation. The client has requested a meeting, so asking about the situation over the phone would not be appropriate. There may not be ample time to get all the information in the call and it would be disruptive to end the assessment abruptly. The material may also be sensitive and the client may feel more comfortable discussing it in person. It is not surprising that the client is raising the issue with the social worker as rapport and trust have already been established between them. Referring to a colleague is not necessary and forces the client to start over by building a relationship with a different professional. The social worker should also not second guess or doubt the client's intentions by attributing the request to problems with termination. Often individuals encounter multiple problems throughout their life course and asking previous social workers for assistance with new issues is understandable as they have been helpful in the past.

Knowledge Area

Unit III—Interventions With Clients/Client Systems (Content Area); Intervention Processes and Techniques for Use Across Systems (Competency); Techniques Used for Follow-Up (KSA)

110. D

Rationale

There are many techniques that are helpful to social workers as they seek to inform and influence organizational and social policy. Kurt Lewin's **force field analysis** was designed to weigh the driving and restraining forces that affect change in organizations. The "force field" can be described as two opposite forces working for and against change. **Driving forces** are those seeking change. **Resisting (restraining) forces** are those seeking to maintain the status quo.

Test-Taking Strategies Applied

This is a recall question on an organizational theory that can be used in indirect (macro) practice. Organizational theory attempts to explain the workings of organizations. Many theories have emerged from varying bodies of knowledge and disciplines. These theories can be useful to social workers in understanding the environments in which they deliver services and the workings of organizations in which clients interact.

Knowledge Area

Unit III—Interventions With Clients/Client Systems (Content Area); Intervention Processes and Techniques for Use With Larger Systems (Competency); Techniques to Inform and Influence Organizational and Social Policy (KSA)

111. A

Rationale

Transference and **countertransference** are terms used to describe reactions of clients and social workers. First discussed by Freud in the 1900s, theories about transference and countertransference and the role that they play in the therapeutic relationship have evolved.

Transference: the feelings a client transfers onto a social worker (and other present relationships), occurring usually unconsciously and focusing around unresolved issues or conflicts in past relationships.

Countertransference: the unconscious feelings or reactions a social worker may have toward a client.

In the past, transference and countertransference were seen as bad. Now, it is believed that transference and countertransference are inevitable and paying attention to them can be helpful. Supervision is an appropriate venue to identify and process these feelings.

Test-Taking Strategies Applied

In this case scenario, the correct answer must be the one that will "appropriately deal with these feelings." Changing the session topic or explaining the grieving process does not "deal with" the issue at hand, which is countertransference. It is not appropriate for the social worker to self-disclose to the client as this admission is not being made in the client's best interest. There is no indication that the client questions the ability of the social worker to understand his feelings.

Transference and countertransference are best addressed in supervision. The social worker must acknowledge to herself that the client's emotions are eliciting a personal reaction due to her own life circumstances. Such reactions must be processed outside of the client session so that they do not interfere with the therapeutic relationship.

Knowledge Area

Unit IV—Professional Relationships, Values, and Ethics (Content Area); Professional Development and Use of Self (Competency); The Impact of Transference and Countertransference in the Social Worker–Client/Client System Relationship (KSA)

112. B

Rationale

The **functions of human or social work services** can be thought of broadly as **social care, social control,** and **habilitation/rehabilitation**. Social care is concerned primarily with changing the situations or environments of clients. It is mainly used to assist those who cannot meet their needs themselves. Public entitlement programs or subsidized housing can be classified as social care. Contrarily, habilitation/ rehabilitation is focused on changing individuals, such as helping them learn new skills or return to prior levels of functioning. Substance abuse and mental health treatment programs are focused on rehabilitation, while employment training upon entering the workforce is aimed at habilitation. The purpose of social control is to monitor or restrict client independence for a specific time because of law violation (such as with those in the criminal justice system). Social control differs from social care in two fundamental ways: who receives the services and under what conditions they receive them. Most recipients of social control are able to care for themselves, but have either failed to do so or have done so in a manner that violates society's norms for appropriate behavior. *Social workers have to put social control over social care or habilitation/rehabilitation when fulfilling their duty to report dangerous client behavior, such as child abuse.*

Test-Taking Strategies Applied

The question contains a qualifying word—PRIMARILY. While reports may lead to safer home environments for abused children (a social care function) or treatment for perpetrators (a rehabilitation function), reporting suspected abuse aims to mostly limit the ability of abusers to continue to harm. This question asks about the act of reporting—not the care of those abused or the treatment of perpetrators.

Social workers must be aware of the core functions of human services and how they may interact with one another. At times, there may be tensions that arise because of their differences. For example, clients may be involuntarily mandated to receive inpatient mental health treatment to protect themselves and/or others from harm (social control). While much of treatment in these settings is aimed at rehabilitation/habilitation, it may also include requirements for the administration of psychotropic medications against the wishes of clients for safety (social control). The limiting of self-determination can also make it difficult for clients to trust workers in these settings, thereby hindering therapeutic alliances that are essential.

Knowledge Area

Unit IV—Professional Relationships, Values, and Ethics (Content Area); Confidentiality (Competency); Legal and/or Ethical Issues Regarding Mandatory Reporting (e.g., Abuse, Threat of Harm, Impaired Professionals, etc.) (KSA)

113. C

Rationale

Cognitive behavioral therapy (CBT) is a hands-on, practical approach to problem solving. Its goal is to change patterns of thinking or behavior that are responsible for clients' difficulties, and so change the way they feel. CBT works by changing clients' attitudes and their behavior by focusing on the thoughts, images, beliefs, and attitudes that are held (cognitive processes) and how they relate to behavior, as a way of dealing with emotional problems. CBT can be thought of as a combination of psychotherapy and behavioral therapy. Psychotherapy emphasizes the importance of the personal meaning placed on things and how thinking patterns begin in childhood. Behavioral therapy pays close attention to the relationship between problems, behaviors, and thoughts.

This approach is active, collaborative, structured, time limited, goal-oriented, and problem-focused. It lends itself to the requirements of managed care companies, including brief treatment, well-delineated techniques, goal and problem-oriented, and empirically supported evidence of its effectiveness.

CBT has been used clinically with almost every client population. There are no strict universal exclusionary criteria for the use of CBT. However, typical exclusion criteria include the presence of a Substance Use Disorder since those who are impaired may be unable to perform the work required; an active psychotic disorder since clients with delusions/hallucinations are not good candidates for most psychotherapies; a crisis state including suicidal ideation or behavior that may distract from CBT and require more immediate attention; and/or permanent or temporary severe cognitive impairment due to organic brain syndrome, intellectual disabilities, depression, and so on, that impairs the cognitive ability to examine thought processes.

CBT is an evidence-based treatment for clients with eating disorders and emphasizes the important role that both thoughts (cognitive) and actions (behavioral) play in maintaining eating disorders. Examples of maintaining factors include cognitive factors (overevaluation of weight and shape, negative body image, core beliefs about self-worth, negative self-evaluation, perfectionism) and behavioral factors (weight-control behaviors including dietary restraint, restriction, binge eating, purging behaviors, self-harm, body checking, and body avoidance). Clients with eating disorders hold negative or distorted views of themselves and their bodies. These highly critical thoughts can result in feelings of shame, anxiety, or disgust that often trigger weight-control behaviors and fuel a cycle of negative self-evaluation. CBT helps clients examine which specific factors are maintaining their disorders.

Test-Taking Strategies Applied

The question contains a qualifying word—NOT. Three of the response choices represent contraindications. The correct answer is a condition that, when present, does not make the use of CBT inadvisable. It is the response choice that names a problem for which CBT can assist.

The exclusion criteria for CBT are similar to those for many other psychotherapeutic interventions. Substance use, psychosis, and severe cognitive disability can greatly interfere with abstract thinking that is required for most "talk" therapies.

Knowledge Area

Unit III—Interventions With Clients/Client Systems (Content Area); Intervention Processes and Techniques for Use Across Systems (Competency); Cognitive and Behavioral Interventions (KSA)

114. D

Rationale

Congress has a central role in shaping the scope and nature of the federal grants-in-aid system. **Block grants** are a form of grant-in-aid. In its deliberative, legislative role, Congress determines its objectives, decides which grant mechanism is best suited to achieve those objectives, and creates **social welfare legislation** to achieve its objectives, incorporating its chosen grant mechanism. It then exercises oversight to hold the administration accountable for grant implementation and to determine whether the grant is achieving its objectives.

Block grants provide state and local governments with a specified amount of funding to assist in addressing broad purposes, such as community development, social services, public health, or law enforcement. Block grant advocates argue that block grants increase government efficiency and program effectiveness by redistributing power and accountability through decentralization and partial devolution of decision-making authority from the federal government to state and local governments. Advocates also view them as a means to reduce the federal deficit. Block grant critics argue that block grants can undermine the achievement of national objectives and can be used as a "backdoor" means to reduce government spending on domestic issues. Block grant critics also argue that the decentralized nature of block grants makes it difficult to measure block grant performance and to hold state and local government officials accountable for decisions.

A **categorical grant** can be used only for a specific program and usually is limited to narrowly defined activities.

Federal match is the share of costs that the federal government contributes to accomplish the purpose of a grant. Any funder may require that a grantee "match" some portion of the funds. Grant agreements may specify what sources of matching funds can be used and the degrees to which types of matching funds are allowed.

A **voucher program** is a cross between in-kind benefits and cash assistance. Vouchers are earmarked for a specific service or commodity, but clients can use them as desired. Choices as to commodities acquired or providers used can be made.

Test-Taking Strategies Applied

This is a recall question that relies on social workers understanding the impact of social welfare legislation on social work practice, including knowing about funding mechanisms for programs. Block grant eligibility is limited to state and local governments (not foreign governments or nongovernmental organizations). Program funds are typically distributed using a formula that is prescribed in legislation or regulations. Unlike categorical programs, which target funds for a specific activity, block grant recipients undertake, at their discretion, a number of activities within a broad functional category to address national objectives.

Knowledge Area

Unit III—Interventions With Clients/Client Systems (Content Area); Intervention Processes and Techniques for Use With Larger Systems (Competency); The Effects of Policies, Procedures, Regulations, and Legislation on Social Work Practice and Service Delivery (KSA)

115. A

Rationale

Amicus briefs are documents that are filed in court by those who are not directly related to cases under consideration. Many are filed by advocacy groups, such as the NASW. The information found in such documents can be useful for judges evaluating cases, and they can become part of official case records. Once amicus briefs are filed, courts decide whether or not to accept them. Briefs may be rejected for any number of reasons.

Social workers have become increasingly involved in the preparation and submission of amicus curiae or "friend of the court" briefs. Such briefs often summarize research relevant to particular legal cases and describe implications for legal issues before a court. These briefs are usually filed by social workers in cases that involve important issues such as the death penalty, gay rights, abortion, child welfare, prediction of dangerousness, and so on. Thus, filing amicus briefs can be an effective technique for influencing social policy.

Briefs can supplement or take the place of expert witnesses as a method for communicating information to the courts. Briefs may have an advantage over expert testimony because they are usually prepared by several individuals, they are reviewed by official groups or organizations, and their sources are documented. Also, brief writers are usually not paid for their work, unlike experts who are hired by one side or the other to testify. Consequently, the courts may have more confidence that briefs represent the profession as a whole.

Test-Taking Strategies Applied

This is a recall question that relies on social workers being aware of legal strategies to influence social policy. Social policies are those that are designed to address social issues, ranging from poverty to racism. Many governments have agencies that formulate and administrate social policies, and governments approach social issues in a variety of ways. Social workers must be aware of ways in which they can create new or modify existing laws or policies in order to promote the mission of the profession.

Knowledge Area

Unit III—Interventions With Clients/Client Systems (Content Area); Intervention Processes and Techniques for Use With Larger Systems (Competency); Techniques to Inform and Influence Organizational and Social Policy (KSA)

116. D

Rationale

Active listening skills can be thought of as existing along a continuum. While simply listening shows a client that a social worker is accepting of his or her feelings, it is often useful for a social worker to speak to demonstrate engagement and that he or she understands what is said. **Repeating** is the most basic way that a client knows that a social worker is listening. By just repeating a client's exact words back to him or her, a social worker makes a crude attempt at letting a client know that he or she is listening. However, using a client's exact words can often appear awkward. **Paraphrasing** involves paying attention and remembering what a client is saying. It involves using similar words and phrases to the ones used by a client. Usually a social worker rearranges the words and phrases. A client feels listened to, because a social worker is able to reword what was said. **Reflecting** is where a social worker actually processes the information heard and summarizes it using his or her own words. Reflecting what a client said entails having empathy, withholding judgment, and describing the world from a client's point of view. This level of listening leads to the deepest connection as a client feels truly understood since a social worker can accurately describe what is felt in his or her own words.

Test-Taking Strategies Applied

The question contains a qualifying word—MOST. While active listening in general is an essential part of building relationships and trust with clients, the correct answer is the one that includes verbal statements that demonstrate understanding of clients' situations by using social workers' own words. Reflection is optimal over listening alone—or with repeated statements or paraphrasing. It shows clients that social workers truly comprehend their circumstances as they are able to accurately describe them.

Knowledge Area

Unit III—Interventions With Clients/Client Systems (Content Area); Intervention Processes and Techniques for Use Across Systems (Competency); Verbal and Nonverbal Communication Techniques (KSA)

117. C

Rationale

Social workers providing clinical services to couples must keep in mind that both members of the couple possess the **right to confidentiality and privilege**. If records from conjoint sessions were maintained in one file, then consent to release the record is needed from both members of the couple. Records of any individual sessions may be released based on consent from the individual client who was the subject of the records. If one party in couples counseling does not consent to disclosure of records, the social worker is obligated to take legal steps to protect confidentiality and to block a subpoena, if issued. A subpoena for a couple's therapy records is generally issued by an attorney for one of the parties in a divorce or child custody matter. Acting diligently to protect the privacy of couples is not only prudent and ethical practice, but it may also avoid legal action on the part of one or more of the individuals involved in the couples therapy.

Test-Taking Strategies Applied

This is a recall question that relies on social workers understanding the legal issues regarding confidentiality when providing couples, family, or group counseling.

Social workers should consider several resources in order to formulate an appropriate response to such requests. These include the 2008 *NASW Code of Ethics* and state social worker–client confidentiality and privilege laws, as well as exceptions to privilege made by the courts in related legal proceedings.

Conjoint (combined) records cannot be released when only one party consents or there is a subpoena. A subpoena and court order are not the same. A subpoena is a request for information and a social worker is mandated to claim privilege on behalf of clients when receiving one. However, when a social worker receives a court order, he or she is legally mandated to release the information. Lastly, third-party payers do not have access to client records without proper consent. In this situation, both parties would need to consent to releasing the record to either insurance company.

Knowledge Area

Unit IV—Professional Relationships, Values, and Ethics (Content Area); Confidentiality (Competency); Legal and/or Ethical Issues Regarding Confidentiality, Including Electronic Information Security (KSA)

118. A

Rationale

Cultural and **linguistic competence** is one of the core values of social work. Cultural competence is defined as the integration of knowledge, information, and data about individuals and groups of people into standards, skills, service approaches and supports, policies, measures, and benchmarks that align with the individual's or group's culture and increases the quality, appropriateness, and acceptability of services and outcomes. *Linguistic competence is the capacity of an organization and its personnel to communicate effectively and convey information in a manner that is easily understood by diverse audiences, including persons of limited English proficiency, those who have low literacy skills or are not literate, and individuals with disabilities.*

Linguistic competence is much broader than just being able tospeak multiple languages. However, as the country becomes more linguistically diverse, linguistic competence within the social work profession becomes more critical for effective service delivery. Individual practitioners and organizations are challenged to develop the capacity to use the verbal, written, and multimedia communications in a manner that supports effective practice, including with those who are not literate or use augmentative/facilitated communication devices as they are nonverbal.

Test-Taking Strategies Applied

The question contains a qualifying word—BEST. While having proficiency in multiple languages assists in communicating with those who are non-English speaking, linguistic competence is much broader as it involves using methods that reach those who have low literacy or are not literate. Thus, materials may need to be verbally explained with jargon-free language that is easily understood. In addition, some individuals may use facilitated communication including devices such as picture boards or sign language.

The correct response choice is broad and captures all of these methods of communication.

Knowledge Area

Unit IV—Professional Relationships, Values, and Ethics (Content Area); Professional Development and Use of Self (Competency); The Dynamics of Diversity in the Social Worker–Client/Client System Relationships (KSA)

119. A

Rationale

Psychological abuse occurs when a person tries to control another in order to manipulate his or her sense of reality or view of what is acceptable and unacceptable. Psychological abuse often contains strong emotionally manipulative content and threats designed to force the victim to comply with the abuser's wishes. Psychological abuse can include humiliating or embarrassing, constant put-downs, hypercriticism, refusing to communicate, ignoring or excluding, use of sarcasm, extreme moodiness, making fun, domination and control, withdrawal of affection, blaming, and so on.

Test-Taking Strategies Applied

The question contains a qualifying word—NOT—that requires social workers to select the response choice that is not an indicator of psychological or emotional abuse. When NOT is used as a qualifying word, it is often helpful to remove it from the question and eliminate the three response choices that are categories. This approach will leave the one response choice that is NOT a category.

All of the response choices are indicators of abuse, but the correct answer is a sign of physical rather than psychological abuse. While physical abuse can also involve threatening, isolation, discrediting, belittling, and so on, all psychological abuse does not result in physical mistreatment.

Knowledge Area

Unit I—Human Development, Diversity, and Behavior in the Environment (Content Area); Concepts of Abuse and Neglect

(Competency); Indicators and Dynamics of Abuse and Neglect Throughout the Lifespan (KSA)

120. B

Rationale

When applying ethics to practice situations, issues arise related to the **payment of services**. For example, social workers should avoid accepting goods or services from clients as payment for services. **Bartering** arrangements, particularly involving services, create the potential for conflicts of interest, exploitation, and inappropriate boundaries in social workers' relationship with clients. Social workers should explore and may participate in bartering only in very limited circumstances when it can be demonstrated that such arrangements are an accepted practice among professionals in the local community, considered to be essential for the provision of services, negotiated without coercion, and entered into at a client's initiative and with a client's informed consent.

Test-Taking Strategies Applied

This is a recall question that relies on social workers understanding the ethical issues regarding payment for services, specifically focused on bartering. In this question, the correct response choice is the one that meets "the needs of the client." *Social workers cannot waive or barter for insurance copayments.* Contracts with insurance companies stipulate that clients are responsible for portions of their service payments, which are referred to as copayments. It is unethical to receive insurance payments without billing clients for their responsible portions. It is also unethical to discontinue services and provide self-help materials if the client is still in need.

Social workers can reduce fees using sliding scales when clients are experiencing financial hardship. However, it appears that this would not remedy the problem in this case scenario as the client may not be able to afford any copayment. To be ethical, the social worker would need to reduce the overall fee charged to the insurance company. If the client is responsible for a percentage of the service charge, his copayment would be reduced. However, if the copayment is a fixed dollar amount, the reduced fee structure would have no impact.

The social worker can ethically meet the client's need by waiving the fees for services (e.g., seeing the client pro bono) to both the insurance company and client until the client is able to pay his copayment again.

Knowledge Area

Unit IV—Professional Relationships, Values, and Ethics (Content Area); Professional Values and Ethical Issues (Competency); Ethical Issues in Supervision and Management (KSA)

121. D

Rationale

Social workers should know diverse styles of communicating, including working with those who use facilitated communication. The visual nature of **sign language interpretation** requires careful thought to be given to the placement of the interpreter. The interpreter should stand in front of and in the direct sight line of the deaf person. It is also critical that the interpreter is located near the person who is speaking so the deaf person can glance back and forth from the speaker to the interpreter to get a flavor of the speaker's mood and manner of expression. Thus, the interpreter should sit or stand as close to the hearing speaker as possible so the deaf person can pick up on facial expressions and body language from his or her hearing counterpart. It is not appropriate to place the interpreter next to the deaf individual or put the interpreter in a location that will be difficult for the deaf person to see both the hearing person and the interpreter without turning his or her head. Deaf people should easily be able to see everything interpreters and hearing people do.

Test-Taking Strategies Applied

The correct answer requires the placement of the interpreter in a location that will "effectively facilitate communication." Social workers must recognize that nonverbal behaviors are equally as important as what is spoken. If a sign language interpreter is standing or sitting next to the client or away from both the social worker and client, the client will need to face the interpreter and will not be able to see the nonverbal messages being communicated by the social worker when he or she is speaking. However, if the client can see both the social worker and interpreter within his or her sight line, both verbal and nonverbal communication will be transmitted simultaneously. In this arrangement, the social worker can also naturally face the client when he or she is signing while hearing clearly while an interpreter is translating.

Knowledge Area

Unit III—Interventions With Clients/Client Systems (Content Area); Intervention Processes and Techniques for Use Across Systems (Competency); The Principles and Techniques of Interviewing (e.g., Supporting, Clarifying, Focusing, Confronting, Validating, Feedback, Reflecting, Language Differences, Use of Interpreters, Redirecting) (KSA)

122. C

Rationale

The **effects of physical abuse** are varied and include both bodily injuries and psychological scars. Often, victims of physical abuse are wary of others, especially adults or caregivers if the victims are children.

In this case scenario, the social worker "has begun" serving an 8-year-old girl who was physically abused. There is no information about the setting in which the social worker is employed or the type of services that are being delivered. As services have recently commenced, the social worker should focus on the beginning of the problem-solving process, namely engagement, followed by assessment, and then planning.

Telling the child that she should discuss her feelings will not be effective as she needs to build trust with the social worker before feeling comfortable enough to do so. It is also premature to ask her about the abuse if she has not mentioned it as she has just begun services. The recent removal from her parent's home may be too painful to discuss at this time. Gathering information about her abuse from others may be useful, but is not directly related to the focal point of the question, which is how to interact with the child.

Test-Taking Strategies Applied

This is a recall question that relies on social workers understanding that building trust is necessary when working with victims of abuse. Social workers should let clients set the pace of treatment and discuss their abuse when they are ready to do so. Engagement in the problem-solving process may take a long time in these situations as clients wrestle with addressing the short- and long-term effects of their abuse.

Knowledge Area

Unit I—Human Development, Diversity, and Behavior in the Environment (Content Area); Concepts of Abuse and Neglect (Competency); The Effects of Physical, Sexual, and Psychological Abuse on Individuals, Families, Groups, Organizations, and Communities (KSA)

123. C

Rationale

Social workers should respect **clients' right to privacy**. Records can only be released with proper client consent, unless court-ordered to do so.

In this case scenario, the client is at the beginning of the problem-solving process as the information is being provided "upon intake." During engagement, the social worker should be finding out why the client is seeking treatment, explaining his or her role and what can be expected, and explaining confidentiality and its limits. It is the client's decision about whether to release his records or discuss what has occurred in the past.

Perhaps asking the client more about his past treatment history and reasons for terminating therapy may be appropriate at a later time during the problem-solving process. The client must trust the social worker before such actions are taken, making them incorrect as current responses.

Test-Taking Strategies Applied

When selecting an appropriate action to a case scenario, it is important to determine when it is occurring in the problem-solving process. Actions that may be appropriate interventions may not be advisable during engagement and vice versa. Each step in the problem-solving process has a different focus. Asking a lot of questions, especially those about sensitive topics, before trust has been established can scare a client and hinder the development of a therapeutic alliance.

Knowledge Area

Unit IV—Professional Relationships, Values, and Ethics (Content Area); Confidentiality (Competency); Legal and/or Ethical Issues Regarding Confidentiality, Including Electronic Information Security (KSA)

124. A

Rationale

Throughout the profession's history, social workers have learned about the importance of skillful "**use of self**." The concept refers to social workers' conscious and deliberate reflections on the ways in which their own personality traits, attributes, values, beliefs, life experiences, and cultural, ethnic, and religious heritage influence their work with clients. *Social workers must understand the influence of their own values on the helping relationship in order to be effective.*

Test-Taking Strategies Applied

This is a recall question that relies on social workers being attuned to how their own traits, attributes, values, beliefs, experiences, and heritage influence relationships with clients. In addition to what they bring to these relationships, social workers must also pay close attention to the feelings that arise throughout their relationships with clients. Social workers should think about their "use of self" and countertransference as they are confronted with client issues and clinical challenges.

Knowledge Area

Unit IV—Professional Relationships, Values, and Ethics (Content Area); Professional Development and Use of Self (Competency); The Influence of the Social Worker's Own Values and Beliefs on the Social Worker–Client/Client System Relationship (KSA)

125. D

Rationale

Behavioral theories focus on explaining observable and measurable interactions between clients and their environments. There are many techniques aimed at changing or eliminating undesired behaviors.

Flooding is a treatment that extinguishes clients' anxiety by prolonged real or imagined exposure to high-intensity feared stimuli. In the case scenario, exposing the client to many dogs that would be at the animal shelter is considered flooding.

Extinction withholds a reinforcer that normally follows a behavior so that it will eventually cease.

Modeling is an instruction that demonstrates a desired behavior.

Aversion therapy reduces the attractiveness of a stimulus or behavior by repeated pairing of it with an aversive stimulus.

Test-Taking Strategies Applied

This is a recall question that relies on social workers knowing specific strategies to alter behavior. While all the response choices are behavioral techniques, flooding is the only one that is based on exposure to the feared stimuli. When studying theories, models, and perspectives, it is essential to also know key terms and concepts/techniques that are associated with each.

Knowledge Area

Unit I—Human Development, Diversity, and Behavior in the Environment (Content Area); Human Growth and Development (Competency); Theories of Human Development Throughout the Lifespan (e.g., Physical, Social, Emotional, Cognitive, Behavioral) (KSA)

126. B

Rationale

Developmental counseling and therapy (DCT) is a counseling approach developed by Allen Ivey for understanding and helping people. It provides a means for social workers to assess clients accurately and incorporate **human development considerations in the creation of an intervention plan** to increase their effectiveness.

DCT is grounded in multiple theories and in the philosophical writings of Plato and the research of Jean Piaget. Both proposed four levels or styles of thinking that are linear and qualitatively different. In DCT, four cognitive-emotional developmental (CED) styles are defined: the sensorimotor, concrete, formal, and dialectic systemic CED styles. These are similar to Piaget's four styles, but differ in that they are not linear, not hierarchical, and not sequential. They cycle over the lifespan in response to new developmental transitions and life experiences. The CED styles are similar to Plato's concepts in that they represent both observable external behaviors and internal ideas.

Each of the four styles is a different way of processing information. A client can function in one style most of the time or in multiple styles. The styles are not mutually exclusive and a client can function in more than one style at the same time. Each client has a preference for a particular style in response to a given issue or set of issues. Problems arise when a client overuses one style or when he or she gets stuck in one style and is unable to see other perspectives in a situation.

Each of the four styles helps clients to understand their world and their experience in different and important ways. All four are important and necessary ways of understanding their experiences. The inability to function in a style is referred to as a developmental block. This is what was referred to earlier as a "blind spot." Developmental blocks can be overcome through counseling.

An advantage of integrative counseling models is that they bring together assessments, interventions, and multiple theoretical approaches so that social workers use assessment results to select interventions most likely to be successful with a particular client in response to a given presenting issue. Examples of the preferred interventions based on the four styles are as follows:

- **Sensorimotor:** bodywork (acupuncture, massage, yoga); exercise (walking, jogging); focusing on emotions in the here-and-now; Gestalt interventions; guided imagery; medication; meditation; relaxation training

- **Concrete:** assertiveness training; behavioral therapy (counts and charts); brief therapy; crisis intervention; decision making and problem solving; psychoeducational skills training

- **Formal:** Adlerian therapy; bibliotherapy; cognitive therapy; dream analysis; narratives and reflecting on stories; person-centered therapy; psychodynamic therapies

■ **Dialectic Systemic (understanding how others think):**
advocacy for social justice; community or neighborhood action; consciousness-raising groups; multicultural counseling; self-help groups

Test-Taking Strategies Applied

The question contains a qualifying word—MOST. While a client might benefit from any of the treatments listed, "concrete" is a key word as the concrete CED style is based in logic and details. Thinking concretely means thinking in terms of linear sequences of events. Often a client with this style can provide extensive detail about events. In the early concrete stage, specific, linear details of events and circumstances are provided. The late concrete stage is characterized by "if-then" thinking. When a client is able to give detailed sequences of events and reflect on those sequences, the next step is to logically see the relationship between antecedents and consequences. Such a developmental style is most responsive to behavioral interventions or treatments that use reinforcement and punishment to change actions. The incorrect answers are better suited for the sensorimotor or formal CED styles.

Knowledge Area

Unit II—Assessment and Intervention Planning (Content Area); Intervention Planning (Competency); The Criteria Used in the Selection of Intervention/Treatment Modalities (e.g., Client/Client System Abilities, Culture, Life Stage) (KSA)

127. A

Rationale

Dementia is a loss of cognitive functioning—thinking, remembering, and reasoning—to such an extent that it interferes with a client's daily life and activities. It is not a disease itself, but a group of symptoms that often accompanies a disease or condition. Some dementias are caused by neurodegenerative diseases such as Alzheimer's disease and Parkinson's disease with dementia. Alzheimer's disease accounts for most cases. Vascular dementia, which occurs after a stroke, is the second most common dementia type. However, dementia also has other causes, some of which are treatable, such as medication side effects, depression, vitamin deficiencies, and so on. Many dementias are progressive, meaning symptoms start out slowly and gradually get worse.

Dementia is caused by damage to brain cells. This damage interferes with the ability of brain cells to communicate with each other. When brain cells cannot communicate normally, thinking, behavior, and feelings are affected.

Test-Taking Strategies Applied

The question contains a qualifying word—TRUE. It is even capitalized to assist with identifying the distinguishing factor of the correct response from the rest. Each statement must be read carefully and evaluated as to its accuracy. The correct answer is identified through a process of elimination, with each false assertion being excluded.

Knowledge Area

Unit II—Assessment and Intervention Planning (Content Area); Biopsychosocial History and Collateral Data (Competency); Symptoms of Neurologic and Organic Disorders (KSA)

128. A

Rationale

The primary purpose of an **ethics audit** is to provide social workers with a practical way to identify pertinent ethical issues in their practice settings, review and assess the adequacy of their current practices, design a practical strategy to modify current practices as needed (including what resources will be needed and when), and monitor the implementation of this quality assurance strategy.

Ethics auditing helps prevent ethics complaints and lawsuits, but it is difficult to measure precisely whether and how much these actions will result in cultural improvements (such as those in morale, service efficiency/effectiveness, turnover, etc.).

Conducting an ethics audit involves several key steps:

1. In agency settings, a staff member should assume the role of chair of the ethics audit committee.

2. The audit committee should identify ethics-related issues on which to focus (specific area versus entire agency).

3. Data may be gathered from documents and interviews. The committee should also review relevant codes of ethics and federal and state statutes and regulations.

4. Once the necessary data are gathered and reviewed, the audit committee should assess the risk levels—no risk (current practices are acceptable); minimal risk (current practices are reasonably adequate; minor modifications would be useful); moderate risk (current practices are problematic; modifications are necessary

to minimize risk); and high risk (current practices are seriously flawed; significant modifications are necessary to minimize risk).

5. An action plan for each risk area that warrants attention, beginning with high-risk issues, should be developed.

6. The committee should identify which staff will be responsible for the various tasks and establish a timetable for completion of each and a mechanism to follow up on each task to ensure its completion and monitor its implementation.

Test-Taking Strategies Applied

The question contains a qualifying word—LEAST. Three of the response choices are essential steps in conducting an ethics audit, making them likely outcomes. It appears logical that employees will be less disgruntled and morale will improve when agency policies are ethical. However, it is impossible to measure these intangible benefits. Attributing any improvements in morale due solely to ethically sound procedures is difficult from a research perspective due to threats to internal validity.

Knowledge Area

Unit IV—Professional Relationships, Values, and Ethics (Content Area); Professional Values and Ethical Issues (Competency); Legal and/or Ethical Issues Related to the Practice of Social Work, Including Responsibility to Clients/Client Systems, Colleagues, the Profession, and Society (KSA)

129. D

Rationale

Often social workers are the primary professionals assisting clients who are developing **advance directives**. Social workers in a variety of treatment settings may interact with clients who have advance directives or other documents related to health care proxy decision making or clients who would benefit from executing such documents. Social workers help clients and their families consider potential scenarios, evaluate options for care, and cope with the emotions that arise during such discussions. The role of social workers can be an important one to assure that clients are informed of their decision-making rights and options and to coordinate the resources available to enhance clients' self-determination about future care and treatment.

It is a generally accepted standard that persons who may benefit directly from clients' decisions or who may be in positions to influence the decisions should not serve as witness signatories to legal documents that formalize those decisions, such as advance directives and powers of attorney. Consistent with the need to avoid conflicts of interest or the appearance of conflicts, it is recommended that clients' family members and health care providers (including employees of a residential facility) avoid serving as witnesses for these documents. While it may be challenging in some circumstances to locate suitable witnesses, it is important that the signed documents meet these standards to withstand later potential legal challenges. *Social workers are generally discouraged from witnessing clients' advance directives.*

Test-Taking Strategies Applied

This is a recall question that relies on social workers knowing about the rights of clients with regard to advance directives. These rights are established legislatively and greatly impact on social work practice. Social workers must be aware of how their actions are viewed and do not want to do anything that results in conflicts of interest, whether real or perceived.

Knowledge Area

Unit III—Interventions With Clients/Client Systems (Content Area); Intervention Processes and Techniques for Use With Larger Systems (Competency); The Effects of Policies, Procedures, Regulations, and Legislation on Social Work Practice and Service Delivery (KSA)

130. A

Rationale

The concept of **informed consent** has always been prominent in social work. Consistent with the principle of client self-determination, informed consent procedures require social workers to obtain clients' permission before releasing confidential information to third parties; allowing clients to be photographed, videotaped, or audiotaped by the media, professionals, or other parties; permitting clients to participate in treatment programs; or permitting clients to participate as subjects in research or evaluation projects. According to the 2008 *NASW Code of Ethics,* in instances when clients are not literate or have difficulty understanding the primary language used in practice settings, social workers should take steps to ensure clients' comprehension. This may include providing clients with a detailed verbal explanation or arranging for qualified interpreters or translators whenever possible.

In order to obtain informed consent, social workers must use clear and understandable language related to service purposes, risks, limits due to third-party payers, time frames, and rights of refusal or withdrawal.

A lack of literacy does not mean that clients are incapable of making decisions for themselves. Most individuals who cannot read are their own guardians and capable of making informed choices related to their care.

Test-Taking Strategies Applied

This is a recall question that relies on social workers understanding informed consent procedures. It tests whether social workers inappropriately make assumptions about the competency of those who cannot read. A lack of literacy does not mean that a client has an appointed guardian or that consent has to be obtained by a third party. However, special care is needed in verbally explaining the purpose, risks, limits, and so on, for those who are not able to read them from agency forms.

Knowledge Area

Unit IV—Professional Relationships, Values, and Ethics (Content Area); Confidentiality (Competency); The Principles and Processes of Obtaining Informed Consent (KSA)

131. B

Rationale

An **influence of culture, race, and/or ethnicity on behaviors, attitudes, and identity** of clients who are Hispanic/Latino is the notion of "familismo" (familism), defined as a strong orientation and commitment toward the family. "Familismo" places a high value on marriage, childbearing, and responsibility toward siblings. Family duties, loyalty, and interconnection to family members in both nuclear and extended families are also consistent with "familismo." The ideology of familism extends beyond blood kin to include extended families of several generations and godparents (compadres), another important cultural practice found among Hispanic/Latino families. The mother, father, grandparents, aunts, and uncles may come to their children's doctor visits, and all may have some say in how the child will be cared for. Grandmothers (la abuela), in particular, often play a strong role in how their grandchildren are cared for, both in what they are fed as well as what remedies are used.

The importance of the extended family in decision making, particularly when discussing serious medical conditions, must be kept in mind. Allowing for family meetings to include important extended family members when discussing serious medical conditions is of utmost importance to ensure that medical decisions, treatments, and plans will be followed.

Test-Taking Strategies Applied

In the case scenario, the social worker must consider the impact of "familismo" when taking action to meet the client's needs. *When words are in quotation marks in questions, they should be considered carefully as they are included for a reason.* They usually relate directly to the KSA being tested or distinguish the correct answer from the incorrect ones. Many of the incorrect response choices, such as ensuring that family members are knowledgeable about the boy's prognosis or finding out who will be providing care, may be appropriate social work actions. However, the response choice that most directly relates to "familismo"—which is distinguished by quotation marks—is that which includes the entire family in meetings about treatment and follow-up.

Social workers must be aware of cultural influences and their impact on behaviors and attitudes. Without understanding the meaning of terms such as "familismo," it will be difficult to pick the correct answer from the incorrect ones as this knowledge is the key to distinguishing between them.

Knowledge Area

Unit I—Human Development, Diversity, and Behavior in the Environment (Content Area); Diversity, Social/Economic Justice, and Oppression (Competency); The Effect of Culture, Race, and Ethnicity on Behaviors, Attitudes, and Identity (KSA)

132. B

Rationale

The beginning of the problem-solving process includes activities aimed at **engagement**. During engagement, several key tasks must occur. It is critical for social workers to find out the nature of clients' problems and why clients have decided to seek treatment now. Social workers should explain their role in the helping process and what clients can expect in treatment. Understanding the process can assist with reducing resistance. Also, social workers should explain the limits of confidentiality so clients are clear about mandatory reporting.

Discussing options for treatment is a planning task. Planning occurs after engagement and assessment in the problem-solving process. Planning is followed by intervention, evaluation, and termination.

Test-Taking Strategies Applied

The question contains a qualifying word—MOST. In order to identify the correct response choice, it is necessary to determine whether the actions are likely not to occur in "an initial meeting." "Not" is also an important qualifying word—even though it is not capitalized. The problem-solving process should be used to order the actions listed. Finding out why the client has come to see a social worker, explaining the helping process, and reviewing the limits of confidentiality should happen immediately as part of engagement. It will not be possible to discuss options for treatment until a thorough assessment has been made about the root cause of the problem. Assessment and planning usually do not occur in the first session.

Knowledge Area

Unit IV—Professional Relationships, Values, and Ethics (Content Area); Professional Development and Use of Self (Competency); The Principles and Techniques for Building and Maintaining a Helping Relationship (KSA)

133. B

Rationale

Intermittent reinforcement increases resistance to extinction. **Extinction** is a process of eliminating a behavior by stopping the delivery of reinforcers responsible for maintaining it. Intermittent reinforcement makes extinction slower or harder to accomplish. The word "intermittent" means not every time. Intermittent reinforcement contrasts with continuous reinforcement. Under conditions of continuous reinforcement, a client is reinforced every time he or she does something. For example, if a client always won when gambling, he or she would likely walk away if winning did not occur after several bets. However, gambling is based on intermittent reinforcement, meaning that a client does not know when he or she will win or lose. A client is used to periods of not being rewarded. Thus, a client is much more likely to keep gambling even when not winning, thinking that eventually the reinforcer (e.g., winning) will occur.

Test-Taking Strategies Applied

This is a recall question that relies on social workers understanding principles of behavioral theory. Operant conditioning is based on the knowledge that antecedents precede behaviors, which, in turn, are followed by consequences. Consequences that increase the occurrence of behaviors are referred to as reinforcements while consequences that decrease the likelihood of such behavior are punishments.

Knowledge Area

Unit I—Human Development, Diversity, and Behavior in the Environment (Content Area); Human Growth and Development (Competency); Theories of Human Development Throughout the Lifespan (e.g., Physical, Social, Emotional, Cognitive, Behavioral) (KSA)

134. C

Rationale

All of the listed diagnoses appear in a chapter on **Obsessive-Compulsive and Related Disorders**, which is new in the *DSM-5*. The creation of this chapter reflects the increasing evidence that these disorders are related to one another in terms of a range of diagnostic validators, as well as the clinical utility. New disorders include **Hoarding Disorder, Excoriation (Skin-Picking) Disorder, Substance/Medication-Induced Obsessive-Compulsive and Related Disorder**, and Obsessive-Compulsive and Related Disorder Due to Another Medical Condition. **Trichotillomania** is not new, but is now termed Trichotillomania (Hair-Pulling Disorder) and has been moved from a *DSM-IV* classification of Impulse-Control Disorders not elsewhere classified to Obsessive-Compulsive and Related Disorders in the *DSM-5*.

Test-Taking Strategies Applied

The question contains a qualifying word—NOT—that requires social workers to select the response choice that is not a new diagnosis in the *DSM-5*. When NOT is used as a qualifying word, it is often helpful to remove it from the question and eliminate the three response choices that are new diagnoses. This approach will leave the one response choice that is NOT a new diagnosis.

Social workers must know new *DSM-5* diagnoses and their corresponding criteria. Social workers must be aware of these additions to ensure that they are appropriately diagnosing clients.

Knowledge Area

Unit II—Assessment and Intervention Planning (Content Area); Assessment Methods and Techniques (Competency); The Use of the Diagnostic and Statistical Manual of the American Psychiatric Association (KSA)

135. B

Rationale

Social workers must respect **cultural considerations in the creation of an intervention plan**. For example, a social worker who has conducted a community intervention that is successful might think about building upon this success and conducting the intervention elsewhere—in a context that could be different culturally or have an entirely different population. The key questions here are (a) whether that intervention will be successful elsewhere and (b) how it can be made most successful. Interventions are not one-size-fits-all.

When the setting is different, interventions may need to be adapted. A well-adapted intervention that accounts for cultural considerations can:

- Show respect for another culture's values and identity
- Improve the ability to connect with the target community
- Increase the relevance of actions
- Decrease the possibility of unwanted surprises
- Increase the involvement and participation of members of other cultural groups
- Increase support by cultural group members
- Increase the chances for success of the intervention (and its community impact)
- Build future trust and cooperation across cultural lines—which should raise the prospects for more successful interventions in the future

The first step in adapting interventions across cultures is to learn as much as possible about beliefs and practices, social norms, political concerns, history, and so on.

Test-Taking Strategies Applied

The question contains a qualifying word—BEST. While the incorrect response choices may be helpful in learning more about the community, the best and only way to "understand the cultural beliefs and practices" is by speaking directly with community members. Government, legislative, and other documents, such as newspapers, will not explicitly state the attitudes, behaviors, and customs of community members that will need to be considered when altering an intervention plan.

Also, simply spending time with key officials will not provide insight into the views of those who will be critical to successful implementation of the intervention. The attitudes of key officials may be very different from those of the larger community.

Knowledge Area

Unit II—Assessment and Intervention Planning (Content Area); Intervention Planning (Competency); Cultural Considerations in the Creation of an Intervention Plan (KSA)

136. C

Rationale

Universalization is a supportive, **verbal communication technique** used by social workers to reassure and encourage clients. **Universalization** *places client experiences in the context of other individuals who are experiencing the same or similar challenges, and seeks to help clients grasp that feelings and experiences are not uncommon given the circumstances.*

Universalization helps social workers reassure clients about the "normality" of their feelings regarding their own situation. This technique is used to demonstrate that client feelings and experiences are shared by others. There are many other verbal communication techniques.

Confrontation *occurs when social workers call attention to clients' feelings, attitudes, or behaviors, often when there is inconsistency in them.* Confrontation can be very effective when there is a need to highlight feelings, attitudes, or behaviors that may be useful to the therapeutic process.

Clarification *uses questioning, paraphrasing, and restating to ensure full understanding of clients' ideas and thoughts, including formulation of the existing problem.*

Reflection *is the process of paraphrasing and restating the feelings and words of clients to show that social workers understand their meaning and to encourage clients to continue talking about them.*

Test-Taking Strategies Applied

The question requires the correct answer to be distinguished from the incorrect ones as it is chosen "to best address the client's isolation." While many of the verbal communication techniques listed may be helpful in the therapeutic process, universalization is distinctly intended to let clients know that they are not alone by informing them that others have undergone similar experiences.

Understanding that rejection often occurs when families learn of same-gender relationships may assist the client in seeing the family's reaction as part of a common process. Knowing that others have been treated in this manner and have been able to work through these issues may instill hope in the client. Thus, universalization is the correct answer as it makes the client feel part of a larger group of individuals, thereby reducing isolation.

Knowledge Area

Unit III—Interventions With Clients/Client Systems (Content Area); Intervention Processes and Techniques for Use Across Systems (Competency); The Principles and Techniques of Interviewing (e.g., Supporting, Clarifying, Focusing, Confronting, Validating, Feedback, Reflecting, Language Differences, Use of Interpreters, Redirecting) (KSA)

137. A

Rationale

Most states with **legal provisions applicable to social workers' records** include these in social work licensing regulations. As state licensing is a requirement specific to individual social work practitioners, it is likely that there is no professional licensure enforcement action available upon the death of a licensed social worker. Enforcement may potentially be available, however, against surviving licensed health practitioners who were co-owners or administrators of a business where a social worker practiced.

If the business entity continues to operate, then it would be appropriate for the records of the deceased social workers' clients to be maintained for the period of time required generally by state mental health records laws. This would serve the interests of former clients who may seek the records based on a reasonable expectation that the corporate entity would retain them.

If a social worker is a solo practitioner, former clients are generally precluded from initiating legal actions against that deceased social worker once his or her estate has been closed, such as through probate. There may be some exception covered by state law pertaining to claims that are covered by insurance.

Test-Taking Strategies Applied

The question contains a qualifying word—BEST. Even when there is no legal obligation, social workers should act in clients' best interests.

In this case scenario, destroying the records would not afford clients the opportunity to request them so they could be used for subsequent treatment. Contrarily, sending them to clients and reviewing them without client consent both have confidentiality concerns. A social worker who is a co-owner of a therapy practice does not automatically have client permission to access all files.

Knowledge Area

Unit IV—Professional Relationships, Values, and Ethics (Content Area); Confidentiality (Competency); Legal and/or Ethical Issues Regarding Confidentiality, Including Electronic Information Security (KSA)

138. D

Rationale

Munchausen syndrome by proxy (MSBP) is a mental health problem in which a caregiver makes up or causes an illness or injury in a person under his or her care, such as a child, an elderly adult, or a person who has a disability. Because vulnerable people are the victims, MSBP is a form of abuse. Often perpetrators of MSBP are mothers and victims are small children. Perpetrators can lie about symptoms, change test results, and/or physically harm to produce symptoms. Victims may get painful medical tests they do not need. They may become seriously ill or injured or may die because of the actions of caregivers.

The cause is not known, but it may be linked to problems during perpetrators' childhoods. Abusers often feel like their lives are out of control. They often have poor self-esteem and cannot deal with stress or anxiety. The attention that caregivers get from having to care for those who are "sick" may encourage their behavior. Caregivers may get attention not only from doctors and nurses, but also from others in their community. For example, neighbors may try to help by doing chores, bringing meals, and/or giving money.

Test-Taking Strategies Applied

This is a recall question that relies on social workers understanding indicators of physical abuse and neglect. MSBP is a mental illness and a form of child abuse. It is also called Factitious Disorder by Proxy.

Knowledge Area

Unit I—Human Development, Diversity, and Behavior in the Environment (Content Area); Concepts of Abuse and Neglect (Competency); Indicators and Dynamics of Abuse and Neglect Throughout the Lifespan (KSA)

139. B

Rationale

Understanding the **influences of culture, race, and ethnicity on behaviors, attitudes, and identity** includes learning about nonverbal behaviors. Memorizing a reference guide for culturally based behaviors and lists of cultural practices is ineffective. Most important is the recognition that interactions between people happen within contexts and, thus, are distinct between groups and encounters. Social workers must always allow for the ambiguous nature of communication between people. *Social workers must observe themselves and become more aware of assumptions made about others' behaviors in order to be less reactive. Nonverbal behaviors do not translate across cultures easily and can lead to serious misunderstanding.* Human behaviors are driven by values, beliefs, and attitudes and it is helpful to consider how these invisible aspects of culture drive behaviors that are seen. Nonverbal behaviors that are culturally based include time management, eye contact, head nodding, taking turns in conversation, use of silence, expressiveness, gesturing, use of humor, smiling, laughter, and so on. Social workers should be self-aware, adjusting their own behaviors based on client leads. Otherwise, social workers may misinterpret client nonverbal behaviors based on their own social, economic, religious, and other norms, which may be very different from those of clients being served.

Test-Taking Strategies Applied

The question is asking about "cross-cultural communication with clients," so the correct response choice must relate to competency in this area. Several of the response choices are not accurate. Nonverbal behaviors are not universal and should be analyzed concurrently with verbal messages, not after. While nonverbal behaviors may come in conflict with expressive communication, this assertion is not unique to "cross-cultural communication with clients" as it also occurs within cultures. Social workers do not need to be a part of the same cultural groups as their clients, but they must have self-awareness in order to understand how their differences can impact service delivery.

Knowledge Area

Unit I—Human Development, Diversity, and Behavior in the Environment (Content Area); Diversity, Social/Economic Justice, and Oppression (Competency); The Effect of Culture, Race, and Ethnicity on Behaviors, Attitudes, and Identity (KSA)

140. C

Rationale

Engagement within the context of a therapeutic relationship is defined as a point at which a client views treatment as a meaningful and important process. It involves developing agreement with a social worker on the broad goals of treatment. Engagement can also be described as the onset of a therapeutic relationship or working alliance that exists between a social worker and client. The therapeutic relationship is structured by the goals of treatment that are created through collaboration. Too often engagement is seen as a step in the problem-solving process that requires little attention. This viewpoint is flawed as engagement is the foundation during which a working alliance forms. This alliance will dictate how a therapeutic relationship will progress.

Test-Taking Strategies Applied

This is a recall question that relies on social workers knowing the meaning of a working alliance. There is also a qualifying word— initiated—though it is not capitalized. While a working alliance must be maintained throughout the problem-solving process, it begins during the first step—engagement.

Knowledge Area

Unit IV—Professional Relationships, Values, and Ethics (Content Area); Professional Development and Use of Self (Competency); The Principles and Techniques for Building and Maintaining a Helping Relationship (KSA)

141. A

Rationale

While *there is currently no federal law protecting elders from abuse,* all states have passed laws specifically dealing with **elder abuse, neglect, and exploitation**. Laws and definitions of terms may vary from one state to another, but all states have set up reporting systems. Adult Protective Services (APS) is designated as the public agency to receive, investigate, and respond to allegations of elder abuse and neglect and for providing victims with treatment and protective services. The long-term care Ombudsman (LTCO) investigates and resolves nursing home, assisted living, and other facility-based complaints.

Suspected elder abuse should be reported to local APS or LTCO offices. *Social workers do not need to prove that abuse is occurring prior to making a report.* Social workers are required to report their suspicions, not to verify that abuse is actually occurring. These suspicions should be investigated by APS or LTCO officials.

The U.S. Department of Health and Human Services has identified six types of elder abuse—physical, sexual, neglect, exploitation, emotional abuse, and abandonment. Abandonment is the desertion of an elderly person by anyone who has assumed the responsibility for his or her care or custody. *The majority of abusers are family members, most often adult children or spouses.* Abuse can also occur at a long-term care facility, such as a nursing home or assisted living residence, by employees who perform direct care.

Test-Taking Strategies Applied

The question contains a qualifying word—NOT—that requires social workers to select the response choice that is not correct. When NOT is used as a qualifying word, it is often helpful to remove it from the question and eliminate the three response choices that are accurate. This approach will leave the one response choice that is NOT true about elder abuse.

Knowledge Area

Unit I—Human Development, Diversity, and Behavior in the Environment (Content Area); Concepts of Abuse and Neglect (Competency); Indicators and Dynamics of Abuse and Neglect Throughout the Lifespan (KSA)

142. B

Rationale

Kohlberg's theory of moral development outlines a series of six developmental stages within three different levels that children go through as they develop morality.

Level 1. Preconventional Morality

> **Stage 1—Obedience and Punishment**
> The earliest stage of moral development is especially common in young children, but adults are also capable of expressing this type of reasoning. At this stage, children see rules as fixed and absolute. Obeying the rules is important because it is a means to avoid punishment.

> **Stage 2—Individualism and Exchange**
> At this stage of moral development, children account for individual points of view and judge actions based on how they

serve individual needs. Reciprocity is possible at this point in moral development, but only if it serves one's own interests.

Level 2. Conventional Morality

Stage 3—Interpersonal Relationships
Often referred to as the "good boy/good girl" orientation, this stage of moral development is focused on living up to social expectations and roles. There is an emphasis on conformity, being "nice," and consideration of how choices influence relationships.

Stage 4—Maintaining Social Order
At this stage of moral development, people begin to consider society as a whole when making judgments. The focus is on maintaining law and order by following the rules, doing one's duty, and respecting authority.

Level 3. Postconventional Morality

Stage 5—Social Contract and Individual Rights
At this stage, people begin to account for the differing values, opinions, and beliefs of other people. Rules of law are important for maintaining a society, but members of the society should agree upon these standards.

Stage 6—Universal Principles
Kohlberg's final level of moral reasoning is based on universal ethical principles and abstract reasoning. At this stage, people follow these internalized principles of justice, even if they conflict with laws and rules.

Test-Taking Strategies Applied

The question contains a qualifying word—MOST. All of the response choices are stages in Kohlberg's theory of moral development. Thus, while Kohlberg is not named explicitly, the correct answer must be the stage that attributes actions primarily to avoid "getting in trouble."

Knowledge Area

Unit I—Human Development, Diversity, and Behavior in the Environment (Content Area); Human Growth and Development (Competency); Theories of Human Development Throughout the Lifespan (e.g., Physical, Social, Emotional, Cognitive, Behavioral) (KSA)

143. A

Rationale

Ecomaps are tools for understanding family history and functioning as part of the assessment process. Ecomaps build upon an ecological approach to practice and outline the relationship of a family as a whole, and its individual members, with the outside world, including cultural systems. They are diagrams that depict families within societal contexts, demonstrating the energy, supports, and resources necessary to maintain specific relationships. Ecomaps are used by social workers to depict a variety of reciprocal influences between the client and those people related to the client, relevant social institutions, and environmental influences. It reflects families at particular points in time, thus providing snapshots in time. In effect, it illustrates family members' relationships within a larger social context, such as schools, health systems, work, and spiritual communities. Ecomaps can demonstrate the flow or lack of resources and supports.

Mental status examinations may be viewed as psychological equivalents of physical exams. Their purpose is to evaluate, quantitatively and qualitatively, a range of mental functions and behaviors at specific points in time.

Genograms are graphic representations that identify emotional relationships and intergenerational family patterns within families. They can be used in concert with ecomaps to understand both the internal repetitive behavioral and hereditary patterns (genograms), as well as families' relationships with outside systems (ecomaps).

Psychological assessments are tests that use a combination of techniques to help arrive at some hypotheses about clients and their behaviors, personalities, and capabilities.

Test-Taking Strategies Applied

This question tests social workers' knowledge about tools that can be used to better understand family history and functioning. Answering correctly requires familiarity with the four assessments listed as response choices.

Knowledge Area

Unit I—Human Development, Diversity, and Behavior in the Environment (Content Area); Human Growth and Development (Competency); Systems and Ecological Perspectives and Theories (KSA)

144. B

Rationale

Empathic communication is a key social work skill that is central to social workers' roles and responsibilities. The basis of empathy is that social workers are nonjudgmental, accepting, and genuine. Empathic communication bridges the gap between social workers and clients as verbal and nonverbal messages are used to assist clients to explore themselves and their problems. It decreases defensiveness and helps clients to process and test new information.

   While sound logic and reasoning may be critical to problem solving, they are not the basis for empathic communication. Empathic responding relates to the manner in which social workers communicate. It is also important not to criticize or condemn client feelings or actions—whether or not they appear logical or reasonable.

Test-Taking Strategies Applied

The question contains a qualifying word—NOT—that requires social workers to select the response choice that is not true of empathic communication. When NOT is used as a qualifying word, it is often helpful to remove it from the question and eliminate the three response choices that are essential principles or true about empathic communication. This approach will leave the one response choice that is NOT correct.

Knowledge Area

Unit IV—Professional Relationships, Values, and Ethics (Content Area); Professional Development and Use of Self (Competency); The Concept of Acceptance and Empathy in the Social Worker–Client/Client System Relationship (KSA)

145. A

Rationale

Social workers often partner with others from various professions. This is known as an interdisciplinary approach or **interdisciplinary collaboration**. Some interdisciplinary teams interface daily, whereas others may only meet periodically. To practice effectively, social workers must be prepared to work with professionals from all other disciplines. Through this process, social work knowledge is influenced by, and in turn influences, other disciplines, including family studies, medicine, psychiatry, sociology, education, and psychology.

Each discipline has its own set of assumptions, values, and priorities. These differences can lead to conflict based on professional norms. Thus, interdisciplinary collaboration is a rewarding, yet challenging, social work activity. It means resolving differences for the betterment of a client. Social workers must understand their own styles, as well as the values and norms of others. Social workers must focus on their behavior as part of a group, rather than simply on how others should change.

Test-Taking Strategies Applied

The correct answer is the one by which "a social worker is more likely to reach an acceptable solution." Informing other team members about social work ethics will not find "common ground," which considers alternatives that are consistent with diverse professional perspectives. Evaluating alternatives in supervision does not directly engage team members in collaborative problem solving. While it is good to have established decision-making protocols, an acceptable solution is best generated by a social worker understanding the reasons for the disagreement based on the unique views that are inherent in interdisciplinary collaboration. This understanding will assist a social worker in finding a solution that would be acceptable to all involved.

Knowledge Area

Unit IV—Professional Relationships, Values, and Ethics (Content Area); Professional Development and Use of Self (Competency); The Concept of Acceptance and Empathy in the Social Worker–Client/Client System Relationship (KSA)

146. B

Rationale

It is a good practice for social workers to give **termination letters** to clients once treatment has ended, regardless of the reasons for termination. Readiness for termination may be appropriate when meetings between social workers and clients seem uneventful and no new ground has been discovered for several sessions in a row. Termination letters provide clarity to clients and help avoid any implication that there are ongoing therapeutic responsibilities. Termination letters should be in the form of business letters and include:

- Clients' names
- Dates treatment began and ended

■ Reasons for the termination (e.g., treatment goals have been met, clients' needs are beyond the scope of social workers' practice or areas of expertise, noncompliance with treatment recommendations, social workers are retiring/closing practices)

■ Summary of treatment, including whether further treatment is recommended, and contact information for all referrals (at least three)

Termination letters should be presented in person whenever possible or sent with delivery tracking and confirmation service and/or certified return receipt. Copies and delivery documentation should be retained in clients' files. Letters should be marked "confidential."

Termination letters should not contain confidential therapeutic treatment information, including diagnoses.

Test-Taking Strategies Applied

The question contains a qualifying word—EXCEPT. Three of the four response choices are essential elements in termination letters. Social workers should read each answer and ask whether it is best practice to include the information in a formal document marking the end of services. If so, the response choice can be eliminated as this question is requiring the one answer that is not essential or appropriate.

Knowledge Area

Unit III—Interventions With Clients/Client Systems (Content Area); Intervention Processes and Techniques for Use With Larger Systems (Competency); The Principles and Processes for Developing Formal Documents (e.g., Proposals, Letters, Brochures, Pamphlets, Reports, Evaluations) (KSA)

147. B

Rationale

Social planning is defined as the process by which a community decides its goals and strategies relating to societal issues. There are many compelling reasons to maximize community participation in this process.

First, community participation makes it more likely that policy solutions will be generated that are effective. Without the knowledge of the history and social structure of the community to which members can contribute, there is a risk of serious error. Attempting to repeat something that did not work in the past, or assuming that particular groups will work together when actually they have been at odds for years, can undermine a community development effort before it starts. Furthermore, community members can inform policy-makers and planners of the real needs of the community, so that the most important problems and issues can be addressed.

Second, community participation leads to ownership and support of whatever initiatives come out of a social planning effort. When community members have a hand in planning and decision making, they feel that whatever plan is implemented is theirs, and therefore they will strive to make it work. The same is rarely, if ever, true about plans that are imposed on a community from outside.

Third, community participation can create relationships and partnerships among diverse groups who can then work together. Involving all sectors of the community can bring together groups and individuals who would normally not have—or might not want—contact with one another, and help them understand where their common interests lie.

Fourth, community participation contributes to institutionalizing the changes brought about by changes in policy. Community members are far more likely to buy into policy that has been created with the participation of all sectors of the community. Their support over time will lead to permanent change.

Lastly, community participation energizes the community to continue to change in positive directions. Once community members see what they can accomplish, they will be ready to take on new challenges. Community participation can change their attitude about what is possible—probably the single most important element to creating change.

Test-Taking Strategies Applied

The question contains a qualifying word—NOT. Three of the response choices represent legitimate justifications for community participation in social planning. Including members of the community based on state and federal grant requirements does not speak directly to the benefits for participants and their communities. While grants may require such participation, social workers should always be justifying their actions by how they help clients—not because they are required or because rules need to be followed.

The correct answers on the examination are always those that most effectively and efficiently directly benefit clients.

Knowledge Area

Unit III—Interventions With Clients/Client Systems (Content Area); Intervention Processes and Techniques for Use With Larger Systems (Competency); Community Organizing and Social Planning Methods (KSA)

148. B

Rationale

The *DSM-5* has a number of changes with regard to **Bipolar and Related Disorders** in addition to putting them in their own chapter. One change is to the main criteria of bipolar manic or hypomanic episodes, which did state the mood must be markedly expansive, elated, or irritable. Added to this list is now, "an emphasis on changes in activity and energy as well as mood." There is no longer a Bipolar Not Otherwise Specified diagnosis; now there is an Other Specified Bipolar and Related Disorder diagnosis. This diagnosis is designed to take into account clients who may, for example, have a history of depression and meet all the criteria of hypomania, except the duration. Similarly, if clients have too few symptoms to meet the bipolar II criteria, but have been symptomatic for more than 4 days, they may also fall under this new diagnosis.

In addition to the typical diagnoses of bipolar mania, hypomania, and depression, further information about the mood can be denoted with a **"specifier."** A specifier is an extension to the diagnosis that further clarifies the course, severity, or special features of the disorder or illness. Specifiers were used in the *DSM-IV-TR*, but not much was ever said about them. The two new specifiers in the *DSM-5* are "with mixed features" and "with anxious distress."

The "with mixed features" specifier denotes a mood that simultaneously contains both manic/hypomanic and depressive symptoms. It can be applied to any mood: manic, hypomanic, or depressed (including unipolar depression). This is a fairly major change as previously mixed moods could officially be diagnosed only in bipolar I mania.

The "with anxious distress" specifier is designed to denote clients experiencing anxiety symptoms that are not part of the Bipolar diagnostic criteria.

Test-Taking Strategies Applied

This is a recall question that relies on social workers understanding diagnostic criteria in the most current *DSM—DSM-5*. There are some substantial overall content and format changes between the *DSM-IV-TR* and the *DSM-5*. Social workers must be aware of these revisions to ensure that they are appropriately diagnosing clients.

Knowledge Area

Unit II—Assessment and Intervention Planning (Content Area); Assessment Methods and Techniques (Competency); The Use of the Diagnostic and Statistical Manual of the American Psychiatric Association (KSA)

149. C

Rationale

If a social worker is being **sued by a client**, he or she has the right to defend himself or herself and may need to release client information as part of this defense. A social worker should limit this disclosure only to information required for defense. It would be inappropriate to provide the court with treatment documents, such as those about past history or current diagnoses, if they are not directly relevant to the allegations in the client's case.

Test-Taking Strategies Applied

The question requires the social worker to choose a correct answer that would "address the matter ethically." Whenever ethical mandates of social workers are the foci of questions, the 2008 *NASW Code of Ethics* must be recalled. The answer that most closely resembles the wording of the 2008 *NASW Code of Ethics* should be selected.

The social worker must be able to defend himself or herself, so it will not be possible to safeguard all client information, including documentation indicating that services were in fact delivered. Sending all treatment records will result in client information that is not relevant to the lawsuit to be known. It is also not advisable to contact the client outside of the legal process once the court is involved. The correct answer is the one that balances the social worker's right to an adequate defense with the client's right to confidentiality by producing only relevant redacted information.

Knowledge Area

Unit IV—Professional Relationships, Values, and Ethics (Content Area); Confidentiality (Competency); Legal and/or Ethical Issues Regarding Confidentiality, Including Electronic Information Security (KSA)

150. D

Rationale

Client suicide brings with it both emotional and ethical issues. A difficult issue that a social worker may struggle with is **appropriateness of sharing client information with a deceased client's family members**. Social workers are sometimes contacted by surviving family members for many reasons. In some cases, merely acknowledging to the family that the client was being treated raises legal considerations. However, there are other cases where the surviving family members knew the social worker was treating a client (e.g., the therapy sessions were paid for by a parent's health insurance).

Social workers must remember that privacy rights continue after the death of a client. Protecting the privacy interests of clients does not end with a client's death. A social worker needs to be aware of the continuing ethical limitations and legal exceptions to be considered in any request for a deceased client's records. A social worker needs to explain to survivors that disclosures about what a client discussed in treatment are limited by privacy laws.

In this case scenario, the client has rights to confidentiality even though a parent's insurance was paying for the treatment. Thus, the record cannot be released.

Instead, the social worker can express sympathy and support for the family, listening and responding to the emotional needs of the grieving family rather than talking. The social worker can also focus on the sadness of the death and the needs of the family rather than the details of treatment. It may be appropriate to provide information about suicide in general rather than specific information about the client. However, the social worker must avoid engaging in therapeutic work with the family, since this would create a dual relationship.

Test-Taking Strategies Applied

This is a recall question that relies on social workers understanding the ethical standards related to releasing confidential information after a client's death. While a social worker feels compassion for a family when a client commits suicide, it is essential that these feelings do not cloud the social worker's judgment and lead him or her to breach confidentiality. There are methods described earlier that can help to comfort the family without disclosing protected client information.

Knowledge Area

Unit IV—Professional Relationships, Values, and Ethics (Content Area); Confidentiality (Competency); Legal and/or Ethical Issues Regarding Confidentiality, Including Electronic Information Security (KSA)

151. A

Rationale

Social workers must know **techniques to establish measurable intervention or service plans**. A goal statement is a quantifiable, time-limited statement of planned results. It has the following characteristics:

- It is relevant to a specific problem.
- It specifies who (or what) will change.
- It specifies what the change will be.
- It specifies how much change is expected.
- It specifies the conditions under which the change can take place (this, however, may depend on the nature of the problem).
- It specifies how long it should take to see the change happen.

Test-Taking Strategies Applied

The question requires identifying the problem with the goal statement that is in quotation marks. The social worker appropriately prioritized the health and safety issue using Maslow's hierarchy of needs. The selection of the safety concern over the isolation is not directly related to concerns about the goal statement provided, making the second choice incorrect. The other issues that may be contributing to her eviction are also irrelevant and questioning the validity of the report by the woman is not appropriate. The stove being on for extended periods is a concern regardless if it is the main contributor to her possible eviction. Lastly, a goal statement does not include the next actions to be taken if desired results are not achieved. Subsequent goal statements can be developed if needed, but each goal statement should focus on a single behavioral or attitudinal change.

The goal statement lacks a schedule for evaluation or when change is to be expected. By adding "for a month" to the end of it, for example, it would provide the first checkpoint for seeing whether the change has happened. The goal statement also does not say under what conditions this behavioral change should occur because, in this instance, it is not acceptable for the stove to be on at any time that it is not in use.

Knowledge Area

Unit III—Interventions With Clients/Client Systems (Content Area); Intervention Processes and Techniques for Use Across Systems (Competency); Methods to Develop and Evaluate Measurable Objectives for Client/Client System Intervention, Treatment, and/or Service Plans (KSA)

152. A

Rationale

Many ethical standards speak to the **professional boundaries** that social workers should maintain with clients. Clearly, social workers should not engage in sexual activities or sexual contact with current clients, whether such contact is consensual or forced. In addition, social workers should not engage in sexual activities or sexual contact with former clients because of the potential for harm to a client.

Social workers also should not provide clinical services to individuals with whom they have had a prior sexual relationship. Providing clinical services to a former sexual partner has the potential to be harmful to the individual and is likely to make it difficult for a social worker and individual to maintain appropriate professional boundaries.

Test-Taking Strategies Applied

This is a recall question that requires understanding of ethical issues that relate to professional boundaries. The case scenario mentions a request by a former girlfriend for the provision of clinical services. Though the relationship ended many years ago, it is not appropriate for a social worker to provide either individual or group counseling as there was a prior intimate relationship. Gathering additional information about the grief would also not be advisable as the individual may confuse this assessment as marking the onset of a therapeutic relationship. The individual will ultimately have to provide this history to a treating professional.

The social worker must provide information about other qualified service providers as a first step in making appropriate referrals for services. The social worker should provide the names and contact information of multiple providers so the individual does not think that one is being recommended by the social worker. The individual must choose the provider who is best suited to meet her own needs without being influenced by the social worker.

Knowledge Area

Unit IV—Professional Relationships, Values, and Ethics (Content Area); Professional Values and Ethical Issues (Competency); Professional Boundaries in the Social Worker–Client/Client System Relationship (e.g., Power Differences, Conflicts of Interest, etc.) (KSA)

153. C

Rationale

The biopsychosocial assessment (also known as the biopsychosocial–spiritual–cultural assessment) is a hallmark of social work, recognizing the *interactional relationship between a client's physical health, psychological functioning, and his or her social environment*. It informs where additional assessment is needed and where the focus of treatment is required.

It recognizes the mutual link between the physical/body, mental/mind, and emotional/social/spiritual aspects of a client. Without data in all these areas, crucial diagnostic information will be left out of the clinical picture.

The **components of a biopsychosocial assessment** include cursory identifying information, presenting problem(s)/issue(s), summary impressions, goals, discharge/transition plan, and diagnostic impression(s). The bulk of the instrument consists of three sections: the biological/medical (including substance-related issues, medical conditions, medications, disability restrictions), psychological (including symptom/problems, mental status, family history of psychiatric issues, risk assessment), and social (including spirituality, cultural issues, educational background, developmental history, legal history, marital/relationship status and history, employment history/aspirations, and needs/abilities/preferences).

Systems theory describes human behavior in terms of complex systems. It recognizes that each client is a system with biological, psychological, social, spiritual, and cultural dimensions that impact upon one another. Client problems in any one area affect functioning in others. In addition, a client is a member of a couple, family, and community, which impact one another reciprocally. A biopsychosocial history looks at physical, psychological, and social functioning as a way to understand a client problem—recognizing that they all contribute and must be considered. Thus, the use of a biopsychosocial history is justified by systems theory.

Transpersonal theory proposes additional stages beyond the adult ego. In healthy individuals, these stages contribute to creativity, wisdom, and altruism. In people lacking healthy ego development, experiences can lead to psychosis.

Rational choice theory is based on the idea that all action is fundamentally rational in character, and people calculate the risks and benefits of any action before making decisions.

Social learning theory is based on Albert Bandura's idea that learning occurs through observation and imitation. New behavior will continue if it is reinforced. According to this theory, rather than simply hearing a new concept and applying it, the learning process is made more efficient if the new behavior is modeled as well.

Test-Taking Strategies Applied

The question requires knowledge of the four theories listed as response choices, as well as the premise of a biopsychosocial assessment.

Knowledge Area

Unit II—Assessment and Intervention Planning (Content Area); Biopsychosocial History and Collateral Data (Competency); The Components of a Biopsychosocial Assessment (KSA)

154. A

Rationale

The Indian Child Welfare Act (ICWA) is a federal law passed in 1978. ICWA is an integral policy framework on which tribal child welfare programs rely. It provides a structure and requirements for how public and private child welfare agencies and state courts view and conduct their work to serve tribal children and families. It also acknowledges and promotes the role that tribal governments play in supporting tribal families, both on and off tribal lands.

The intent of Congress under ICWA was to "protect the best interests of Indian children and to promote the stability and security of Indian tribes and families." ICWA defines an "Indian child" as "any unmarried person who is under age eighteen and is either (A) a member of an Indian tribe or (B) is eligible for membership in an Indian tribe and is the biological child of a member of an Indian tribe." Under federal law, individual tribes have the right to determine eligibility, membership, or both. ICWA does not apply to divorce proceedings, intra-family disputes, juvenile delinquency proceedings, or cases under tribal court jurisdiction. While "Indian child" is defined in the legislation, other terms such as "American Indian," "Native American," "Alaska Native," and/or "Indigenous" child are also used to describe a covered youth.

When ICWA applies, a child's tribe and family have an opportunity to be involved in decisions affecting services. *A cornerstone is active and early participation and consultation with a child's tribe in all case planning decisions.* A tribe or a parent can also petition to transfer jurisdiction of the case to a tribal court. ICWA sets out federal requirements regarding removal and placement of Indian children in foster or adoptive homes and allows children's tribes to intervene. States are required to provide "active efforts" to families, and courts will be asked to determine whether active efforts have been made. The definition of "active efforts" is left open in the ICWA to accommodate individual case decisions. However, federal guidelines do exist that mandate states make active efforts to:

- Provide services to families to prevent removal of Indian children from their parents or Indian custodians
- Reunify Indian children with their parents or Indian custodians after removal

Test-Taking Strategies Applied

This is a recall question that relies on social workers understanding federal legislation that applies to child abuse and neglect. The examination will never require knowledge about state or local laws as they apply only to social work practice within their respective jurisdictions. The examination is used by social work regulatory bodies in the United States, Canada, and other international locations. Social workers in the United States must be aware of the impacts of federal social welfare legislation on practice as these standards apply universally, regardless of state.

There are always a handful of questions on every Association of Social Work Boards (ASWB) examination that ask about information that may not be familiar. In this case scenario, the "unique factor" must be identified "according to federal legislation." All answers mention the relevancy of the child being American Indian. It seems unlikely that the definition of abuse or requirements for investigations would be different for these children. There may be some children who are American Indian who do not have biological family members with whom to place them. Through elimination, the correct answer can be identified even when there is no direct knowledge of ICWA.

Knowledge Area

Unit III—Interventions With Clients/Client Systems (Content Area); Intervention Processes and Techniques for Use With Larger Systems (Competency); The Effects of Policies, Procedures, Regulations, and Legislation on Social Work Practice and Service Delivery (KSA)

155. D

Rationale

After assessment, social workers must determine which **intervention modality** is best to meet client needs. Such decisions may evaluate individual versus group therapy, as well as short-term versus long-term treatment. The issue of short-term versus long-term treatment has been the focus of much controversy with merits for each. Often accessibility or payment for services can limit ongoing availability.

Many factors are considered when working in a short-term model or setting such as staying focused on the immediate goals of treatment, learning new ways to problem solve, improving coping skills and becoming more aware of adverse situations, and determining how to manage those situations differently. In short-term treatment, clients must be actively involved and take responsibility for the change process.

Short-term treatment is not appropriate for all client situations as some problems are better addressed via long-term treatment.

Test-Taking Strategies Applied

The question contains a qualifying word—PRIMARY—that indicates that there may be multiple answers that should be considered. All of the incorrect response choices are important for effective client services, but not related or unique to "time-limited treatment." Ensuring ongoing availability of service access, that goals are based on client priorities, and supports are provided to sustain progress should occur with all clients, regardless of treatment length.

The correct answer is the only one that addresses the short period to achieve goals, thereby necessitating that progress be made quickly. It is not appropriate to tackle long-term complicated client situations when only brief treatment is possible. Interventions must be realistic and feasible within the sessions available to clients.

Knowledge Area

Unit II—Assessment and Intervention Planning (Content Area); Intervention Planning (Competency); The Criteria Used in the Selection of Intervention/Treatment Modalities (e.g., Client/Client System Abilities, Culture, Life Stage) (KSA)

156. D

Rationale

A **social work interview** is always purposeful and involves verbal and nonverbal communication between a social worker and client, during which ideas, attitudes, and feelings are exchanged. The actions of the social worker aim to gather important information; therefore, the actions of a social worker during the interview must be planned and focused. Questions in a social work interview should be tailored to the specifics of a client, not generic, "one size fits all" inquiries. The focus is on a client and his or her unique situation.

The purpose of the social work interview can be informational, diagnostic, or therapeutic. The same interview may serve more than one purpose. Communication during a social work interview is interactive and interrelational. A social worker's questions will result in specific responses by a client that, in turn, lead to other inquiries. The message is formulated by a client, encoded, transmitted, received, processed, and decoded.

The importance of words and messages may be implicit (implied) or explicit (evident). There are a number of techniques that a social worker may use during an interview to assist clients including **universalization**, **clarification**, **confrontation**, **interpretation**, **reframing**, and **relabeling**.

Test-Taking Strategies Applied

This is a recall question that relies on social workers understanding interviewing techniques. Confrontation is not inherently punitive or judgmental. It means calling attention to something.

In this case scenario, the client's reaction to her husband's disinterest in having a ceremony to renew their vows and a party to celebrate the occasion would not be expected given her desire to end her marriage. Thus, the social worker must respond by pointing out this incongruence in order to gain a better understanding of the situation. None of the incorrect response choices allow the social worker to gain insight into the client's emotional reactions.

Knowledge Area

Unit III—Interventions With Clients/Client Systems (Content Area); Intervention Processes and Techniques for Use Across Systems (Competency); The Principles and Techniques of Interviewing (e.g., Supporting, Clarifying, Focusing, Confronting, Validating, Feedback, Reflecting, Language Differences, Use of Interpreters, Redirecting) (KSA)

157. B

Rationale

Gender roles are socially and culturally defined prescriptions and beliefs about the behavior and emotions of men and women. Many theorists believe that perceived gender roles form the bases for the development of gender identity. Some prominent theories of gender role and gender identity development include evolutionary theory, object-relations theory, gender schema theory, and social role theory.

Evolutionary theories of gender development are grounded in genetic bases for differences between men and women. They propose that men and women have evolved differently to fulfill their different and complementary functions, which are necessary for survival.

In contrast, **object-relations theories** focus on the effects of socialization on gender development. Whereas boys must separate from their mothers to form their identities as males, girls do not have to endure this separation to define their identities as females. The devalued role of women is a product of the painful process men undergo to separate them from the female role.

Gender schema theory focuses on the role of cognitive organization in addition to socialization. This theory postulates that children learn how their cultures and/or societies define the roles of men and women and then internalize this knowledge as a gender schema or unchallenged core belief. The gender schema is then used to organize subsequent experiences.

Social role theory suggests that the sexual division of labor and societal expectations based on stereotypes produce gender roles. Behavior is strongly influenced by gender roles when cultures endorse gender stereotypes and form firm expectations based on those stereotypes.

Test-Taking Strategies Applied

The question required choosing a correct answer based on the use of "an ecological perspective." The ecological perspective is rooted in systems theory, which views roles as resulting from transactional processes that reflect the "person-in-environment" relationship. Thus, the correct answer considers both the genetic physical predispositions, which are central to evolutionary theory, as well as the social and cultural influences, which are the basis of object-relations, gender schema, and social role theories.

Knowledge Area

Unit I—Human Development, Diversity, and Behavior in the Environment (Content Area); Diversity, Social/Economic Justice, and Oppression (Competency); Gender and Gender Identity Concepts (KSA)

158. C

Rationale

The purpose of **clinical supervision** is to ensure that clients receive treatment or habilitation which is consistent with accepted standards of practice and their needs. While supervision does increase social workers' capacity to work more effectively, to provide work contexts conducive to productivity, and to help social workers take satisfaction in their work, it only attempts to reach these objectives as means to an end—namely, enhanced client well-being. Social workers can use supervision as a method of professional development, but only with the goal of improved practice.

Test-Taking Strategies Applied

The question contains a qualifying word—PRIMARY. Unlike other questions, the qualifying word in this question is not capitalized.

Qualifying words may be capitalized or not, so it is important to read questions carefully. While the incorrect response choices may be done as part of or achieved by clinical supervision, its most important purpose is to guarantee the provision of quality services.

In actual practice, social workers often view supervisory functions as they relate to assisting practitioners to enhance their skills or make difficult decisions. Supervisors are hands-on instructors, especially for students in field settings. Despite how helpful supervision may be for social workers themselves, the ultimate goal of this essential activity must not be forgotten. Supervisors assist and develop social workers only so that they can provide better client services. Enhanced client welfare must always be considered and is critical to distinguishing the correct answer from the incorrect ones.

Knowledge Area

Unit IV—Professional Relationships, Values, and Ethics (Content Area); Professional Values and Ethical Issues (Competency); Professional Development Activities to Improve Practice and Maintain Current Professional Knowledge (e.g., In-Service Training, Licensing Requirements, Reviews of Literature, Workshops) (KSA)

159. A

Rationale

Structured decision-making is an important concept in child welfare as it assists social workers in promoting the ongoing safety and well-being of children. It uses structured assessments and tools to improve the consistency and validity of each decision. Structured decision-making includes clearly defined service standards, mechanisms for timely reassessments, methods for measuring workload, mechanisms for ensuring accountability and quality controls, and so on. *The primary goal of structured decision making is to bring a greater degree of consistency, objectivity, and validity to child welfare case decisions in order to help focus limited resources on cases at the highest levels of risk and need.* Structured assessment tools are used at various points in the case decision-making process (e.g., initial responses to allegations, child removals, case openings/closings, and reunifications). Each tool incorporates decision protocols—based directly on assessment results—to guide responses to families. One key assessment tool is a research-based risk assessment that classifies families according to their likelihood of continuing to abuse or neglect their children. Structured decision making also focuses on how case management decisions are made and how resources can best be directed.

Test-Taking Strategies Applied

The question contains a qualifying word—PRIMARY—that indicates that structured decision-making may be used for more than one of the reasons stated. However, understanding that it is based on using standardized tools to guide processes assists in picking out the main justification for its use—reliability (i.e., consistency).

Knowledge Area

Unit II—Assessment and Intervention Planning (Content Area); Assessment Methods and Techniques (Competency); Risk Assessment Methods (KSA)

160. A

Rationale

In any situation where there is a decision about whether a client's record is to be released, it is a social worker's obligation to ensure that **client consent** is informed. In order to accomplish this, a client needs to be fully aware of the content of the record that is to be disclosed. It is not unusual for clients to have little awareness of the information that has been documented in the course of therapeutic sessions. After a discussion or review of the contents of a clinical record with a social worker, a client will be in a better position to determine whether to agree to a potential release of information. This procedure should be done even when a release was signed prior to the onset of treatment. A client may not be aware of the information contained in a record and may want to revoke or modify an authorization that has already been signed.

Test-Taking Strategies Applied

The question contains a qualifying word—BEST. The correct answer is the response choice that "will BEST assist the client in deciding whether the assessment should be released." The ability to review the document prior to making a decision ensures that the client is informed about what will be received by the insurance company. The other answers will not be most helpful in decision making with regard to release of the document.

Knowledge Area

Unit IV—Professional Relationships, Values, and Ethics (Content Area); Confidentiality (Competency); The Use of Client/Client System Records (KSA)

161. C

Rationale

Social workers may limit **clients' right to self-determination** when, in social workers' professional judgment, clients' actions or potential actions pose a serious, foreseeable, and imminent risk to themselves or others (*NASW Code of Ethics, 2008—1.02 Self-Determination*).

Test-Taking Strategies Applied

The question contains a qualifying word—NOT. Three of the response choices represent criteria that must be present in order for a social worker to limit a client's right to self-determination as per the 2008 *NASW Code of Ethics*. The correct answer is the one that is not required.

When client action violates the rights of another person or persons, it does not have to be stopped as these behaviors may not be serious, foreseeable, and imminent, all of which must be present to prevent the client from acting.

Knowledge Area

Unit IV—Professional Relationships, Values, and Ethics (Content Area); Professional Values and Ethical Issues (Competency); Techniques for Protecting and Enhancing Client/Client System Self-Determination (KSA)

162. A

Rationale

In the child welfare field, the practice of including children and families as part of the decision-making team has grown tremendously. Several distinct practice models use child- and family-centered principles to bring children and families "to the table" to discuss and solve problems and to support each other.

A basic assumption is that all families can harness their strengths and capabilities to enter into partnership with formal child welfare agencies and courts in order to make decisions that protect and nurture their children. Prior to the advent of child and family meetings, child welfare agencies often made decisions about children and families with little or no input from them. However, when key family and community members, formal and informal supports, and child welfare agency representatives join together in mutual respect, better decisions and integrated plans result.

The purpose of a **Child and Family Team** is to engage and partner with all people who surround a family to build a support network. A Child and Family Team includes family members and community members who come together to create, implement, and update a plan with a youth and family. The plan builds on the strengths of a youth and family and addresses their needs, desires, and dreams.

Test-Taking Strategies Applied

Social workers must understand the importance of informal supports in the lives of clients. A core social work function is to assist clients to build and mobilize support systems. *Optimally clients should be able to solve their own problems and rely on unpaid staff for support.*

In identifying informal supports to be on a Child and Family Team for a youth entering the child welfare system, it is not the decision of treating professionals. The family is a partner in the process and is best suited to know who should be included. Often informal supports are neighbors, religious or spiritual leaders, school personnel, sports or club organizers, and so on. Informal supports do not need to be knowledgeable about the abuse or neglect. They also do not need to be at all meetings, but should be committed to assisting the child and family in some way.

Knowledge Area

Unit II—Assessment and Intervention Planning (Content Area); Intervention Planning (Competency); Methods to Involve Clients/Client Systems in Intervention Planning (KSA)

163. C

Rationale

Social workers must take reasonable steps to prevent client access to social workers' personal social networking sites to maintain **professional boundaries** and avoid confusion with regard to inappropriate dual relationships. Social workers shall maintain separate professional and personal social media and websites in order to establish clear boundaries and to avoid inappropriate dual relationships.

In addition, social workers must refrain from accepting "friend" or contact or blog response requests from clients on social networking sites. Exceptions can be made only when such contact is an explicit component of a service-delivery model and meets prevailing standards regarding use of digital technology to serve clients.

Test-Taking Strategies Applied

The proliferation of social workers' use of digital and other electronic technology has created new ethical challenges. The standards of care that have historically protected social work clients in the context of in-person relationships apply to electronic communication.

In the case scenario, the social worker has already blurred the boundary lines by posting agency events and awareness activities on her personal social networking site. However, accepting the parent as a "friend" may provide access to personal information about the social worker that is not relevant to services or volunteering. Even though the parent is not a client, the social worker has a professional relationship with him or her as the guardian of a current service recipient. Thus, access to the social worker's social networking site is not appropriate and leads to boundary confusion.

Knowledge Area

Unit IV—Professional Relationships, Values, and Ethics (Content Area); Professional Values and Ethical Issues (Competency); Professional Boundaries in the Social Worker–Client/Client System Relationship (e.g., Power Differences, Conflicts of Interest, etc.) (KSA)

164. D

Rationale

Disruptive Mood Dysregulation Disorder (DMDD), a new diagnosis for children in the *DSM-5*, is characterized by severe and recurrent temper outbursts that are grossly out of proportion in intensity or duration to the situation. These occur, on average, three or more times each week for 1 year or more. Between outbursts, children with DMDD display a persistently irritable or angry mood, most of the day and nearly every day, that is observable by parents, teachers, or peers. A diagnosis requires the previously noted symptoms to be present in at least two settings (at home, at school, or with peers) for 12 or more months, and symptoms must be severe in at least one of these settings. During this period, the child must not have gone 3 or more consecutive months without symptoms. The onset of symptoms must be before age 10, and a DMDD diagnosis should not be made for the first time before age 6 or after age 18.

Test-Taking Strategies Applied

The question contains a qualifying word—MOST. While the *DSM-5* does include two diagnoses with related symptoms to DMDD, Oppositional Defiant Disorder and Bipolar Disorder, the symptoms described in DMDD are significantly different than those two diagnoses. Oppositional Defiant Disorder is an ongoing pattern of anger-guided disobedience, hostilely defiant behavior toward authority figures that goes beyond the bounds of normal childhood behavior. Bipolar Disorder also has similar symptoms, but they occur in an episodic, rather than constant, way.

Knowledge Area

Unit II—Assessment and Intervention Planning (Content Area); Assessment Methods and Techniques (Competency); The Use of the Diagnostic and Statistical Manual of the American Psychiatric Association (KSA)

165. A

Rationale

DSM-5 advances the evolution of the practice of cultural psychiatry with the **Cultural Formulation Interview** (CFI), which was based on the *DSM-IV's* Outline for Cultural Formulation (OCF). The CFI is an evidence-based tool composed of a series of questionnaires that assist social workers in making person-centered cultural assessments to inform diagnosis and treatment planning. It recognizes the influences of culture, race, and ethnicity on behaviors, attitudes, and identity. The CFI facilitates the evocation of a client's own narrative of illness. In addition, it explicitly inquires about the views of members of a client's social network, to better place him or her in the context of a community and help a client and his or her support system engage more fully in the treatment process.

The CFI can be used in assessment with all clients, not just with cultural minorities or in situations of obvious cultural difference between social workers and clients. All social workers bring their own cultures, values, and expectations to encounters, including often invisible influences on how to approach specific aspects of care.

Test-Taking Strategies Applied

The question contains a qualifying word—MOST. While the information gathered by the CFI can be helpful throughout the problem-solving process, it is a tool to gather information, making it extremely beneficial when doing assessments. Social workers wanting to perform culturally appropriate assessments now have sample questions upon which to draw. For example, some questions focus on determining the cultural definition of the problem and perceptions of cause, context, and support. By asking clients how they would describe their problem to their family, friends, or others in their community, it is possible to see how their issues would be viewed within their cultural context. Other questions focus on finding out clients' thoughts about why problems are occurring.

Such questioning is the hallmark of assessment as engaging focuses on relationship building and planning/intervention occur after the problem is clearly understood.

Knowledge Area

Unit I—Human Development, Diversity, and Behavior in the Environment (Content Area); Diversity, Social/Economic Justice, and Oppression (Competency); The Effect of Culture, Race, and Ethnicity on Behaviors, Attitudes, and Identity (KSA)

166. B

Rationale

Drugs used to treat mental disorders can have serious **psychopharmacological side effects**. A "black box warning" is the strictest warning put on the labeling of prescription drugs or drug products by the Food and Drug Administration (FDA) when there is reasonable evidence of an association between a serious hazard and use of the drug. It is basically a warning with a black box around it, hence the name. Having the black box around the warning means an adverse reaction to the drug may lead to death or serious injury.

Sometimes a black box warning is necessary at the time a new drug is approved. More commonly, however, it is added after the drug has been approved and the FDA has received reports of adverse events. After the FDA confirms the serious risk, then depending on the severity of the adverse events (and in collaboration with the pharmaceutical company), a boxed warning is implemented. This does not mean the drug is contraindicated in any way, but it is a means of communication from the FDA to clients and service providers to highlight the risk. As with any drug, there are associated risks and benefits. The black box warning is to alert to the potential risk of taking this drug so it can be taken into consideration.

For example, the FDA issued a black box warning on antidepressants indicating that they were associated with an increased risk of suicidal thinking, feeling, and behavior in young people. In addition, in an attempt to help slow the prescription drug abuse epidemic, immediate-release opioid painkillers such as oxycodone and fentanyl now have to carry a "black box" warning about the risk of abuse, addiction, overdose, and death.

Test-Taking Strategies Applied

This is a recall question that relies on social workers understanding the side effects, especially the serious ones, of psychotropic medications. While these medications can have many side effects, it is the serious ones that are sometimes asked about on the ASWB examination.

Knowledge Area

Unit II—Assessment and Intervention Planning (Content Area); Biopsychosocial History and Collateral Data (Competency); Common Psychotropic and Nonpsychotropic Prescriptions and Over-the-Counter Medications and Their Side Effects (KSA)

167. B

Rationale

The impact of stress, trauma, and violence can be physical and emotional/psychological. Physical symptoms of trauma can be insomnia, nightmares, racing heartbeat, aches, pains, fatigue, muscle tension, and so on. Victims of violence can suffer serious health problems as a result of being physically assaulted. Emotional and psychological symptoms of trauma include shock, denial, anger, guilt, shame, depression, hopelessness, anxiety, fear, withdrawal, and so on. There are both short- and long-term effects of stress, trauma, and violence.

In intimate partner abuse, a person being abused will not leave until the benefits of leaving outweigh the costs or risks (**social exchange theory**). The **cycle of abuse** starts with tension building until battering occurs. After a battering incident, an abuser is often apologetic and attentive as part of a honeymoon period until tension builds again.

Test-Taking Strategies Applied

The question contains a qualifying word—FIRST. There may be more than one appropriate response choice, but the order in which they are to occur is critical, with the most immediate or urgent needing to happen before the others. The correct answer is the one that best meets "this woman's needs." Using Maslow's hierarchy of needs to help prioritize, safety needs must be addressed before emotional ones (e.g., intimacy, esteem, and self-actualization). While it may be useful to find out why she stayed in this relationship for so long and assure her that information is confidential and she will not be judged, these actions will not directly help "meet this woman's needs," which is the focus of the question.

Maslow's hierarchy of needs is rarely explicitly stated in questions, but is a useful tool for prioritization of needs for any KSA.

Knowledge Area

Unit I—Human Development, Diversity, and Behavior in the Environment (Content Area); Human Growth and Development (Competency); The Impact of Stress, Trauma, and Violence (KSA)

168. A

Rationale

The issues surrounding **parental consent to a child's treatment** can be thorny, especially when a child is often presented for treatment by one parent who may be separated or divorced from the other (second) parent. An inquiry by a social worker before treatment begins about the terms of a separation, a divorce decree, and a child custody order is the first step to avoid issues later. By requesting a copy of the temporary and/or final custody and divorce decree, a social worker may be able to identify the rights accorded to each of the parents regarding the mental health treatment for a child. At a minimum, a review of these documents should establish whether a presenting parent has legal custody regarding a child and can make medical or mental health decisions independent of the other parent. *If the documents are not clear and do not establish each parent's decision-making authority for health care decisions including mental health, requesting written consent from the two parents who each have legal custody is preferred and a better course of action prior to beginning treatment with a child.* If unable to obtain a consent form signed by both parents, social workers may request that the consenting parent sign a statement confirming that he or she has the legal right to consent to a child's treatment without the consent of any other individuals. However, this attestation should not be sought until consent from both parents has been requested.

All documents related to the issue of custody and consent for treatment should be maintained in a client's file.

A social worker assumes a risk of treating a child without full consent if there is no written document signed by a presenting parent that confirms her/his right to obtain treatment for a child without the consent of the other parent. This has both potential ethical and legal concerns.

Test-Taking Strategies Applied

The question contains a qualifying word—NEXT. Its use indicates that the order in which the response choices should occur is critical. Social workers must know the steps required in obtaining informed consent. Consent for treatment of minors, especially when parents are separated or divorced, can be complex.

In this case scenario, initially, the social worker has appropriately asked for and reviewed the custody decree, but it does not provide critical information needed. When there is a question about the ability of one parent to legally consent to treatment of a minor, best practice is to next request consent from both parents. Only if such consent is not possible should the social worker ask the consenting parent to sign a statement confirming that he or she has the legal right to consent to the child's treatment without the consent of others.

Knowledge Area

Unit IV—Professional Relationships, Values, and Ethics (Content Area); Confidentiality (Competency); The Principles and Processes of Obtaining Informed Consent (KSA)

169. B

Rationale

The 2008 *NASW Code of Ethics* explicitly acknowledges social workers' **ethical obligation to address professional impairment**. Professional impairment occurs when personal problems, psychosocial distress, legal problems, substance abuse, or mental health difficulties affect professional performance. In these instances, social workers must consult with and assist colleagues who are manifesting symptoms of impairment.

Social workers should not allow their own personal problems, psychosocial distress, legal problems, substance abuse, or mental health difficulties to interfere with their professional judgment and performance or to jeopardize the best interest of people for whom they have a professional responsibility (*NASW Code of Ethics*, 2008—4.05 Impairment). If social workers' problems do interfere, they should immediately seek consultation and take appropriate remedial action by seeking professional help, making adjustments in workload, terminating practice, or taking any other steps necessary to protect clients and others.

Test-Taking Strategies Applied

The question states that the correct answer should be chosen "to appropriately protect clients." In the case scenario, the social worker is "experiencing a lot of personal issues" that include marital, and subsequent financial, problems. Such distress can certainly impact professional judgment. Limiting her practice to only single adults and children will not protect against incompetent practice that can result from impairment. Impairment can lead to lapses in sound decision making, regardless of the population served.

Not addressing or suppressing thoughts and feelings will not help the social worker to take appropriate actions to protect clients. Unfortunately social workers who suffer from the effects of mental illness, stress, or substance abuse are like everyone else; they are often the worst judges of their behavior, the last to recognize their problems, and the least motivated to seek help. Hiding or avoiding behavior will lead to adverse outcomes. Treatment should be delivered by qualified professionals, not supervisors, as turning to them for treatment results in dual or multiple relationships.

Knowledge Area

Unit IV—Professional Relationships, Values, and Ethics (Content Area); Professional Development and Use of Self (Competency); Social Worker Self-Care Principles and Techniques (KSA)

170. D

Rationale

Cultural competence is essential in the creation of an intervention plan. It is achieved by identifying and understanding the needs and help-seeking behaviors of individuals and families. In addition, culturally competent organizations design and implement services that are tailored or matched to the unique needs of individuals, children, families, organizations, and communities served. Practice is driven in service delivery systems by client-preferred choices, not by culturally blind or culturally free interventions.

Cultural competence recognizes that family is defined differently by different cultures. Family as defined by each culture is usually the primary system of support and preferred intervention. Family/consumers are the ultimate decision makers for services and supports for their children and/or themselves. Communities determine their own needs.

Thus, cultural competence involves working in conjunction with natural, informal support, and helping networks within diverse communities (e.g., neighborhood, civic, and advocacy associations; local/neighborhood merchants and alliance groups; ethnic, social, and religious organizations; and spiritual leaders and healers).

Test-Taking Strategies Applied

The correct answer must focus on the hallmark of cultural competence, namely that individuals and families make different choices based on cultural forces and effective services are those that are tailored or matched to their unique needs. Family, as defined by each culture, is the primary system of support and preferred unit of intervention. Thus, culturally competent social work practice involves working in conjunction with natural, informal support and helping networks within culturally diverse communities (e.g., neighborhood, civic, and advocacy associations; ethnic, social, and religious organizations; and where appropriate, spiritual healers).

Two of the incorrect response choices view informal supports as supplemental or secondary to services by professionals. This view does not accept a client as competent to solve his or her own problems. In addition, while informal supports can serve as collateral informants to understand problems more clearly, this notion is not directly related to the major principles of cultural competence. Thus, the answer that sees the major value of informal supports as helping social workers to understand problems is not correct.

Knowledge Area

Unit II—Assessment and Intervention Planning (Content Area); Intervention Planning (Competency); Cultural Considerations in the Creation of an Intervention Plan (KSA)

Evaluation of Results

These tables assist in identifying the content areas and competencies needing further study. Within each of the competencies, there are specific Knowledge, Skills, and Abilities (KSAs) that social workers should reference to assist with locating appropriate study resources. As there is tremendous overlap in the material that could be contained across the KSAs within a given competency, all KSAs for the competency should be reviewed to make sure of an adequate breadth of knowledge in the content area. A listing of the KSAs for each content area and competency can be found in Appendix A.

The results of this evaluation should be the basis of the development of a study plan. Social workers should get to a level of comfort with the material so that they can summarize relevant content, including key concepts and terms. Social workers do not need to be experts in all of the KSAs, but should understand their relevancy to social work practice. They should be able to describe how each of the KSAs specifically impact assessment, as well as decisions about client care.

Appendix B provides useful information on learning styles that can assist when determining the best ways to study and retain material. Success on the Association of Social Work Boards (ASWB®) examination does not require a lot of memorization of material, but rather the ability to recall terms and integrate multiple concepts to select the best course of action in hypothetical scenarios. Thus, time is best spent really understanding the KSAs and not just being able to recite definitions.

	Analysis of Masters Practice Test Unit I: Human Development, Diversity, and Behavior in the Environment (27%)				
Competency	Question Numbers	Number of Questions	Number Correct	Percentage Correct	Area Requiring Further Study?
1. Human Growth and Development	1, 3, 13, 20, 26, 27, 29, 30, 44, 49, 55, 71, 73, 77, 89, 91, 100, 103, 104, 105, 125, 133, 142, 143, 167	25	___/25	___%	
2. Concepts of Abuse and Neglect	6, 70, 74, 92, 119, 122, 138, 141	8	___/8	___%	
3. Diversity, Social/ Economic Justice, and Oppression	11, 18, 31, 34, 39, 66, 72, 78, 102, 131, 139, 157, 165	13	___/13	___%	

Analysis of Masters Practice Test					
Unit II: Assessment and Intervention Planning (24%)					
Competency	Question Numbers	Number of Questions	Number Correct	Percentage Correct	Area Requiring Further Study?
4. Biopsychosocial History and Collateral Data	17, 23, 33, 40, 45, 48, 51, 60, 63, 88, 98, 99, 107, 127, 153, 166	16	__/16	__%	
5. Assessment Methods and Techniques	10, 36, 53, 54, 57, 58, 59, 62, 80, 93, 94, 134, 148, 159, 164	15	__/15	__%	
6. Intervention Planning	41, 50, 67, 82, 106, 126, 135, 155, 162, 170	10	__/10	__%	

Analysis of Masters Practice Test Unit III: Intervention With Clients/Client Systems (24%)					
Competency	Question Numbers	Number of Questions	Number Correct	Percentage Correct	Area Requiring Further Study?
7. Intervention Processes and Techniques for Use Across Systems	28, 37, 47, 52, 68, 79, 81, 83, 86, 87, 109, 113, 116, 121, 136, 145, 151, 156	18	—/18	—%	
8. Intervention Processes and Techniques for Use With Larger Systems	4, 5, 9, 16, 21, 22, 24, 35, 38, 46, 64, 84, 85, 96, 97, 108, 110, 114, 115, 129, 146, 147, 154	23	—/23	—%	

	Analysis of Masters Practice Test				
Unit IV: Professional Relationships, Values, and Ethics (25%)					
Competency	Question Numbers	Number of Questions	Number Correct	Percentage Correct	Area Requiring Further Study?
9. Professional Values and Ethical Issues	12, 15, 32, 42, 90, 101, 120, 128, 152, 158, 161, 163	12	__/12	__%	
10. Confidentiality	7, 8, 14, 19, 25, 69, 112, 117, 123, 130, 137, 149, 150, 160, 168	15	__/15	__%	
11. Professional Development and Use of Self	2, 43, 56, 61, 65, 75, 76, 95, 111, 118, 124, 132, 140, 144, 169	15	__/15	__%	

Overall Results of Masters Diagnostic Practice Test				
	Content Area	Number of Questions	Number Correct	Percentage Correct
Unit I (27%)	Human Development, Diversity, and Behavior in the Environment	46	__/46	__%
Unit II (24%)	Assessment and Intervention Planning	41	__/41	__%
Unit III (24%)	Interventions With Clients/Client Systems	41	__/41	__%
Unit IV (25%)	Professional Relationships, Values, and Ethics	42	__/42	__%
Overall Knowledge	ASWB® Masters Examination	170	__/170	__%

Appendix A

Content Areas, Competencies, and KSAs for the ASWB® Masters Examination

Human Development, Diversity, and Behavior in the Environment (Content Area)

1. Human Growth and Development (Competency)

KSAs
Theories of human development throughout the lifespan (e.g., physical, social, emotional, cognitive, behavioral)
The indicators of normal and abnormal physical, cognitive, emotional, and sexual development throughout the lifespan
Theories of sexual development throughout the lifespan
Theories of spiritual development throughout the lifespan
Theories of racial, ethnic, and cultural development throughout the lifespan
The effects of physical, mental, and cognitive disabilities throughout the lifespan
The interplay of biological, psychological, social, and spiritual factors
Basic human needs
The principles of attachment and bonding
The effect of aging on biopsychosocial functioning
The impact of aging parents on adult children

Gerontology

Personality theories

Theories of conflict

Factors influencing self-image (e.g., culture, race, religion/spirituality, age, disability, trauma)

Body image and its impact (e.g., identity, self-esteem, relationships, habits)

Parenting skills and capacities

The effects of addiction and substance abuse on individuals, families, groups, organizations, and communities

Feminist theory

The impact of out-of-home placement (e.g., hospitalization, foster care, residential care, criminal justice system) on clients/client systems

Basic principles of human genetics

The family life cycle

Family dynamics and functioning and the effects on individuals, families, groups, organizations, and communities

Theories of couples development

The impact of physical and mental illness on family dynamics

Psychological defense mechanisms and their effects on behavior and relationships

Addiction theories and concepts

Systems and ecological perspectives and theories

Role theories

Theories of group development and functioning

Theories of social change and community development

The dynamics of interpersonal relationships

Models of family life education in social work practice

Strengths-based and resilience theories

The impact of stress, trauma, and violence

Crisis intervention theories

Theories of trauma-informed care

The impact of the environment (e.g., social, physical, cultural, political, economic) on individuals, families, groups, organizations, and communities

The effects of life events, stressors, and crises on individuals, families, groups, organizations, and communities

Person-in-environment (PIE) theory

Communication theories and styles

Psychoanalytic and psychodynamic approaches

The impact of caregiving on families

The dynamics and effects of loss, separation, and grief

2. Concepts of Abuse and Neglect (Competency)

KSAs
Indicators and dynamics of abuse and neglect throughout the lifespan
The effects of physical, sexual, and psychological abuse on individuals, families, groups, organizations, and communities
The indicators, dynamics, and impact of exploitation across the lifespan (e.g., financial, immigration status, sexual trafficking)
The characteristics of perpetrators of abuse, neglect, and exploitation

3. Diversity, Social/Economic Justice, and Oppression (Competency)

KSAs
The effect of disability on biopsychosocial functioning throughout the lifespan
The effect of culture, race, and ethnicity on behaviors, attitudes, and identity
The effects of discrimination and stereotypes on behaviors, attitudes, and identity
The influence of sexual orientation on behaviors, attitudes, and identity
The impact of transgender and transitioning process on behaviors, attitudes, identity, and relationships
Systemic (institutionalized) discrimination (e.g., racism, sexism, ageism)
The principles of culturally competent social work practice
Sexual orientation concepts
Gender and gender identity concepts
Social and economic justice
The effect of poverty on individuals, families, groups, organizations, and communities
The impact of social institutions on society
Criminal justice systems
The impact of globalization on clients/client systems (e.g., interrelatedness of systems, international integration, technology, environmental or financial crises, epidemics)

Assessment and Intervention Planning (Content Area)

4. Biopsychosocial History and Collateral Data (Competency)

KSAs
The components of a biopsychosocial assessment
The components and function of the mental status examination

Biopsychosocial responses to illness and disability
Biopsychosocial factors related to mental health
The indicators of psychosocial stress
Basic medical terminology
The indicators of mental and emotional illness throughout the lifespan
The types of information available from other sources (e.g., agency, employment, medical, psychological, legal, or school records)
Methods to obtain sensitive information (e.g., substance abuse, sexual abuse)
The indicators of addiction and substance abuse
The indicators of somatization
Co-occurring disorders and conditions
Symptoms of neurologic and organic disorders
The indicators of sexual dysfunction
Methods used to assess trauma
The indicators of traumatic stress and violence
Common psychotropic and nonpsychotropic prescriptions and over-the-counter medications and their side effects

5. Assessment Methods and Techniques (Competency)

KSAs
The factors and processes used in problem formulation
Methods of involving clients/client systems in problem identification (e.g., gathering collateral information)
Techniques and instruments used to assess clients/client systems
Methods to incorporate the results of psychological and educational tests into assessment
Risk assessment methods
The indicators and risk factors of the client's/client system's danger to self and others
Methods to assess the client's/client system's strengths, resources, and challenges (e.g., individual, family, group, organization, community)
Methods to assess motivation, resistance, and readiness to change
Methods to assess the client's/client system's communication skills
Methods to assess the client's/client system's coping abilities
The indicators of the client's/client system's strengths and challenges
Methods to assess ego strengths
Placement options based on assessed level of care
The use of the Diagnostic and Statistical Manual of the American Psychiatric Association

The indicators of behavioral dysfunction
Methods to develop, review, and implement crisis plans
The principles and features of objective and subjective data
Basic and applied research design and methods
Data collection and analysis methods
Methods to assess reliability and validity in social work research

6. Intervention Planning (Competency)

KSAs
Methods to involve clients/client systems in intervention planning
The indicators of motivation, resistance, and readiness to change
Cultural considerations in the creation of an intervention plan
The criteria used in the selection of intervention/treatment modalities
    (e.g., client/client system abilities, culture, life stage)
The components of intervention, treatment, and service plans
Psychotherapies
The impact of immigration, refugee, or undocumented status on service
    delivery
Discharge, aftercare, and follow-up planning

Interventions With Clients/Client Systems (Content Area)

7. Intervention Processes and Techniques for Use Across Systems
    (Competency)

KSAs
The principles and techniques of interviewing (e.g., supporting, clarifying,
    focusing, confronting, validating, feedback, reflecting, language differ-
    ences, use of interpreters, redirecting)
The phases of intervention and treatment
Problem-solving models and approaches (e.g., brief, solution-focused
    methods or techniques)
Methods to engage and motivate clients/client systems
Methods to engage and work with involuntary clients/client systems
Methods to obtain and provide feedback
The principles of active listening and observation
Verbal and nonverbal communication techniques
The concept of congruence in communication
Limit setting techniques
The technique of role play
Role modeling techniques

Techniques for harm reduction for self and others
Methods to teach coping and other self-care skills to clients/client systems
Client/client system self-monitoring techniques
Methods of conflict resolution
Crisis intervention and treatment approaches
Methods and approaches to trauma-informed care
Anger management techniques
Stress management techniques
Cognitive and behavioral interventions
Strengths-based and empowerment strategies and interventions
Client/client system contracting and goal-setting techniques
Partializing techniques
Assertiveness training
Task-centered approaches
Psychoeducation methods (e.g., acknowledging, supporting, normalizing)
Group work techniques and approaches (e.g., developing and managing group processes and cohesion)
Family therapy models, interventions, and approaches
Couples interventions and treatment approaches
The impact of out-of-home displacement (e.g., natural disaster, homelessness, immigration) on clients/client systems
Permanency planning
Mindfulness and complementary therapeutic approaches
The components of case management
Techniques used for follow-up
The elements of a case presentation
Methods to develop and evaluate measurable objectives for client/client system intervention, treatment, and/or service plans
Techniques used to evaluate a client's/client system's progress
Primary, secondary, and tertiary prevention strategies
The indicators of client/client system readiness for termination
Methods, techniques, and instruments used to evaluate social work practice
Evidence-based practice
Case recording for practice evaluation or supervision
Consultation approaches (e.g., referrals to specialists)
The process of interdisciplinary and intradisciplinary team collaboration
The basic terminology of professions other than social work (e.g., legal, educational)
The principles of case recording, documentation, and management of practice records

8. Intervention Processes and Techniques for Use With Larger Systems (Competency)

KSAs

Methods to establish program objectives and outcomes

Methods to assess the availability of community resources

Methods of service delivery

Theories and methods of advocacy for policies, services, and resources to meet clients'/client systems' needs

Methods to create, implement, and evaluate policies and procedures that minimize risk for individuals, families, groups, organizations, and communities

Concepts of social policy development and analysis

Techniques to inform and influence organizational and social policy

The principles and processes for developing formal documents (e.g., proposals, letters, brochures, pamphlets, reports, evaluations)

Methods to establish service networks or community resources

Community organizing and social planning methods

Methods of networking

Techniques for mobilizing community participation

Governance structures

Theories of organizational development and structure

The effects of policies, procedures, regulations, and legislation on social work practice and service delivery

Quality assurance, including program reviews and audits by external sources

The impact of the political environment on policy-making

Leadership and management techniques

Fiscal management techniques

Educational components, techniques, and methods of supervision

Methods to identify learning needs and develop learning objectives for supervisees

The effects of program evaluation findings on services

Methods to evaluate agency programs (e.g., needs assessment, formative/summative assessment, cost effectiveness, cost–benefit analysis, outcomes assessment)

Professional Relationships, Values, and Ethics (Content Area)

9. Professional Values and Ethical Issues (Competency)

KSAs

Legal and/or ethical issues related to the practice of social work, including responsibility to clients/client systems, colleagues, the profession, and society

Professional values and principles (e.g., competence, social justice, integrity, and dignity and worth of the person)

Techniques to identify and resolve ethical dilemmas

Client/client system competence and self-determination (e.g., financial decisions, treatment decisions, emancipation, age of consent, permanency planning)

Techniques for protecting and enhancing client/client system self-determination

The client's/client system's right to refuse services (e.g., medication, medical treatment, counseling, placement, etc.)

Professional boundaries in the social worker–client/client system relationship (e.g., power differences conflicts of interest, etc.)

Self-disclosure principles and applications

Legal and/or ethical issues regarding documentation

Legal and/or ethical issues regarding termination

Legal and/or ethical issues related to death and dying

Research ethics (e.g., institutional review boards, use of human subjects, informed consent)

Models of supervision and consultation (e.g., individual, peer, group)

Ethical issues in supervision and management

Methods to create, implement, and evaluate policies and procedures for social worker safety

The supervisee's role in supervision (e.g., identifying learning needs, self-assessment, prioritizing, etc.)

Accreditation and/or licensing requirements

Professional development activities to improve practice and maintain current professional knowledge (e.g., in-service training, licensing requirements, reviews of literature, workshops)

10. Confidentiality (Competency)

KSAs

The elements of client/client system reports

The principles and processes of obtaining informed consent

The use of client/client system records

Legal and/or ethical issues regarding confidentiality, including electronic information security

Legal and/or ethical issues regarding mandatory reporting (e.g., abuse, threat of harm, impaired professionals, etc.)

11. Professional Development and Use of Self (Competency)

KSAs

The components of the social worker–client/client system relationship

The client's/client system's role in the problem-solving process

The social worker's role in the problem-solving process

Methods to clarify the roles and responsibilities of the social worker and client/client system in the intervention process

The principles and techniques for building and maintaining a helping relationship

The concept of acceptance and empathy in the social worker–client/client system relationship

The dynamics of power and transparency in the social worker–client/client system relationship

Ethical issues related to dual relationships

The impact of transference and countertransference in the social worker–client/client system relationship

The impact of domestic, intimate partner, and other violence on the helping relationship

The dynamics of diversity in the social worker–client/client system relationship

The effect of the client's developmental level on the social worker–client relationship

Social worker self-care principles and techniques

Burnout, secondary trauma, and compassion fatigue

The components of a safe and positive work environment

Professional objectivity in the social worker–client/client system relationship

The influence of the social worker's own values and beliefs on the social worker–client/client system relationship

Time management approaches

The impact of transference and countertransference within supervisory relationships

The influence of the social worker's own values and beliefs on interdisciplinary collaboration

Appendix B

Learning Styles

The following are some suggested techniques for each learning style that can help to fill in content gaps that may exist.

VISUAL LEARNERS

Visual learners learn best through what they see. Although lectures can be boring for visual learners, they benefit from the use of diagrams, PowerPoint slides, and charts.

- Use colored highlighters to draw attention to key terms
- Develop outlines or take notes on the concepts
- Write talking points for each of the Knowledge, Skills, and Abilities (KSAs) on separate white index cards
- Create a coding schema of symbols and write them next to material and terms that require further study
- Study in an environment that is away from visual distractions such as television, people moving around, or clutter

AUDITORY LEARNERS

Auditory learners learn best through what they hear. They may have difficulty remembering material, but can easily recall it if it is read to them.

- Tape-record yourself summarizing the material as you are studying it—listen to your notes as a way to reinforce what you read
- Have a study partner explain the relevant concepts and terms related to the KSAs
- Read the text aloud if you are having trouble remembering it
- Find free podcasts or YouTube videos on the Internet on the content areas that are short and easy to understand to assist with learning
- Talk to yourself about the content as you study, emphasizing what is important to remember related to each KSA

KINESTHETIC OR HANDS-ON LEARNERS

Kinesthetic learners learn through tactile approaches aimed at experiencing or doing. They need physical activities as a foundation for instruction.

- Make flashcards on material because writing it down will assist with remembering the content
- Use as many different senses as possible when studying—read material when you are on your treadmill, use highlighters, talk aloud about content, and/or listen to a study partner
- Develop mnemonic devices to aid in information retention (e.g., EAPIET or *EAt PIE T*oday is a great way to remember the social work problem-solving process [Engaging, Assessing, Planning, Intervening, Evaluating, and Terminating])
- Write notes and important terms in the margins
- Ask a study partner to quiz you on material—turn it into a game and see how many KSAs you can discuss or how long you can talk about a content area before running out of material